A Faculty Guidebc for Effective Shareu Governance and Service in Higher Education

A Faculty Guidebook for Effective Shared Governance and Service in Higher Education bridges the gap between training and work experience, offering a blueprint for academic workers' effective participation in service and governance in higher education. Unpacking skills of problem solving, critical analysis, politicking, negotiation, coalition building, and emotional labor, this book provides flexible, adaptable strategies that are relevant across institutional settings and that draw from research, experience, and multiple perspectives.

The principles in the book will guide faculty in developing policies and implementing practices to better serve students, colleagues, communities, and the larger mission of postsecondary education. With an emphasis on shared governance and committee service that advances equity, inclusion, access, and justice, this book pushes back on the view that service is not worth our time and offers specific recommendations for doing governance work effectively. Chapters provide strategies for policy development, implementation, and assessment, as well as tools for navigating common roadblocks to accomplishing sustainable and progressive faculty leadership. This accessible book demystifies a critical part of the academic workload, and is designed for instructors, faculty, and academic advisors at any stage of their career who want to advocate for and create better conditions in higher education.

Kirsti Cole is Professor of Rhetoric, Composition, and Literature at Minnesota State University.

Joanne Baird Giordano is Associate Professor of English, Linguistics, and Writing Studies at Salt Lake Community College.

Holly Hassel is Professor of English at North Dakota State University.

A Faculty Guidebook for Effective Shared Governance and Service in Higher Education

Kirsti Cole, Joanne Baird Giordano and Holly Hassel

Routledge
Taylor & Francis Group

NEW YORK AND LONDON

Designed cover image: © Getty Images

First published 2023
by Routledge
605 Third Avenue, New York, NY 10158

and by Routledge
4 Park Square, Milton Park, Abingdon, Oxon, OX14 4RN

Routledge is an imprint of the Taylor & Francis Group, an informa business

ISBN: 978-1-032-19171-3 (hbk)
ISBN: 978-1-032-19170-6 (pbk)
ISBN: 978-1-003-25797-4 (ebk)

DOI: 10.4324/9781003257974

Typeset in Perpetua
by Apex CoVantage, LLC

This book is dedicated to the legions of academic workers who have forged ahead with equity work in service and shared governance even as rewards were few and validation scarce. We hope this book makes that labor visible and provides tools for improving the conditions of all academic workers.

Contents

CONTENTS

Preface

We wrote this book because so much in the current culture of higher education feels broken. Across the settings we have worked in, we have seen faculty trying to do good work and bring about change, only to stumble, fall, or flounder. Faculty run up against barriers of multiple kinds: incompatible administrative values, territorial colleagues, resource limitations, challenging workloads—the list goes on. They try to push back against status quo-ism and disingenuous what aboutisms. Over and over they encounter the common default of the academy: "We've always done it this way." These obstacles can feel insurmountable. Even the best efforts to move good work forward can lead to disengagement and despair.

The academy is now functioning in the aftermath of scrambling mode, as a result of the COVID-19 pandemic, and compounded by longitudinal inequities in academic labor. As such, it is so easy to become frustrated with higher education service, governance, and change work. The underfunded and market-driven university, and overreliance on contingent labor, also asks faculty and staff to do more with increasingly fewer resources. It might feel impossible to do anything at all, especially activities and initiatives that would improve conditions for working, teaching, and learning.

However, this book is meant to give a blueprint to counter hopelessness. We have witnessed firsthand how effective governance and service work can be in bringing about important changes that improve the quality and experience of what happens in higher education for faculty, staff, and students. We have seen new, inclusive governance structures created. We have witnessed practices of evaluating student learning or faculty performance updated to align values with processes. We have participated in work as big as structuring equity, diversity, and inclusion into the fabric of an organization, or as small as increasing stipends for graduate students or compensating non-tenure-track instructors for service participation. Service efforts make our academic workplaces more just. By focusing on equity efforts across shared governance contexts we can improve all of our working conditions.

Our hope for this book is that it might make service and shared governance a less mystifying and less frustrating part of the academic workload. We also hope that viewing shared governance and service not as burdens but as tools will inspire readers to take up initiatives for equity, inclusion, access, and justice in their own contexts.

–Holly, Kirsti, and Joanne

Foreword

A Faculty Guidebook for Effective Shared Governance is a timely and far-reaching contribution to the national dialogue on higher education. Written as a handbook for faculty and drawing from an on-the-ground recognition of the subject's complexity, Kirsti Cole, Joanne Giordana, and Holly Hassel make a compelling argument that successful shared governance is not only possible but is essential to the success of our colleges and universities.

Shared governance is under attack from all sides, variously dismissed as inefficient or impossible to achieve. On the one hand, we are told by the "business model mind set" that shared governance is a drag on institutional agility. Trying to engage multiple voices and perspectives in decision making inevitably slows down the pace of change, leaving higher education unable to respond to rapidly changing market conditions.

On the other hand, the "mission mind set" insists that the fate of higher education should be in the hands of those most closely tied to its educational mission and most deeply engaged in the day-to-day practices of teaching and intellectual engagement. Disciplinary—and maybe interdisciplinary knowledge—should guide everything from curriculum to admissions to policy lest higher education devolve into a valueless theme park of mere entertainment.

The authors of this Guidebook wisely refuse this binary, locating the essence of shared governance in the culture of higher education and showing that, when properly engaged with, shared governance is our best method for ensuring that institutions remain both responsive and important. Mission and Business model. Faculty and Administrators. Leaders and Students. All must come together for success.

Shared governance has much to recommend it. We regularly witness the ways that ego-driven, top-down, corporate leadership has the power to unravel even successful companies overnight.[1] Moreover, we know that the so-called stodgy sector of higher education executed its COVID pivot faster and better than almost any other industry. Clearly there is something to learn from the ways a culture of shared governance can, and often does, lead to sturdy institutional success. Like democracy, shared governance is messy, always partial, sometimes inefficient, and better than any of its alternatives.

I have inhabited many roles with the academy, including faculty member and president. From all of this experience, four elements strike me as particularly salient for the success of shared governance and ultimately for the success of higher education:

A shared commitment to understanding the financial and market realities of the business model. Without adequate information, the various constituencies are unable to provide meaningful advice or good decisions. Presidents and other leaders must practice transparency, providing timely and meaningful information. Faculty and staff, on the other hand, must pay attention and spend time learning about the industry in which they work. Many faculty find this a drag since their professional identities privilege discipline membership over their work within a higher education ecosystem grounded in undergraduate learning that include both public and private funding sources. One aim of the Guidebook is to encourage faculty to see the value of broadening their professional identities and engaging in the work of shared governance with gusto.

A shared commitment to understanding the mission and its enactment. Colleges and universities are not best understood as businesses. If anything, they are perhaps more like small towns. But whatever analogy is used, the mission of student learning and knowledge production should be at the center of every decision. Those who do not enter the classroom or engage in other ways with students have to pay close attention to the practical knowledge gained by those who do. At the same time, faculty have to see the mission in terms broader than "my class," "my subject," or "my majors." The Guidebook is particularly effective in making the case for how and when faculty can take up a truly institutional perspective.

A culture of trust. Formal handbook language about who is responsible for various decisions and who must be consulted or advised is important but is ineffective without a basic foundation of trust. This isn't merely a mandate to reduce tension between "the faculty" and "the administration." Many of the so-called failures of shared governance are really failures within—rather than among—constituencies. This occurs when, for example, faculty do not have confidence in their own elected representatives or when deans are pitted against each other to fight for resources. As the Guidebook shows in detail, faculties have to get their own house in order to ensure that they can responsibly engage, communicate, compromise, and come to a position in a timely manner if they are to play a significant role in the institution's broader governance.

Inclusive teams and committees. Much of the faculty cynicism toward shared governance flows from experience with myopic leadership or committees. The Guidebook pays special attention to ensuring that minority viewpoints are considered and that diverse members of the institution have an opportunity to play meaningful roles in decision making. When diversity is added as an afterthought, it is rarely effective. Diversity at every level—from the board to the cabinet to the faculty and staff committees—leads to better decisions and greater buy-in and collaboration.

Cole, Giordano, and Hassel have produced a true guidebook. The book rewards active engagement, so I encourage the reader to carry out the exercises and thought experiments included in the chapters. There is much here as well that could be used to foster discussion within a faculty and between faculty and leadership.

For all its challenges, faults, and problems, higher education remains a bright hope for a better future for individuals, communities, and societies. All of us who build careers within it owe it to our students, our colleagues, and our neighbors near and far to make the best use of our power and shared resources that we can. *A Faculty Guidebook for Effective Shared Governance* is a timely and trusted friend to that goal.

By Dr. Marjorie Hass, President, Council of Independent Colleges and past president, Rhodes College.

NOTE

1 As we write this, the news is full of the decline of both Twitter and FTX due to the unrestrained decision making of their CEOs.

Acknowledgments

We are grateful to the contributors who shared vignettes in this chapter about their experience and knowledge with service and shared governance. Without their voices, this book would be incomplete. We are also thankful for the colleagues with whom we have worked on a variety of levels and types of projects who have helped us develop the advice and strategies that we outline in the book, some as object lessons, some colleagues, some as cautionary tales. We also acknowledge the commitment that has been made by the public higher education systems in the states we have taught and served. Without a robust and stable college and university system, there can be no democracy.

Chapter 1

Introduction
You Have a Job in Higher Education, Now What?

For workers new to higher education, entering the environment is a different experience from the one that many faculty and staff had as college students. What seems, for example, like a comfortable and supportive resource center actually required years of proposals for staffing, annual budgets, and accountability reports. An exciting new major or minor program that classmates added on to their degree by filling out a form was actually years in the making—going through multiple levels of planning, research, curricular approval, and advocacy by various campus stakeholders. The campus activity that takes up hours of a student's life—music, the campus newspaper, a student club—requires oversight, sponsorship, and management by staff, student governance, and faculty advisors. The research grant or lab sponsored by a faculty member that gives undergraduate student's hands-on research experience has research, scientific, ethical, and hiring processes that are governed by university policy. In other words, a career in higher education involves pulling back the curtain on the operations of a college or university that are invisible (yet essential) to most students, and that are, ultimately, part of every academic worker's experience.

The governance of a college and university happens in the examples provided in the previous paragraph, but it is much more. Shared governance and service include many elements of the work of the institution, all in the service of an institution's mission. This might include:

- University committees on evaluation, curriculum, grievances and appeals
- Campus groups working on diversity, equity, inclusion, and access issues for students, faculty, and staff
- Staff, student, or faculty senates/councils
- Committees involved in department governance like scholarship, curriculum, outreach, graduate admissions, bylaws, promotion/tenure, or specific programs
- Union or bargaining units within the institution or system

feministkilljoy
@SaraNAhmed   ...

Counter-institutional work in feminist hands is also
housework with the drudgery & repetition that word
implies, painstaking work, administrative work, also
care work, because if we need to transform institutions
to survive them we need to survive what we are trying
to transform.

10:04 AM · Mar 7, 2021

174 Retweets   **29** Quote Tweets   **799** Likes

Tweet your reply   Reply

Art Blake @ArtMBlake · Mar 7, 2021   ...
Replying to @SaraNAhmed
Yes. It's even worse than vacuuming and gets me more tired and cranky.
And it comes with a whole slew of critics unplugging the vacuum, denying
the place needs cleaning, not helping, not moving their feet, and then
saying what a crap job I've done.

                                                        11

Figure 1.1 Sarah Ahmed tweet on service work.

- Representation to system or university boards, including boards of trustees
  or regents, or president's cabinets
- Search and screen or hiring committees
- Committees involving budgets at multiple levels, including funding for
  research, professional development, travel, and campus resources
- Groups and committees with responsibility for cocurricular activities, such
  as athletics, student publications, arts, music, or theater
- Groups responsible for ethical conduct, such as the institutional review
  board or academic misconduct review committees
- Task forces, committees, or other groups focused on student success,
  retention, or conditional admissions

- Service to professional organizations, such as elected or appointed roles in governance, on awards committees, conference planning, or grants
- Committees at multiple levels of governance for programs like general education, writing across the curriculum, educational programs for preservice teachers, or other cross-disciplinary programs warranting faculty oversight

Unfortunately, very few future faculty or academic staff have opportunities to experience these kinds of activities during graduate school, which means that they must develop the skills, dispositions, and institutional knowledge to effectively do this work on the job.

The goal, then, of *A Faculty Guide to Effective Shared Governance and Service in Higher Education* is to fill the gap between training and work experience, offering a blueprint for effective participation in service and governance. Though no single guidebook can prepare readers for every service situation, we aim to provide flexible, adaptable strategies that are portable across institutional settings. This book can help readers tackle some of the following issues:

1. Common attitudes about service work in academia (see figure 1.1)
2. Material conditions that complicate service work in academia
3. Labor practices in academia that need to change to accommodate necessary service work
4. Misconceptions that new faculty have as they begin to participate in service work
5. How faculty can undertake service responsibilities effectively
6. The "need to know" basics that new faculty require as they move from a student to a faculty position
7. Specific issues that academic staff and nonteaching staff should be aware of as they approach service and governance responsibilities
8. What non-tenure-track instructors need to know as they take on new service responsibilities
9. What marginalized or multimarginalized faculty may encounter as they take on shared governance responsibilities

Though it is impossible to provide definitive answers to all these questions, *A Faculty Guide to Shared Governance and Service* draws from research, experience, and multiple perspectives to offer a toolkit for faculty.

SHARED GOVERNANCE AND SERVICE: WHAT THEY ARE AND WHY THEY MATTER

As three faculty members with decades of experiences in higher education, including roles in institutional and program governance groups, national organizations, and union leadership, we have observed firsthand the ways that governance can function effectively for the purposes of bringing about equity and positive change. We have also witnessed how it can flounder in dysfunction, ego, and rudderlessness, unable to effectively move work forward. Shared governance is a complex, complicated, multifaceted, and changeable topic. It is hard. The work of shared governance can feel thankless and grueling, but it is our contention in this book that is the primary and most effective way to effect change in an organization. In Chapter 2, we elaborate on shared governance activities—what they are, and how they look in higher education. However, we offer this short definition of governance: *a collaborative decision-making process that meaningfully involves all groups with a stake in decisions that affect their educational and work environment.*

Achieving this aspirational definition, let alone offering a blueprint for doing this kind of work effectively is challenging because there is so much variation across institutional and governance structures. The casualization of labor (with greater reliance on nontenure line positions, adjunct faculty, and teaching-track lines that may not necessarily include service as a component of the contract) has made it increasingly difficult for effective participation by faculty in shared governance. These issues can make it feel like addressing shared governance, let alone participating in it, is impossible. But it's not. We want to assure our readers that taking the time to locate, understand, and participate in your own labor in higher education is one of the best things you can do. In the rising call to think of a job as a job and not as a vocation, labor spent in organizing and investing in an understanding of the workplace environment is an essential element of fighting for equitable, humane, kind, and livable work.

The surge of labor activism since 2020—including union activism at even large corporate conglomerates like Amazon, Wal-Mart, and Starbucks—has shown that even the previously union-proof corporate cultures are now contending with empowered workers. Higher education is no different. The *Washington Post* recently covered the growth and expansion of faculty labor organizing (Marcus 2022):

> About 120 new faculty union chapters have won recognition since 2013, with more than 36,000 members, according to the National Center for the Study of Collective Bargaining in Higher Education and the Professions at Hunter College. That includes 65 at private, nonprofit institutions, where faculty have historically been slower to unionize.

It is in this context that we write—to encourage participation in academic governance because while many stakeholders across campus argue that they are committed to the quality of the student experience and the mission of the university, the primary way to move such efforts forward is through the collaboration across and among groups. A way to think about shared governance is as *quality control*, that is, ensuring that all sites of decision making are directed by those with expertise and experience in a higher education issue or practice.

Our own view, that service and shared governance are valuable and worth the time and attention of faculty, is not necessarily shared across higher education. For example, philosopher Jason Brennan, commenting in book published through Johns Hopkins University Press, argues: "For one, most service work is not worth doing, period, by anyone. Most committees accomplish little to nothing but consume lots of time" (Jaschik 2020). Later in 2020, Lance Fusarelli argued "As for service, do the minimal amount necessary to be considered a good citizen but no more. Service is another one of those metrics that has value only in the negative. Doing twice as much service as others and saying yes to every service opportunity will kill you and your career" (Fusarelli 2020). Meanwhile, there are ubiquitous *Chronicle of Higher Ed* and *Inside Higher Ed* stories like "Who Needs a Faculty Senate" and "Why Can't My Faculty Senate Do More?" along with ongoing news stories about tensions between administrators and governance, inequities in service labor, and eroding protections for faculty in higher education.

This book intends to push back on the view that service is not worth our time. More than ever before, shared governance groups need to cultivate a collective voice—one that represents the diverse and varied constituencies that make colleges and universities work—students, tenure-line or continuing-contract faculty, lecturers and adjunct instructors, academic and university staff, student governance representatives. As we first began conceptualizing this project in 2020, decisions about the teaching and learning environments facing students, non-tenure-track faculty, and tenure-line faculty were debated (or being made with little consultation) in the midst of a pandemic—the actual life and death situation for many stakeholders that administrators have used to frame budget cuts for years. And yet the role and authority of governance groups remains murky in many institutions. In part, this is because those who begin new positions as faculty receive little to no preparation to participate in governance. When elected to serve, they may receive only a link to bylaws and a constitution, with perhaps some brief conversations between colleagues about "how senate meetings go." For many institutions, such governance meetings can be assumed to be long, not very interactive, focused heavily on determining how processes work, and with the voices of a few assertive faculty members dominating the conversation.

We set this context in order to highlight two things. First, the gap between "how governance works" in many institutions and "what academics come prepared to do" is yawning. Second, in our experience, simply knowing how things work is not the same as being able to do things within that structure. Last, many governance structures simply do not work that well, and shared governance work requires accomplishing points one and two before any individual or group can take the steps to make change happen in ways that ensure full and robust functioning of a governance process.

We address this issue by noting that the premise that service is unpaid labor is a false construct to begin with. Service is part of most contractual full-time positions in higher education (we will talk about the erosion of such positions at length). As a contractual expectation it is, by nature, paid labor. Research by Jones, et al. (2017) showed that, in their scan of Research 1 institutions, fully 85% of academic senates/councils had structured eligibility for full-time, non-tenure-line faculty to participate in elected shared governance (513), though it should be noted that "nearly 90% of highest research doctoral universities excluded part-time NTTF from faculty senate eligibility" (516). Certainly, the ratios are different in two-year colleges and less-selective four-year or comprehensive universities, which readers should investigate and consider in their own institutional context.

What we argue in this book is that service is a crucial part of having functional institutions and disciplinary organizations; it is sometimes actively discouraged because it is not intellectual labor that we are taught to value. We argue that doing minimal or no service work is an employment strategy that only a privileged few can make. And if these privileged few are being mentored away from doing service work, they are being told, quite simply, not to do their job. When they do not do their job, they leave colleagues, usually white women and people of color, to pick up their slack (see June 2018; Flaherty, "Undue Burden" 2019; Kezar, et al. 2021).

LOCATING OUR IDENTITIES: THE AUTHORS

Holly has two decades of experience in governance and institutional service work across multiple states and institutions. She has chaired committees on assessment, writing programs, general education, the status of women, promotion and tenure, bylaws, accreditation, inclusive excellence, dual credit courses, online program development, and many other topics. She has a decade of service in faculty senates, with three of those years as chair of her previous institution's senate during a turbulent set of years involving board of regents–level changes to tenure and shared governance. She spent six years as chair of a multidisciplinary and multicampus women's and gender studies program, was a senate executive committee member, and co-coordinated the reaccreditation self-study for her institution over a two-year process. She has also served as a senate member at her current institution. She has worked at two-year colleges, regional comprehensives, and research-intensive institutions. She has held both adjunct and full-time faculty positions, with eight years of professional service at the national level through several national disciplinary organizations, most specifically as chair of multiple task forces and committees for the Two-Year College English Association and the Conference on College Composition and Communication.

Kirsti has 22 years of shared governance experience, 7 in a right-to-work state, and 15 in a union environment. She has served as a campus college representative, on curriculum committees at the department, college, and university levels, chaired an institutional assessment committee, was on the leadership team for accreditation, served as a statewide representative for the faculty union, and trained as a grievance officer. She chaired an international conference, sits on three editorial and review boards, chaired and cochaired multiple feminist committees and commissions on the status of women in the profession at two institutions.

Joanne has 18 years of shared governance and institutional service experience, with 10 years' experience coordinating a statewide open-access literacy program and mentoring two-year college instructors. She has won two national program excellence awards and has 10 years' experience chairing a student-led campus multicultural resource center. She serves as an elected leader of a disciplinary organization and participates in three related national executive committees. She has chaired a statewide academic policy committee, served on a statewide committee that developed policies for contingent faculty and academic staff, chaired two national professional conferences, served on a state system placement committee, served on three editorial boards, chaired national task forces and committees, and served on three national disciplinary research committees. At her community college, she currently coordinates the integrated reading and writing program through a shared governance committee; serves on institutional placement and equity committees, cofacilitates an inclusive teaching practices faculty development program, leads a project to develop a writing literacy support program, and cochairs a departmental assessment committee.

We share these condensed service resumes to highlight the breadth of our backgrounds in places, topics, and roles while also outlining the varied ways in which faculty engage in higher education governance and service. At the same time, we know that our own positionalities as white, cis, women faculty within particular institutional contexts have limits. We have sought to represent additional perspectives throughout this handbook by integrating what we call vignettes, insights from faculty across different identities, positions, and institutions.

We address this issue from a feminist and equity perspective. Holly wrote a recent blog post that talks about the significance and value of service work, "Service, Activism, and Writing Teachers," which argues that some of the most important equity work to be done must take place through service and governance. For example, advocating for changing the rewards attached to particular kinds of work typically involves revising promotion and tenure or merit evaluation documents, which is the responsibility of governance groups. Other examples include spelling out service expectations, processes for managing the curriculum, procedures for assigning courses, or the criteria by which teaching is evaluated. All of these activities that create equity and transparency are discussed and decided *through shared governance, committees, and service.* Which is to say service is an avenue for change and for having a say and stake in our working conditions, particularly in contexts where union membership is not the way that employment conditions are established.

In the context of feminist equity, we know that BIPOC, LGBTQIA+ individuals, and women take on a disproportionate responsibility for the work of managing the institution and the greater good of colleagues and students. Identity is central to the principles we will discuss in this book. But the crux of our argument is this: people simply need to care AND do their fair share. One point that we will emphasize throughout the book is that service and governance responsibilities are a social justice issue. It is no accident that the majority of the voices who advise against doing "unpaid labor" tend to be white men at selective institutions or other groups with a variety of class, race, and gender privilege that enables them to opt out of unglamorous but essential responsibilities. The loudest voices railing against doing service work are the ones who see it as having no pay off, literally or figuratively. But it bears repeating that if an individual has a contract at an institution, service work of this kind is part of what they are paid to do. This dismissive attitude emerges from the privilege of occupying a system designed to work for them and people like them. This book directly pushes back against those underlying, implicit expectations about the value and status of governance and service and will offer a game plan for doing the work (and holding others accountable for doing it).

LOCATING THE CONVERSATION

Myths about higher education abound. The myth of mobility (Cole, et al. 2017), for example, is the notion that most faculty are positioned to negotiate for new and higher status positions on the tenure line. Though this may have been true in the past (if it ever was), today's faculty member is most likely to be working off the tenure track and in a teaching-intensive institution, not a member of the "academic star system" where the portable currency of research, grants, and publications are bargaining chips for higher teaching loads and more money.

Likewise, the idea that "shared governance" is embedded in and available to most college instructors is accurate in some areas and less accurate in others. For example, Derek Bok, in 2013, notes that "In two large surveys of professors asking identical questions about governance in 1970 and again in 2001, the results indicated that faculty influence had in fact increased substantially over this period—most obviously in matters of teaching, curriculum, and faculty appointments, but even with respect to such sensitive questions as choosing deans and setting salary scales" (Bok 20). The most recent (2021) version of the same survey

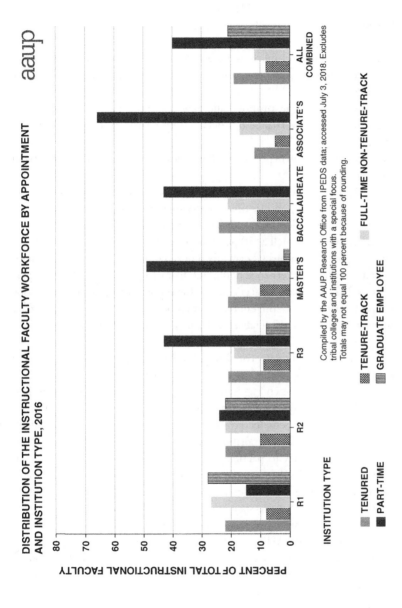

Figure 1.2 Distribution of the instructional faculty workforce by appointment and institution type, American Association of University Professors, 2020.

surfaces some new insights. As the American Association of University Professors (AAUP) data report, there was an increase in the number of institutions that have a faculty senate or council as a governing body, reaching 90% (Flaherty, "Faculty Governance" 2021). The 2021 AAUP Report on Shared Governance concluded the following based on a national survey of shared governance leaders:

- "two-thirds of institutions now have a formal mechanism for direct faculty communication with the governing board, such as through a faculty senate or a joint committee"
- "the percentage of institutions allowing part-time faculty members full participation in governance has declined by nearly six percentage points since 2001"
- "faculty participation in presidential searches also declined, from 94 percent to 88 percent"
- "the 2021 survey found that at 76 percent of four-year institutions with a senate or council, all full-time faculty members on contingent appointments can vote in elections, and that contingent faculty members can serve on the senate or council at 70 percent of institutions"
- "the share of institutions where only tenured or tenure-track faculty members may vote in governance bodies fell from 17 percent in 2001 to 7 percent by 2021, suggesting, according to the report, 'that policies supporting the participation of contingent faculty members in governance have become more widely adopted'" (Flaherty, "Faculty Governance").

A summary of this snapshot is provided in the AAUP report, which notes that faculty authority persists at the level that has been deemed acceptable by the organization in the areas of curriculum, teaching assignments, faculty searches, selection of department chairs, and promotion and tenure. Tiege notes that, in fact, faculty authority has actually *increased* in these areas. In the areas of budget, determining approval of faculty positions, and facilities, "the faculty has little or no meaningful opportunity to participate" (93–94) and, as Tiege observes, this has decreased since the 2001 survey. We prefer in this book to focus on the highly significant number of areas that academic workers—faculty, often whether tenure-line or non-tenure line—have to shape many areas of their labor conditions.

At the same time, shared governance and service do not exist in a vacuum. Even as organizations like AAUP work to define the realities of shared governance within institutions, the type of institution in which one works can and does shape the influence and status one has, just as the kind of position an individual faculty or staff member has can dictate how they are able to participate in this part of the academic portfolio of job tasks. For example, the COVID-19 pandemic offered an opportunity for AAUP to update its shared governance data collection, gathering results on how much influence faculty had during the transitions necessitated by the pandemic. The survey's goal was to understand how influential faculty had been in decision making at their institutions both before and after the onset of the COVID-19 pandemic. While the greatest increase was in the category of "not influential at all" (10%, from 5%), the next most common response was "extremely influential," which was 6.6%, from 5.4% ("Survey Data"). Though about a quarter of respondents said that faculty had less influence during this time, a strong majority reported there was no change in influence (61.7%); to speak to disparate influence, though, the data noted that "There were differences in reported levels of increased influence by institutional type: at doctoral institutions, 24.2 percent of governance leaders reported increased influence, compared to 14 percent at master's institutions and 7.1 percent at bachelor's institutions" ("Survey Data" 2021). It should also be noted that two-year colleges and associate's degree institutions are not even represented in either of the shared governance surveys conducted by the AAUP.

In this way, an institutional type can shape how any given institution extends governance rights and responsibilities to its faculty and staff, and the individual positionalities and identities of those faculty and staff shape their experience in these sites. As rhetoric scholars Ore, Wieser, and Cedillo (2021) write:

> Many of us came to this space idealizing the academy as the bastion of liberal thought in America, but we didn't realize that thinking is just that—thinking. Much of what the academy supports in theory is thwarted in practice precisely because racism IS systemic, and the academy is not as divorced from the rest of society as the "Ivory Tower" metaphor would have us think—unless we totally rethink that metaphor to realize that White Privilege is the structure that has upheld it all along.
>
> (602)

It is difficult to ameliorate let alone redress the exclusionary spaces that are central to how colleges and universities operate; and yet, without critical and reflective approaches to the work of service and governance, incremental cultural and practical changes will only serve as Band-Aids.

Identities other than race and ethnicity also shape the level of influence and experience that academic workers will have navigating spaces outside the classroom. These include but are not limited to gender identity, dis/ability, sexuality, veteran status, religious identity, and more. For example, as the *Harvard Business Review* recently reported, "women in leadership positions are perceived just as—if not more—competent as their male counterparts," noting that on the 19 indicators, women "were thought to be more effective in 84% of the competencies that we most frequently measure" (Zenger and Folkman 2019). These include measures such as initiative, resilience, self-development, integrity, bold leadership, and a number of others. Despite such empirical findings,

"Only 4.9% of Fortune 500 CEOs and 2% of S&P 500 CEOs are women. And those numbers are declining globally." The authors note the influence of stereotypes, cultural biases that influence hiring and promotion decisions, though they do not acknowledge some of the material conditions (particularly in the United States) that can influence women's ability to engage in leadership roles, such as poor support for caregiving responsibilities and gendered wage gaps. Empirical research by Misra, et al. (2021) demonstrate that women of color have high mentoring workloads and engage more substantively in diversity work, which is simultaneously undervalued by institutions (361).

When it comes to shared governance and service, which requires participation in often uneven or unscheduled ways as well as work outside of structured meetings (if done right), these inequities can become intensified. A search committee chair will not only organize meeting agendas but also perhaps manage documents, communicate with candidates, and engage in particular forms of reporting required by the institution; an effective senator or union representative will not only attend meetings but also prepare in advance for them, and inform those stakeholders about the consequences of past or upcoming decisions. This is to say, there is considerable discretion about *how* to take on this work, and investment in the outcome of it can incentivize already marginalized or underrepresented members to take on a disproportionate amount of labor. There are also differential consequences for refusing to take on such labor, as well, as O'Meara, Kuveava, and Nyunt observe in "Asked More Often: Gender Differences in Faculty Workload in Research Universities and the Work Interactions that Shape Them" (2017): "Women received more requests to be engaged in teaching, student advising, and professional service than men. Thus, women began with more time allocated to non-research-related activities and then received more requests to be engaged in even more of this work" (1177). Curcio and Lynch (2017) in "Addressing Social Loafing in Committees" also point out that the willingness of some faculty (the number of whom have committee service as part of their employment obligation continues to shrink) to serve and serve well is an "unsustainable model." They explain: "Moreover, those who have been willing to step up in the past, if now overburdened by even more unrewarded work and with even less time for scholarly endeavors [*or teaching responsibilities, as relevant to the faculty position and institution type, emphasis added*] may rationally decide to withdraw from participating in a system that penalties them for their institutional citizenship" (248). So many faculty, however, especially those who have committed to the success of particular kinds of students or initiatives in their institutions know that "just saying no" or "saying no more" (the social and professional effects of which are documented by Hack, et al. 2013 among others) know that simply dropping an activity has consequences for others beyond their own curriculum vita.

We provide this data and context to acknowledge that expectations and effort around participation in this part of academic work are variable. Whenever possible, we acknowledge how positionalities and identities shape how any given academic worker might navigate a particular situation. We also want to call on those allies for equity with varieties of privilege salient to a particular situation to step up and do not just their fair share but *more* when possible. We cannot simply continue to leave the low-status but crucial activity of making academia equitable to those who have been routinely oppressed. Whether it is white privilege, male privilege, institutional privilege, tenure privilege, able-bodied privilege, or some other unearned advantage, nearly every reader has some salient characteristic where they can show up for justice in the academy.

Such material contexts strongly influence who and how academic workers can participate in service and governance. The practical working conditions for faculty in higher education vary, and have evolved since the zenith of college and university hiring in the 1960s. According to results prepared by the AAUP research department based on Integrated Postsecondary Education Data System (IPEDS) data, in 2019, 10.5% of appointments were tenure track, 26.5% tenured, 20% full-time contingent, and 43% part-time contingent (Tiede 2022). And yet, numbers across graduate programs continue to grow. Students are still encouraged to attend college as a way to enhance their opportunities and future financial security.

To address the real threats to higher education's access and success (austerity, casualization of labor, corporate online contractors and textbook companies that shape the curriculum through corporate lenses, and more), collective effort that draws from the power and authority already vested in faculty is a path toward maintaining the values of higher education: free inquiry, pursuit of knowledge, building human capacity and realized potential, and the other traditions of the academy that are increasingly the primary way to a middle-class lifestyle and engaged electorate in the 21st century. This is the kind of service and governance we address in this book.

INTRODUCTION TO CONTRIBUTORS

We recognize based on our positions and identities that our stories and experiences simply cannot match the stories and experiences of the vastly diverse members of the professoriate. As such, we have sought to include the voices of contributors from a broad range of institutions and backgrounds to provide their own stories about engaging in governance work.

- **Kathryn Blakeman** is secretary to the Common Council at the University of Wisconsin-Stevens Point. A native of Northern Virginia she is well versed in government and bureaucracy. She has worked at several universities, including the University of Virginia and Baylor University.
- **David M. Grant** is an associate professor in the department of Languages & Literatures at the University of Northern Iowa. He is coeditor of *Decolonial Conversations in Posthuman and New Material Rhetorics* (University

of Pittsburgh) and is currently exploring the rhetorical role of consideration in working across incommensurability and difference.

- **Sheila Amin Gutiérrez de Piñeres** is dean of the Burnett Honors College at the University of Central Florida and professor of public administration. Dr. Piñeres joined UCF in May of 2018 following her role as
executive vice president for academic affairs and dean of faculty at Austin
College in Sherman, Texas. She is a founding member of the University of
Texas System Academy of Distinguished Teachers.

- **Marjorie Hass** is the first female president in the 65-year history of The Council
of Independent Colleges. Hass began her tenure as president of Rhodes College
in 2017. Previously, she was president of Austin College for eight years and provost of Muhlenberg College (Pennsylvania), where she spent more than 16 years
as a member of the philosophy faculty. She is the author of *A Leadership Guide for
Women in Higher Education* (2021). Hass earned bachelor's, master's, and doctoral degrees in philosophy from the University of Illinois at Urbana-Champaign.

- **Kate McCahill** is assistant professor of English at the Santa Fe Community College, and serves as faculty advisor for the *Santa Fe Literary Review,*
SFCC's nationally and internationally distributed literary magazine. McCahill is an alumna of Wellesley College (BA) and the Vermont College
of Fine Arts (MFA, Writing). Her book is *Patagonian Road: A Year Alone
Through Latin America*. Her fiction, poetry, and nonfiction have been published in *Vox, The Millions,* and elsewhere.

- **Seth Kahn** is a professor of English at West Chester University of Pennsylvania, where he teaches writing and rhetoric courses, does union work for
the Association of PA State College and University Faculties, and researches
academic labor organizing. Recent publications include "From Activism to
Organizing; from Caring to Care Work" with Amy Lynch-Biniek (*Labor Studies Journal*, July 2022); "What Do We Mean by Academic Labor (in Rhetorical Studies)?" with Amy Pason (*Rhetoric and Public Affairs*, July 2021); and "We
Value Teaching Too Much to Keep Devaluing It" (*College English*, July 2020).

- **Isaac Kamola** is an associate professor of political science at Trinity College,
Hartford, Connecticut. His research examines critical globalization studies, the
political economy of higher education, and African anticolonial theory. He is
author of *Free Speech and Koch Money: Manufacturing a Campus Culture War* (with
Ralph Wilson, 2021) and *Making the World Global: US Universities and the Production of the Global Imaginary* (2019). He is the creator of Faculty First Responders,
a program that monitors right-wing attacks on academics and provides resources
to help faculty members and administrators respond to manufactured outrage.

- **Nerissa Nelson** is a librarian/professor at the University of Wisconsin-
Stevens Point. She just completed her two-year term as chair of the campus
governance body, the Common Council, and has spent 20 years in various
shared governance roles.

- **Molly Secor**, PhD, RN, FSAHM is the associate dean for research and professor in the Mark and Robyn Jones College of Nursing at Montana State University. Prior to this role, she served on the School of Nursing and Department of Health faculty at North Dakota State University. While there she served as faculty senate president, cochaired the university Strategic Planning Committee and was active in other faculty governance leadership roles. In recognition of her leadership and contributions in the field of adolescent health research, she is a fellow in the Society for Adolescent Health and Medicine.

CHAPTER BY CHAPTER OVERVIEW

The chapters in this book walk through of the most basic and most important aspects of shared governance. We begin by defining what shared governance actually is, as that can be opaque in its own right. Chapter 2, "Shared Governance: An Overview," offers a series of clear and practical definitions of what shared governance looks like in different environments, with an overview of the principles and values of shared governance serving as the foundation. Following that definition is a clear explanation of some typical variations, including the differences between institutional governance structures. For example, some institutions follow a traditional faculty senate model, while others might include an integrated senate with faculty, staff, and students, and still others rely on a formal union as a bargaining unit for working conditions while simultaneously employing a senate or governance group for discussion of institutional policies that fall outside workload.

In Chapter 3, "Doing Governance Work," we explore what this kind of work actually looks like and how to do it. The principled practicalities of doing governance work tend to stymie even the most experienced person working in higher education because there are not only so many different ways to do shared governance work, but also so many types of such work. Distinguishing between the kinds of activities and activism required by those who are serving in leadership roles and those who may be new to governance, this chapter offers strategies for involvement, representation, gathering and disseminating information, and the importance of aligning governance work with individual areas of expertise and competence. We highlight strategies for figuring out how to get work done, and how to collaborate across groups. We also delve into the often-invisible labor of shared governance, and the complications of what is invisible and what institutions or workers in those institutions want to remain invisible. If anything, the ongoing pandemic has exposed the fault lines that exist in these processes, which can ultimately be productive, if work is done to remedy those fault lines, rather than cover them back up.

In Chapter 4, "Developing Effective, Equitable, and Transparent Policies," we dig into the most technical aspects of shared governance—policy. Policies guide and drive institutions but they are also created by members of that institution with specific and evolving contexts that include extra-institutional stakeholders. Strategies for creating equitable policies within an institution, department, program, or disciplinary organization are embedded in multiplexity but, when procedures at institutions are well-understood, policy work can be a smooth process. Effective, carefully designed policies provide a framework for shared values, transparent decision making, accountable leadership, and functional collaboration within and across units in higher education. This chapter provides both principles and strategies for effective policy development processes, emphasizing policy development work as an inclusive and recursive process that accounts for the needs of diverse stakeholders.

In Chapter 5, "Engaging in Shared Governance Work to Support Educational Opportunities," we discuss strategies for participating in shared governance work that closes educational opportunity gaps for students within the constraints and resources of varied local higher education contexts. Whether one works at a selective private liberal arts college, an elite Ivy League, or an open-admissions community college, campuses have an obligation to support equitable outcomes for students from diverse cultural, racial, social, linguistic, and educational backgrounds. This chapter offers flexible strategies for developing equity-minded and student-centered shared governance practices that are specific to a campus mission and student population.

In Chapter 6, "Strategies for Implementing and Assessing Change," we discuss strategies for monitoring and assessing the implementation of policies, new initiatives, and other institutional changes. We describe strategies for developing assessment plans that create ethical and transparent processes for implementing a change, determining its outcomes, and working toward ensuring that changes don't create inequities for students and employees.

Chapter 7, "Conflicts in Shared Governance and Policy Development," focuses on conflict, one of the hallmarks of any organizing effort, whether it be internal or external. With an introduction that frames how policies interact with conflict and conflict resolution, this chapter outlines change-making practices, managing conflict indirect or backchannel environments, responding to crises, and the ways in which it is vital to maintain integrity through the process. We describe how conflict can foment positive change but it must be treated with care, compassion, and respect.

Chapter 8, "Conclusion: Collective Action, Individual Effort," concludes the book by situating shared governance and service within the larger national higher education landscape. We summarize how to participate effectively in your organization, what the responsibilities are that accompany participation, and how to create an environment that is responsive, proactive, and ready to meet the demands and changes facing higher education in the United States.

HOW TO USE THIS BOOK

Each chapter of this book focuses on key dimensions of shared governance and service within various sectors of the academy. Chapters include vignettes from contributors to add a scenario or set of insights to the topic, and each chapter closes with brief activities for individuals or groups and application exercises, and questions for consideration. Each chapter begins and ends with questions that are meant to function as heuristics. We ask the first set of questions to provide a contextual scope for the chapter. We ask the second set to prompt readers to consider how their thoughts might have changed and how they might apply shared governance principles to their own higher education situations. Readers can use the chapter questions and application activities to engage in reading circles and initiate discussions with colleagues about how to assess existing governance practices in their institutions or programs and plan for changes that create more effective, equitable, and inclusive governance processes. The book and accompanying activities can also be used in graduate programs and courses to prepare students for higher education service and governance work. The transfer of knowledge to different contexts requires recursive engagement and reflection—we hope to prompt that activity in the formatting of these chapters. Last, the book does not need to be read in sequence or as a whole. We have structured the text so that readers can identify a stage or key issue that they are facing and use that chapter as a free-standing guide.

WORKS CITED

Bok, Derek. "What Is Shared Governance." *Trusteeship Magazine*, Sept.–Oct. 2013, pp. 19–23.

Cole, Kirsti, Holly Hassel, and Eileen Schell. "Remodeling Shared Governance: Feminist Decision-Making and Resistance to Academic Neoliberalism" by Kirsti Cole, Holly Hassel, and Eileen Schell." In Surviving Sexism in Academia: Strategies for Feminist Leadership. Routledge, 2017.

Curcio, Andrea, and Mary Lynch. "Addressing Social Loafing on Faculty Committees." *Journal of Legal Education*, vol. 67, no. 1, Autumn 2017, pp. 242–62.

Flaherty, Colleen. "Undue Burden." *InsideHigherEd*, 4 June 2019, www.insidehighered.com/news/2019/06/04/whos-doing-heavy-lifting-terms-diversity-and-inclusion-work.

———. "Faculty Governance: What the Data Say." *InsideHigherEd*, 14 Oct. 2021, www.insidehighered.com/news/2021/10/14/more-data-faculty-role-shared-governance.

Furstenberg, Francois. "The Era of Artificial Scarcity: Administrators Have Rushed to Embrace Austerity Measures. The Faculty Should Call Their Bluff." *The Chronicle of Higher Education*, 8 Apr. 2021, www.chronicle.com/article/the-era-of-artificial-scarcity.

Fusarelli, Lance. "If I Only Knew: Reflections for New Faculty Members." *InsideHigherEd*. 6 August 2020. https://www.insidehighered.com/advice/2020/08/06/seasoned-faculty-member-reflects-what-he-wishes-hed-known-new-professor-opinion.

Hack, Tay, et al. "Warmth Trumps Competence in Evaluations of Both Ingroup and Outgroup." *International Journal of Science, Commerce, and Humanities*, vol. 1, no. 6, Sept. 2013, pp. 99–105.

Jaschik, Scott. "Good Work if You Can Get It: Author Discusses His New Book on Graduate School and Academic Careers." *InsideHigherEd*. 30 April 2020. https://www.insidehighered.com/news/2020/05/01/author-discusses-his-book-graduate-school-and-academic-careers.

Jimenez, Miguel F., et al. "Underrepresented Faculty Play a Disproportionate Role in Advancing Diversity and Inclusion." *Nature Ecology & Evolution*, June 2019, https://doi.org/10.1038/s41559-019-0911-5.

Jones, Willis, et al. "Shared Governance Among the New Majority: Non-Tenure Track Faculty Eligibility for Election to University Faculty Senates." *Innovative Higher Education*, vol. 42, 2017, pp. 505–19.

June, Audrey Williams. "Professors Are the Likeliest Mentors for Students, Except Those Who Aren't White." *The Chronicle of Higher Education*, 30 Oct. 2018, www.chronicle.com/article/Professors-Are-the-Likeliest/244955.

Kezar, Adrianna, et al. *Shared Equity Leadership: Making Equity Everyone's Work*. American Council on Education, 2021, www.acenet.edu/Documents/Shared-Equity-Leadership-Work.pdf.

Marcus, Jon. "The Nation's Next Union Battlefield May Be on Campus." *The Washington Post*, 28 Mar. 2022, www.proquest.com/newspapers/nations-next-union-battlefield-may-be-on-campus/docview/2643851999/se-2.

Misra, Joya, et al. "Gendered and Racialized Perceptions of Faculty Workloads." *Gender and Society*, vol. 35, no. 3, June 2021, pp. 358–94.

O'Meara, KerryAnn, et al. "Asked More Often: Gender Differences in Faculty Workload in Research Universities and the Work Interactions That Shape Them." *American Educational Research Journal*, vol. 54, no. 6, Dec. 2017, pp. 1154–86.

Ore, Ursula, et al. "Symposium: Diversity Is Not Justice: Working Toward Radical Transformation and Racial Equity in the Discipline." *College Composition and Communication*, vol. 72, no. 4, June, 2021, pp. 601–20, https://library.ncte.org/journals/ccc/issues/v72-4/31443.

Peck, Janice. "(Neo)Liberalism, Popular Media, and the Political Struggle for the Future of US Public Education." *European Journal of Communication*, vol. 30, no. 5, Oct. 2015, pp. 587–603, https://doi.org/10.1177/0267323115597853.

Stein, Mark. "The End of Faculty Tenure." *Inside Higher Ed*, 25 Apr. 2022, www.insidehighered.com/views/2022/04/25/declining-tenure-density-alarming-opinion.

"Survey Data on the Impact of the Pandemic on Shared Governance." *American Association of University Professors*, 2021, www.aaup.org/report/survey-data-impact-pandemic-shared-governance.

Tiede, Hans-Joerg. "The 2022 AAUP Survey of Tenure Practices." *American Association of University Professors*, May 2022, www.aaup.org/file/2022_AAUP_Survey_of_Tenure_Practices.pdf.

Zenger, Jack, and Joseph Folkman. "Research: Women Score Higher Than Men in Most Leadership Skills." *Harvard Business Review*, 25 June 2019, https://hbr.org/2019/06/research-women-score-higher-than-men-in-most-leadership-skills?.

Chapter 2

Shared Governance
An Overview

GUIDING QUESTIONS

1. What are the "need-to-know" issues for academic workers who begin to participate in service and governance?
2. What are important differences between institution types that shape the governance culture at those campuses?
3. What are the major barriers to effective service and governance in higher education, particularly those factors that are within the control of those bodies?
4. What barriers are out of the control of individual committees or governing bodies at a campus level?
5. Why are communication and transparency essential for effective leadership and shared governance?
6. How might difficult shared governance conversations bring about change?

WHAT IS SHARED GOVERNANCE?

The former president of Harvard, Derek Bok, opens a 2013 article aimed at an audience of governing boards with the following claim: "Shared governance has few defenders, or at least, few people who support it publicly" (19). Bok observes that some administrators, college presidents, and boards find shared governance to be slow and unable to respond to urgent situations, touting the need to be "nimble" and "agile" over being deliberative or strategic. In contrast, faculty and staff may believe that shared governance operates as window dressing, with committee and senate work taking up many hours of research, report writing, and meetings, only to result in a field report or an ignored request. The goal of this

DOI: 10.4324/9781003257974-2

19

Statement of Policy

We have examined the manifesto
And established the following:
The decision to eliminate
Every third administrator
Cannot be taken seriously.
(The entire governing body
Is two.)
Likewise the desire to relocate
Displaced members of the
Black community.
(The university has no
Building fund.)
Women's rights is a questionable demand.
(Those demonstrating are known lesbians.)
However,
Capitulation of the administrative offices
To the dissident factions
Will be effected
Only too gladly.
(There are no toilet facilities.)
In summation, therefore,
The ruling powers
After due deliberation,
Yield.

Martin S. Gilderman
Temple University

Figure 2.1 Poem from the AAUP Bulletin, Spring 1970.

chapter is not to debate how or whether shared governance is broken, but rather to define it, to outline how it can work in functional and meaningful ways, and to provide strategies for effecting change through governance and service work. Because whether or not shared governance is broken, it is absolutely necessary for functional and equitable work in higher education.

What most people in academia consider to be the gold standard for defining shared governance is the "Statement on Government of Colleges and Universities," issued by the American Association of University Professors (AAUP) in 1966:

The variety and complexity of the tasks performed by institutions of higher education produce an inescapable interdependence among governing board, administration, faculty, students, and others. The relationship calls for adequate communication among these components, and full opportunity for appropriate joint planning and effort.

This statement builds on the previous foundational definitions of other pillars of higher education, academic freedom and tenure, established by the AAUP's "1940 Statement of Principles on Academic Freedom and Tenure" and many additional documents from the flagship organization that establishes professional standards for academic work.

Joint effort in an academic institution will take a variety of forms appropriate to the kinds of situations encountered. In some instances, an initial exploration or recommendation will be made by the president with consideration by the faculty at a later stage; in other instances, a first and essentially definitive recommendation will be made by the faculty, subject to the endorsement of the president and the governing board. In still others, a substantive contribution can be made when student leaders are responsibly involved in the process. Although the variety of such approaches may be wide, at least two general conclusions regarding joint effort seem clearly warranted: (1) important areas of action involve at one time or another the initiating capacity and decision-making participation of all the institutional components, and (2) differences in the weight of each voice, from one point to the next, should be determined by reference to the responsibility of each component for the particular matter at hand. As noted in the AAUP Red Book (2015), "The ideal . . . is to fuse together administration and the educational tasks of the university as respectively means and end. . . . There can be no question of claiming democracy at the cost of efficiency. The claim that, except by agencies representing the common convictions of the teaching profession, there can be no university government which is in any larger sense efficient" (115). Lack of efficiency does not translate to ineffectiveness.

Though this definition has served to emphasize the value of "joint effort" and the "initiating capacity and decision-making participation of all the institutional components" (AAUP), we, instead, read this as a useful statement of values. One of the primary challenges that all kinds of institutions face is the amorphous nature of this definition and how it is actualized in a range of situations. We know that labor practices in the academy are cyclical and economy dependent. We know that a lot has changed between 1966 and 2022, including funding models at the federal and state levels, the numbers of students enrolled in colleges and universities, the student populations that higher education serves, the overreliance on temporary faculty, and a global pandemic. The past 50 years and more are full of headline-making conflicts between faculty and presidents or chancellors, between institutions and governing boards, between students and administration, between administration and state legislators.

The watchword of "shared governance" appears regularly as a part of the stories told about these conflicts, but we understand these conflicts as emerging because of the ambiguity in the boundaries set out for "the responsibility of each component for the particular matter at hand" (AAUP Statement on Government of Colleges and Universities, 1966, 2a.2). Within institutions of higher education, stakeholders often don't have any agreement on exactly who—students, faculty, staff, administration, a governing board—is responsible for what. Most institutions can agree that faculty are responsible for curricular matters, and yet multiple instances in state systems or individual institutions have centered on an external or internal administrative entity trying to influence what can or cannot be taught. For example, when the University of Wisconsin system changed tenure policies (the policy on Program Discontinuance and the policy on Post-Tenure review), a significant part of the discussion focused on whether or not the revised board policy would have language that allowed for program discontinuance for either educational or fiscal reasons. The process was fraught because no one had primary responsibility for such decisions, and the boundaries between stakeholders were contested.

The Association of Governing Boards and Universities offers another definition of shared governance, as "the process by which various constituents (traditionally governing boards, senior administration, and faculty; possibly also staff, students, or others) contribute to decision making related to college or university policy and procedure" ("Shared Governance," 2017, 3). And in *The Will to Govern Well: Knowledge, Trust, and Nimbleness* (2010), the Center for Association Leadership asserts that "governance in associations refers to the decision-making units of the organization and the relative powers, authorities, and responsibilities that each possesses as well as to the composition of each unit and how individuals are selected to participate in each" (3). All of these definitions capture at least some dimensions of the underpinnings of effective organizational and institutional governance.

For the purposes of this book, we offer a definition of shared governance as a principle, but also a recommendation for what specific institutions or groups should keep in mind when determining the boundaries, responsibilities, and processes that uphold that definition. Shared governance in contemporary higher education depends upon the collaboration and respect between the stakeholder groups of the university or college. It includes students, staff, faculty, administrators, and governing boards. The purview of shared governance is normally explained in the governing documents (bylaws, constitutions, mission statements, and board policy) of a given institution or system. The effective and responsive functioning of the institution requires that the roles of each group are defined, as are boundaries around who is responsible for what. However, that also means naming and carefully attending to those contested and collaborative spaces where each stakeholder groups' interests converge. Those spaces, in particular, are the ones that require intentional planning for communication and negotiation if shared governance is to be effective. We define shared governance as: *a collaborative decision-making process that meaningfully involves all groups with a stake in decisions that affect their educational and work environment.*

Collaboration is necessary in any shared governance situation, but it is not sufficient. Our definition applies to all shared governance situations, but we believe that transparency is also a value that is essential to best practices of shared governance. Transparency is an ideal that we embrace and hold; however, it is not central to or a guarantee of shared governance. Transparency makes shared governance more equitable and inclusive. Shared governance happens in environments that are not transparent, but those situations are far more difficult to navigate, and typically far less equitable and inclusive.

Operationalizing this definition also requires a clear understanding of what shared governance is not:

- A decision made by a single group or stakeholder, especially one that affects others
- Informing stakeholders about decisions without an opportunity for feedback or a voice in the decision-making process
- Autocratic imposition of a decision that affects others onto groups perceived to have lower status or stature within the university
- A set of tasks or work that takes place outside a governance body that is then imposed and imported on a governing group, with the expectation that it will be automatically approved
- A way for administrators to justify decisions as consultative that are actually autocratic
- Faculty, staff, or students engaging in resistance and feet-dragging in the name of academic freedom
- A quick fix
- A waste of time
- An ego boost
- A site for temper tantrums
- Less valuable than teaching or research
- A way for one stakeholder to get their way or win

Shared governance can be nimble. Shared governance can respond quickly. Shared governance can meet the needs of the stakeholders, but only if the goal of the individuals involved is respectful and productive compromise through clearly articulated decision-making processes.

We want to emphasize that shared governance goes beyond what might be a traditional definition or assumption that governance equals college and university senates or councils. In fact, most of the service obligations that instructors, faculty, and staff in higher education engage in are governance work. For example, work with student groups often also requires faculty and staff to use governance principles as they mentor students in becoming leaders and working together productively. The work that staff members do on committees or in conjunction with faculty on committees or other settings also use governance principles. Committee work is governance and also service. Staff councils are also governance. Union bodies are also governance. Governance happens in multiple locations, in multiple ways.

In addition to the slipperiness and imprecision of what shared governance is and who participates in it, we often see a gap between what the ideals of shared governance are and how it is operationalized. There is very little or no formal training that introduces most faculty, staff, or students to the work of serving in committees or in councils and senates. Governance bodies require an understanding of practices for doing distributed labor, facilitating conversation, and setting priorities. This is often not a part of graduate training or employee orientations.

In many institutions, there tends to be an assumption that committee work, service, and governance can simply be done. Because of this assumption, a kind of lore is sometimes developed and handed down by the most senior member of a group. This kind of legacy leads people to say things like, "That's how it's always been done," which is a false assertion that depends upon a sort of constructed self-evident process. We have been on enough dysfunctional service bodies to know that often the lore that is passed down is simply not accurate. How things have been done is not always how things should be done. Likewise, we have been on enough ineffective committees that couldn't identify goals, distribute work, figure out how to build support for actions or proposals, and communicate effectively to stakeholders. The principles in this and subsequent chapters are intended to provide both philosophical and practical recommendations for making shared governance work for everyone.

STRUCTURES OF GOVERNANCE

One of the challenges of defining governance is rooted in the range of structures that universities and community colleges have created to do this work. The varying architectures of decision-making bodies within higher education are created through different mechanisms and endowed with authority differently. In this section, we say a little about how governance structures *can* look, and why it is important to understand the operations of authority within an institution in order to have the ability to get things done within those structures.

Institutional Literacy

To frame this overview, we introduce the term *institutional literacy* to account for how to develop an understanding of governance structures, and how they are established and maintained in a local context. Though many faculty make their careers at a single institution, there has been a historical emphasis on mobility and an assumption that academic superstars will climb to newer, better positions at more prestigious institutions. In the age of neoliberalism, a lack of federal and state funding in conservative legislatures, austerity, and the COVID-19 pandemic, the myth of mobility is even more pernicious and potentially impossible (Hassel et al.).

Within this commonplace, many university faculty are committed primarily to their research and scholarship, sometimes their teaching, and their quality is measured by their attractiveness to other programs or campuses. To be attractive, they should marshal portable academic currency: articles, books, and grant funding. Leaving aside the increasingly predatory nature of journals and academic book publishers, and the nature of pay-to-play publishing that privileges faculty with money, portable academic currency is part of the myth that keeps faculty from engaging in the on-the-ground, sometimes frustrating, often unrewarding, day-to-day change work that supports student, staff, and faculty success. In such jobs (for example at high-research activity campuses with doctoral programs and low teaching loads), new faculty are actively discouraged (sometimes "protected") from participating in governance and committees. At other institution types like two-year colleges or open-access teaching-intensive campuses, however, service is valued equivalently with and potentially at a greater level than scholarship or professional activities that take place on a more disciplinary level. For new faculty at such institutions, it can be a shock to find out that the time they imagined they would spend on research and publication is actually necessarily reallocated to committees, institutional initiatives, senate participation, mentoring students, advising clubs, or other service-related tasks.

Further, a position might be designated as non-tenure-track full time or part time in which an equal but opposite proposition holds true—the primary responsibility of such instructors is teaching, and engagement in service work (committees, mentoring, advising, representative councils or senates) is presented as irrelevant to the primary work responsibility. Many institutions do not grant even the right to be represented in governance bodies to adjunct faculty (or those who are employed below a certain percentage of a full-time load), and in many institutions, those who work off the tenure track may occupy an amorphous institutional location between tenure-line faculty, academic staff, or a general "staff" title.

These rigid definitions of academic labor can be barriers to developing what we term *institutional literacy* and can shut down any significant participation from faculty in the governance of their institution. The National Council of Teachers of English offers this definition: "Literacy has always been a collection of communicative and sociocultural practices shared among communities" (2019) and we see no reason not to apply that definition with slightly more specificity to our institutions. As a site of structures, ideologies, symbolic codes, and written and unwritten processes, institutions require their own type of literacy to move through them, to understand how they operate, and to effect change within them. *Institutional literacy* is knowledge of the institutional communicative and sociocultural practices, as well as understanding of structures, processes, and policy architecture that shape a higher education institution. (See "Do the Homework," Chapter 3.)

Departments, Programs, and Colleges

In a typical public institution, governance starts at a local scale specific to a disciplinary or campus functional unit (for example, academic departments or student services units). An academic department or program might have a structure that imbues a department chair with a great level of individual autonomy to make determinations about issues such as course schedule, appointments, tenure and promotion, merit evaluation, or other areas of departmental work. By contrast, some departments have a robust set of structures that make fairly binding decisions around curriculum, promotion and tenure, or other operations. Whatever the organizational structure, we define governance groups as *any formally constituted body with jurisdictions outlined in bylaws and/or a constitution that has oversight and decision-making authority about a specific university function, policy, or process.*

We also distinguish between stakeholders, who are "any person or constituency group who is affected by university decisions" and constituencies who are "employee groups defined in an institutional document who are represented by governing bodies" (see Appendix C). In the case of local departments, these might be defined by employment class, such as tenure-line faculty, lecturers at different ranks, graduate students, academic staff, or contingent faculty, each of which may be a constituency represented on decision-making bodies (for example, a curriculum committee, executive committee that has decision-making responsibility for a department, or advisory board). Even within smaller governance structures, committees or groups are often structured in such a way that members will have a representative role; they are expected to channel the interests of those who are affected by the decisions around that group's charge and jurisdiction.

For readers, we note that it's important to take stock of what the structures of governance are within one's specific context. Some private universities and community and technical colleges have no structure for academic governance, or at least not one that has decision-making authority about major issues affecting faculty and students. They might have different names such as a "faculty association" or "academic council." Other institutions may have a union contract that is highly rigid and does not include extensive additional opportunity for organizing a governance structure beyond the parameters of the contract.

In union settings, programmatic and departmental work tends to mirror the standing structures in governing documents. At institutions like this, faculty members might divide up every few years onto committees that govern particular areas like scheduling, curriculum, department outreach, and personnel. Departments make administrative decisions about their own leadership, their curriculum, their activities, and schedules, as well as the initial processes in hiring, promotion, and tenure, but all of those decisions are subject to approval through a union-mandated process.

Institutions

Institutional bodies operate at a level beyond a department or unit (like a disciplinary department or an office on campus). They include cross-institutional representation, and these groups are most typically what we might understand as representative bodies, such as a college senate, council, or faculty union. They operate much like some legislative groups in a political system, with defined numbers and types of representatives, diversification rules about who can and should serve, and terms of service. They are largely elected, except in the case that "ex officio" membership has been determined or an administrative appointment is made. For example, someone in a particular role on campus whose expertise is seen as relevant to the work of a governance group can be part of the group in order to provide necessary information. After an individual in a position has fulfilled their term of appointment, they sometimes move to ex officio status within a group to support a transition to new leadership. Shared governance at an institutional level can be any group, elected or appointed, with representation from across a wide range of units on campus. For example, a senate might have a committee focused on the status of women, general education, curriculum, faculty affairs, or appeals and grievances. Those committees include representation from groups that have been determined to have a stake in their outcomes. Their processes are defined by bylaws or a constitution (each of these with their own rhetorical function; see Gindlesparger).

College governance (for institutions that are organized in this way) has similar structures: committees are often organized to *represent* the interests of people who are elected or appointed to serve them (whether that's a tenure review committee or a policy revision committee). In this way, even college and department-level governance groups operate in a model of shared governance in which they have a stated jurisdiction, set of responsibilities, and constituency-representation function.

The governance group that is most often associated with shared governance is the elected academic senate or council (sometimes divided into constituency groups like faculty, staff, and students, sometimes a unified senate with different representative bodies within it). Administrators typically don't have voting responsibilities in institutional governance groups like senates or councils because they either hold a decision-making role beyond the responsibilities of senates or councils (and as such do not need to have their interests represented within the group) or, in some cases, their priorities may be unaligned with faculty priorities. However, there can be committees within institutions that would be considered part of shared governance and may or may not have voting representation from campus leaders in administrative positions (for example, around advising, placement testing, curriculum committees, etc.).

27

It is more than common for management not to be included in union/worker decision making. This holds true in higher education. Miller, Smith, and Nadler in "Debate and Discourse: The Role of the Faculty Senate on the Modern American Campus," (2016) in their review and analysis of 10 university senate minutes, observe that:

> Faculty governance units, typically referred to as academic or faculty "senates" or "councils," generally function on a model of representative democracy, although their structures and practices vary greatly. Some institutions make use of a formal election, with strict regulations on who can vote and what can be spent on campaign materials. Other institutions make use of rosters of faculty signatures, where a faculty member can create an independent constituency by garnering a set number of faculty signatures. Some allow for part-time faculty representation, while others limit participation to those who hold full time, tenure-track positions.

We suggest that, to fully and meaningfully participate in (and effect change through) governance, it is essential that participants have a clear and careful understanding of the governance groups that represent them in their institution. For example, though Miller, et al. found in their research that the senate examined "had good attendance levels and worked on issues that were directly related to the faculty and academic experience of higher education," the representative function that we describe as important here was unclear: "the apportionment of senators was 1:21, yet none of the faculty senate documents analyzed indicated whether or not these senators worked to understand their constituents and represent their interests" (28). This research confirms our own institutional experiences that, without careful attention to the operational competence of institutional groups, they can become largely "a communicative tool by administrators. In almost every instance, a significant portion of the faculty senate meeting was used to present announcements or addresses from senior institutional leaders such as presidents, chancellors, and provosts" (28).

In union settings, institutional governance may have requirements like membership in the union, and may include larger union membership beyond the institution. In the Minnesota State University system, for example, the Inter-Faculty Organization (IFO) is the statewide union to which all faculty (nontenured, tenure track, and tenured) can belong if they become a dues-paying member. The statewide IFO governing body is made up of elected faculty from each university and college campus, and includes an IFO president, treasurer, and legal council. Each major campus, then, has a Faculty Association (FA), with an elected executive committee that includes the president (who serves on the IFO board), treasurer, secretary, a representative for each academic unit (college), and a faculty chairperson for each university committee (assessment and evaluation, budget, curriculum, etc.). Individuals can also be elected to serve on statewide committees or in statewide roles such as negotiator, salary equity, and government relations. Elections are held every two to four years, and all members of the FA are able to vote. The structure of the statewide and campus union bodies is governed by a constitution and bylaws that define the roles, rights, and responsibilities of participating members. In many union settings, the contract under which all faculty are hired is also overseen, in negotiation, by the faculty association.

Union settings can be more formal and more structured than some faculty senate settings because there may be state and federal laws that govern certain activities. In 2018 the U.S. Supreme Court decided *Janus v. AFSCME,* ruling that public employee unions cannot make workers pay for collective-bargaining costs because some employees claimed that leaving their union and stopping dues payments are harder than it should be. The *Janus* decision could have had catastrophic impacts on the ability for unions to function because they are largely dues dependent. In Minnesota, however, despite the Supreme Court ruling, union membership remains steady, and in some cases has seen an uptick because employees recognize the value of union protection and the participatory process. This seems to be pointing to a national trend around labor organizing (see efforts at mega-corporations like Starbucks and Amazon).

State Systems

State- or system-level structures of governance that affect public systems of higher education are often significantly less representative compared to governance within an institution. State-level governing groups can include boards of trustees, boards of regents, a state board of higher education, or even legislative committees, depending on the context and organization of university systems (including distinctions between public and private institutions, or two-year colleges and universities). These groups have tremendous influence over the shape of higher education within a given system or state, and they can be highly interventionist or fairly hands off. Some state systems also have faculty and academic staff groups with representation from each institution that advise system leaders or do statewide governance work. State systems can include additional governance groups with representation from across the state to focus on particular tasks or areas of shared interest (for example, placement, faculty development, equity and inclusion, or transfer articulation).

An important consideration to keep in mind is that state-level governance groups have specific levels of power and areas of influence. For example, some states we have worked in exert a great deal of authority over issues like credit transfer between institutions and transfer articulation agreements. Some states may have common course numbering across all public institutions in the lower division, or agreements about students' fulfillment of General Education requirements and how they transfer between all campuses within a system. Others let individual campuses make determinations about their curricular structure and processes, or they have state-level boards with only a limited role in establishing those policies. In some states, state systems have power over institutions' access to resources because they are responsible for allocating and distributing state funding. In other states, individual institutions receive their funds directly through the state government, and state systems have less control over amounts of and uses for public funding.

Unlike other governance structures, state systems can be difficult to change. First, higher education stakeholders typically have less control over what happens at a state level because power is more concentrated in system leadership and in appointed governing boards. Second, the governing documents and decision-making processes for public institutions at the statewide level are typically determined through legislation and state statutes. For instance, until 2016, the language governing the rights, responsibilities, and jurisdiction for the University of Wisconsin System was codified in state statute but was removed by an act of the legislature and relocated to Board of Regents policies—which make them much easier to change, requiring a vote of the board (18 members, 16 of whom are appointed by the governor) than the previous requirement of an action by state congress. By contrast, the state higher education system governance structure in North Dakota is codified in the state constitution, and change requires a referendum voted on by all voters in the state, which simultaneously makes change more difficult but more democratized. We provide links and annotations to each state/territories governing board authority in Appendix A.

In many states, understanding state system structures, policy-making processes, governing documents, and policies is an essential part of doing every other type of governance work. State system guidelines and related legislation can dictate and define how shared governance processes work, who has a stake in governance, what can and can't happen with institutional policy development work, and the consequences of not following state-level requirements. For instance, Florida, Texas, and California passed legislation that establishes very narrow criteria by which students can be required to take developmental education courses before enrolling in credit-bearing coursework and how related academic programs operate (see Hassel, et al., "TYCA White Paper" 2015). In these states, legislation mandates how faculty in developmental education do program-level work in addition to essentially taking authority away from faculty in every discipline to make determinations about levels of academic preparation for students to enroll in their programs and areas of study.

National Disciplinary Organizations

National disciplinary organizations and associations (or whatever term is used appropriate to disciplinary or affiliate groups) also use structures, documents, and principles of shared governance. These groups typically have governing documents like bylaws and a constitution, as well as governing policies that apply to specific issues or considerations within the organization (funding, awards, convention planning, elected roles, etc.). For college instructors hoping to participate in service or governance at the national level within their disciplines, the governance principles we describe in this book are also relevant.

The need for consultation among and between groups at various levels of disciplinary or other organizations is as great as those at local or institutional levels, and yet those strategies of effective governance can be even more challenging when working at a national level and across constituency groups. Certainly this is exacerbated by the challenges of communicating through distance technologies, as is often the case, as well as what can feel like an ancillary set of responsibilities to teaching and service obligations on their own campuses that individual faculty may feel more strongly pulled toward. Likewise, even though disciplinary organizations are governed by their own documents and policies, members may bring less up-front knowledge of the governance structures and processes within the organization because they operate at a level distant from their day-to-day work in the classroom or committees at their home campus. One of the major challenges of disciplinary organizations is that they bring together faculty and/or academic staff from a wide range of diverse institutions and local contexts without the shared experiences that people have who do governance work within a community of colleagues at the same institution.

At the national level, shared governance can require a commitment to collaboration and transparency that is often difficult to implement and easy to ignore. The stakes for national disciplinary service work are high yet not necessarily direct and immediate. Doing governance work at the national level can bring rewards to an individual's career but also greater professional risks because the outcomes of governance work can have a farther reach than local institutional work. For instance, creating professional standards or writing white papers on disciplinary issues can have consequences for members of a profession and shape the direction of a field while also creating controversy or even hostility. Professional organizations may be called upon to respond to a notable current event (for example, statements on violence at the US capitol by the American Anthropological Association, the American Historical Association, and the Conference on College Composition and Communication). Such fast-moving but high-impact composing, collaborating, and gathering of approvals can require governance strategies on fast-forward.

At every level, regardless of the context and the stakeholders, however, there are a number of characteristics that lead to more effective and ethical shared governance. In the next section of this chapter, we discuss these characteristics and give examples of some of the more common missteps that can undermine effective governance processes.

CHARACTERISTICS OF EFFECTIVE AND ETHICAL GOVERNANCE PROCESSES

There are core values that undergird shared governance, including deliberation, representation of multiple relevant stakeholders in decision making, and inclusion of diverse voices and perspectives. However, in practice, governance groups can struggle to meaningfully actualize these values. Shared governance requires moving beyond conversations that can center exclusively on *who has the power* to make decisions and instead focusing on what process will be used to achieve the best outcome for all stakeholders. Whether it's a decision about holding an annual convention, a new administrative hire, a mode of assessment, budget reductions, an attendance policy, or some other issue that influences an academic environment, inclusive decision-making process make it more likely that the impact of that decision will be positive and well received by those who are affected by it.

Inclusive Leadership Is A Commitment to Substantive and Intentional Equity

This book is meant to provide guidance to effective shared governance processes. These can include the mechanics of decisions, structuring processes, and how to write policies that are clear and applicable across a range of contexts. However, the most central characteristic of effective shared governance is *inclusive decision-making* processes, which can only be achieved through *inclusive leadership practices*. Inclusive leadership means "doing things with people, not doing things to people" and "promotes fairness of input and output to all" (Hollander 2009, 3). However, as Kugelmass (2003) points out, though the focus of shared governance is increasingly on inclusion, "Inclusion is increasingly seen as a key challenge" (4).

In some of the most notable scholarship on inclusive leadership, the principles and practices recommended are the same, summarized by Hollander as the "4R's": "Respect, Recognition, Responsiveness, and Responsibility, both ways" (3). Hollander provides a nice summary, but it is far too simplistic. In the National College for School Leadership study, authors found that, "The development of inclusive approaches did not emerge as a mechanical process . . . . Rather, the evidence suggested that the development of an inclusive culture required a shared commitment by [stakeholders] to processes that produced an overall enhancement in participation" (12). The rhetoric of most organizational leadership nearly always involves some language on inclusion and yet, many organizations and their leaders fail to live up to this ideal.

Although prominent leadership theories have evolved and increasingly reflect changing social contexts, they often still fail to incorporate issues of equity, diversity, and social justice in their conceptualizations (Chin 2010, 150). Gallagos suggests that adherence to past practices can be a barrier (2004), while Ryan suggests that emancipatory leadership is a strategy for overcoming an attachment to the status quo (2005). What does this mean in practice? That any inclusive leadership initiative like shared governance must focus not only on end goals, but also on the processes used to reach those goals. Ryan explains that "dialogue is crucial" and must not involve "heroic individuals" but rather "collective and equitable processes" (para. 13).

In this section we explain some of the common leadership pitfalls within shared governance, as well as why we can and should aspire to better, more inclusive, and ultimately emancipatory, leadership practices. Without these, what is at stake is the very integrity of our institutions. The *integrity of an institution* is the degree to which its stated values are aligned with the decisions that administrators, faculty, and staff make. We take *integrity* to be perhaps even more literal in its etymology. *Integrity* evolved from the Latin word *integer* which means *intact*. When the whole of an institution is not reflected in the principles and practices of its governance, then those decisions inadequately represent the interests of influential perspectives from the body of that institution. For example, in many colleges and universities, contingent faculty in a range of employment positions (full-time lecturer, instructor, or some other status) are long-term employees but are prevented from meaningful participation in governance. This is at odds with the AAUP's 2015 recommendation that "Faculty members who hold contingent appointments should be afforded responsibilities and opportunities in governance similar to those of their tenured and tenure-track colleagues" (200). Including the voices of nontenure line faculty in decisions related to curriculum, academic policies, and departmental or institutional vision is not just a matter of moral responsibility. Without those voices, institutional leaders simply do not have a complete picture of the needs of the institution or functional unit. If one of the key principles of shared governance is that collaboration and dialogue reveal the multiple perspectives that make up an organization, then excluding instructors who (in most institutions in the United States) have primary responsibility for the instruction of students in the lower division will produce an enormous gap for the purposes of responsive decision making.

Noninclusive leadership is ultimately less effective because consultation, shared leadership, transparency, and broad information gathering support better and more informed decision making. Marjorie Hass observes in *A Leadership Guide for Women in Higher Education* (2021) that:

> Leadership is hard in part because it is inherently relational. A strong personality with a lot of structural power can demand change and issue orders. But those changes are unlikely to outlast that individual's time in office. Only by inspiring others to believe in and enact new ways of doing things can a leader make a fundamental change in an institution.
>
> (73)

Process is an important goal in and of itself because the vetting of questions and concerns allows potential problems to surface in advance of implementation. When the voices of those who are affected by decisions are missing from the conversation, then subsequent decisions are uninformed. Failing to vet questions or plans broadly means that those whose voices are excluded, typically those who are vulnerable, marginalized, or have the least amount of power within an organization, are more likely to be harmed. The loudest voices in governing bodies are often not the voices most familiar with the needs of students, staff, and faculty. For example, without a deliberate attention to power, privilege, and vulnerability, meetings and policy drafting within governance can be myopic. Students, staff, and faculty—particularly those who are most likely to be ill-served by the institution—can be harmed by governance processes that do not include and prioritize their voices. Policy writers on senates or committees may see clearly how the implications of a decision play out for them or those in their employment position, but they are not equipped to understand the implications of a decision from every perspective, including staff, non-tenure-line instructors, various student groups, or even administration. As the sunsetted 1970 AAUP statement on student participation asserts, "Most importantly, joint effort among all groups in the institution—students, faculty, administration, and governing board—is a prerequisite of sound academic government." Isaac Kamola of Trinity College describes a professional commitment to strategic participation that pushes back against noninclusive governance.

BOYCOTTING "CONSULTATION THEATER"

ISAAC KAMOLA, TRINITY COLLEGE

Service work is important work, especially for those of us who desire to work in a democratically run university. After all, democracy requires the work of governance, which includes committees, meetings, writing reports, and mobilizing our colleagues. Democracy requires showing up. However, lately, most service work at my institution has become "consultation theater" (a term coined by one colleague in response to yet another ad hoc advisory committee that the president was pulling together). In fact, consultation theater became so normalized that the President justified her appointment of a Dean of Faculty, without conducting a formal search, based on having "consulted" with a number of faculty and concluding that the acting dean had support and therefore should be made permanent. No elected committees were asked to weigh in, just some informal conversation in a handful of faculty members.

Prior to this decision I had long reminded the administration that a college works when faculty and staff give more to the institution than we are compensated for. However, faculty and staff will not continue to give and give unless we also feel empowered to meaningfully participate in the governing of our institutions. The biggest threat academic institutions face—especially teaching institutions—is for the faculty and staff to feel so alienated that we simply do the bare minimum expected of us. We come to work and simply punch the clock.

After the dean's unilateral appointment, I decided that, rather than once again pointing out the long-term effects of continuously undermining meaningful governance, I would instead quietly engage in a personal "consultation boycott." I decide that I would only engage in service where my participation and decision-making (and therefore my time) had a direct effect on the outcome. I continued to serve on a committee that plays an important role in making key decisions regarding faculty governance (including, in normal times, appointing faculty to serve on a dean search). Likewise, I took on work co-directing an interdisciplinary initiative in which my decisions would directly determine which speakers were invited to campus. And I continued attending faculty meetings where important matters facing the faculty (and the institution as a whole) were debated and vote on. However, I stopped attending faculty meetings dedicated to hearing updates from the administration. I stopped participating in surveys and feedback sessions, except when organized by faculty committees as part of their oversight work. I stopped going to events related to the strategic planning or giving feedback about the new branding strategy. Not only did I avoid these, I also didn't feel guilty about not attending them (as I would have previously).

For me, the concept of a consultation boycott has proven incredibly helpful in clarifying what kind of service I will participate in, and which I will actively avoid (and encourage others to avoid as well). Furthermore, I think that, rather than a quixotic individual crusade, such a boycott could also be effective as part of an organized campus strategy. After all, if there are no faculty, no staff, and no students to perform in the Consultation Theater then there's much more space to demand that governance actually takes place in elected committees, formally empowered to make important governing decisions on behalf of the campus community.

As Kamola observes, it is all too easy to call something "shared governance" that is in fact a fully committed course of action expected to be rubber stamped.

The role and responsibilities of administrators has evolved in the last several decades, which can offer some insight into how "consultation theater" becomes a practice in higher education. University administrators, for example, are subject to an increasing number of external pressures and influences, which even in 2003, William Waugh observed:

> university presidents are under increasing pressure to meet performance standards, usually measured by the number of students enrolled and the credit hours generated, but increasingly measured by evidence of reputation and endowment growth (or occasionally by the success of the sports teams). In great measure, the pressure comes from politicians who know little about leading or running academic institutions and see the institution only in terms of its statistical profile. The pressure also comes from business and government leaders who do not understand the unique nature of academic institutions.
>
> (88)

Such pressures on higher education leaders have only intensified. As different stakeholders work to navigate their respective responsibilities, the challenges become more complex and there are more opportunities for friction to emerge.

Within the context of inclusive leadership, we offer six characteristics that function as the best practices for supporting effective shared governance. This book is written to encourage readers to ask themselves questions about practices and processes that do and do not work in their own settings. In this section we offer a heuristic, a range of strategies, that can function as temperature taking, a diagnostic, and a resource. They are meant to ground any decision-making process and can be returned to multiple times over the course of that process to determine effectiveness.

- *Process matters to the outcome*
- *Authority is both shared and rarned*
- *Clear communication supports ethical processes and decisions*
- *Transparency is more important than efficiency*
- *Create the conditions for stability but not calcification*
- *Difficult conversations are sometimes necessary for change*

Process Matters to the Outcome

Commentators like Scott Cowan in "Shared Governance Does Not Mean Shared Decision-Making" (2018) argue for a narrow definition of shared governance: "A first step is to make sure that everyone understands that the sharing in "shared governance" isn't equally distributed, nor does it imply decision-making authority. That authority is held by the president and the board, the ones who are accountable for both results and shortcomings" (Cowan). It is true that not everyone shares the consequences of a decision equally. This is why some college and university administrators may argue for a greater level of latitude in making decisions, even those with significant implications for the educational and working conditions of academic workers. We, too, recognize that there are not equal or shared consequences for every stakeholder in a decision. At the same time, it benefits groups or individuals who do bear the consequences to understand the full landscape of issues (through conversations and deliberations with all stakeholders) before a decision—because they then understand the full range of possible consequences.

The value of process is in the dividends it pays in stakeholder understanding, buy in, and satisfaction. The benefit of transparent and collaborative shared governance conversations about an issue is that, even if one individual's or group's perspective does not prevail, they know that they were heard and understand the perspectives that *did* prevail. We would argue that in many cases *the process is the payoff*. That is, discussions in and of themselves are an accomplishment because they (1) enhance understanding of multiple perspectives on an issue, (2) surface assumptions or beliefs that may be preventing forward movement, and (3) when done well, establish an environment of trust that multiple perspectives are valued.

A more practical cost of limited-perspective decision making is the failure of implementation. Whether it's a formal policy, an initiative or effort, or new process, decisions emerging from governance processes that do not build on inclusive decision making are more likely to fail. For example, when stakeholders are not invested in or informed about how a decision has emerged, implementing that decision will be that much more difficult and may even encounter significant resistance. If curriculum revision or reform efforts, say, start among a small group of committee members or leaders but never expand out in a strategic and scaled way that seeks feedback from the entire program, then the process likely won't build disciplinary knowledge or create buy-in from instructors who actually will be using the revised curriculum.

As another example, the COVID-19 global pandemic created situations on many campuses in which format and mode for instruction were determined quickly and without consultation with stakeholders (including students, staff, and faculty). As many of us experienced, or read about in the higher education trade news publications, campus leadership teams were subsequently met with a range of responses, from public backlash to votes of no confidence by faculty and student governing groups. In this specific instance, the conditions that emerged in the global pandemic met with the constraints of time to make decisions about how to ensure continuity of instruction while simultaneously balancing multiple other health, safety, economic, and social factors. And this trend is ongoing—leading in healthy organizations to open dialogue and planning, and in unhealthy organizations to lip service to consultative leadership or authoritative actions that will face consequences.

Authority Is Both Shared and Earned

In most organizations, there is a fundamental assumption that an individual is in a position of authority because they have earned it, and they are equipped, by default of their position, to make decisions accurately, easily, and about a broad variety of issues that may arise (see Chamorro-Premuzic, 2019; Guillen, et al. 2018; van Esch, et al. 2018). This is simply not the case. All too often, individuals are in positions of authority because no one else volunteered, because they want to change the context in which they work, because they think they might be good at leadership, or because search committees chose a safe option. People in organizations are also "failed up"—moved into a position of authority to remove them from a situation in which they are causing problems.

This is not to say that decisions do not need to be made, or that clear lines of authority do not exist. Higher education is deeply hierarchical. It is also not to say that everyone in a position of authority failed up to get there. It is, however, of key importance to understand that every position has a significant learning curve, and one of the major missteps in shared governance is an organization-wide misunderstanding of what constitutes competence. There is no predetermined Venn diagram that joins formal leadership positions, authority, and competence.

Often, work is allocated to or assumed by individuals or bodies that do not have the necessary expertise (and who may not have the capacity to recognize those limitations; see Pennycook, et al. 2017). Assessment of capacity is a necessary and useful way to begin a functional governance process and should include knowledge, background, jurisdiction, and workload. As readers might guess, leaders who are less interested in authority and more interested in impact are more likely to welcome conversation and less likely to be aggressive or territorial—these can be important cues about the people with whom you work.

Clear Communication Supports Ethical Processes and Decisions

Communication between stakeholders is not a zero sum game, but getting the stakeholders to listen to each other is a difficult task. This relationship is further complicated because in many cases state and federal funding models require negotiation with and communication between legislators, administration, and faculty. Kenneth Bruffee touches on this disconnect in his article on collaborative learning. Faculty, particularly those in the humanities and social sciences, deeply value and are trained in collaborative learning. Though his work is focused on the classroom, important lessons can be gleaned from his argument about nonfoundational understandings of knowledge. Bruffee (1999) argues that education, and by extension, authority, are conversations, and must be viewed as such to be productive and fruitful. Instead of seeing themselves, according to Bruffee, as purveyors of knowledge, individuals in positions of authority can seek consensus through communication, understanding that past practices and knowledge evolve as organizations grow and as new individuals fill their ranks. This is something to be celebrated, and communication is a deeply embedded aspect of inclusive leadership.

Transparency Is More Important than Efficiency

A commonplace about governance processes is that they are inefficient, or that squabbling in senate or department meetings prevents meaningful work from getting done in a "nimble" way. In a 2018 *Chronicle of Higher Education* article, Scott Cowan writes: "Over the course of my career, I've observed two speeds of governance: foot-on-the-brake for everyday business and pedal-to-the-metal for existential decisions. I've also grappled with how to honor the process of shared governance without slowing decision-making to a crawl, especially in situations that require immediate action." The ultimate premise of Cowan's column—one we don't necessarily agree with—is reflected in the article title: "Shared Governance Does Not Mean Shared Decision Making." But we do think that the observation that shared governance processes can go quickly or be a protracted and sluggish process is a meaningful one.

The tension between the desire to make decisions quickly and move them forward and the desire for consultation is a hallmark of shared governance, one that can be tested in moments of crisis, of which there are increasingly more and more. In the last decade, budget crises and reductions can call for quick decisions about hard issues (programs to cut, services that students, faculty, and staff rely on to be eliminated or reduced). Certainly the 2020 COVID-19 pandemic and accompanying difficult decisions—how and whether to bring students back to residential four-year universities, whether to require all instruction to be offered in a particular mode (online, HyFlex, etc.), have tested the bounds and jurisdiction of shared governance stakeholders. What we want to emphasize here is that the consequences of rushed and nonconsultative decision making can be greater than the value of a decision quickly made. As Elaine Maimon reminds us in her book, *Leading Academic Change* (2018), leadership requires the ability to distinguish between "speed" and "haste," noting that speed, "requiring responses in real time" differs from "haste," which, she argues "can actually slow things down because of the time and effort necessary to repair the damage of acting without appropriate information or necessary processes" (12).

The dividends of a productive and effective governance process extend beyond formal decision-making bodies like senates or councils. Returning to our anchoring definitions of the key terms in this book, the definitions of shared governance ("a collaborative and transparent decision-making process that meaningfully involves all groups with a stake in decisions that affect their educational and working conditions") and transparency ("visibility of the rationale, thinking, and information that is considered as part of institutional decision making to the greatest extent possible within the context of policy") we would argue, are deeply relevant to multiple sites. For example, department chairs or academic deans can adhere to these guiding definitions as they approach decisions about staffing, budgets, curriculum, new programs, a vision or strategic planning exercise, salary adjustments, and beyond. Committee chairs who are proposing changes to policy or embracing new views that will infuse the culture of the department or unit can turn to these definitions to achieve a flexible, iterative decision-making process because the integrity of a decision is valid when those who are affected by it understand why it was made.

Create the Conditions for Stability but Not Calcification

It is sometimes assumed that depth and length of experience is a benefit to a governed body—whether it is a provost, a department chair, or a senate leader. We suggest the benefits of continuity can be outweighed by calcification—the consequences of a single individual in a leadership position, whether a department chair, provost, or committee chair. The rotating leadership cycle at the upper administration level is often the source of complaints (with new provosts or presidents arriving and going at three- to five-year intervals). We don't comment here necessarily on the executive leadership level but rather on the leadership roles typically held by faculty or staff members in governance roles who have a significant impact on practice, culture, and policy: department chairs, associate deans, program coordinators, or chairs and members of major committees with heavy workloads (for example, curriculum, tenure, promotion, equity and inclusion, or hiring). This can also include service work that has a representational or research and writing component, such as faculty senators or union representatives, as well as roles within governing bodies that shape the ecology of a campus. (See our previous edited collections for additional commentary on ecologies of academia, Cole and Hassel, 2017; Hassel and Cole, 2019.)

Rotation of leadership responsibilities in these, typically elected, roles offers significant benefits not the least of which is fresh perspectives, experience, and approaches. We think of the multiple examples of departments in one of our university employers that reelected the same department chair for two decades. On the other hand, there are examples in one of our departments of someone doing the job because no one else wanted to, using the position as an awkward attempt to garner power, and getting removed from the position by force. There is no one wrong way. Though, in the first example, the department enjoyed continuity and stability in processes and vision, it ultimately faced significant problems in updating its curriculum and strategic planning to maintain relevance to the larger field and to the university's priorities as it changed around them.

In the second example, the individual in question was removed from their position in the first three weeks of the semester, which left the department and the new chair scrambling, and the discovery that the former chair's time in that position had effectively poisoned administration and union leadership against the department as a whole. Likewise, a standing senate committee on the status of women in one of our universities that was chaired for over a decade by a white male faculty member in the sciences. At the time of the committee's launch, this leadership was important for gaining traction and momentum in a largely STEM and agriculture-focused university, but over time, the importance of having the voices of marginalized faculty at the helm should have taken precedence.

Difficult Conversations Bring About Change

The coauthors of this book have all lived at varying points in parts of the United States in which directness and conflict are assiduously avoided (the upper midwest, specifically). But such cultural norms can be not just regional but also professional—the academy itself can struggle to engage in face-to-face negotiations through contrasting opinions. While many faculty are comfortable advancing positions or supporting claims in their scholarly work, the context of interpersonal negotiation of different perspectives can be less comfortable, particularly in an environment like the academy where hierarchies are deeply entrenched, whether between faculty ranks, between faculty and administration, faculty and students, or adjuncts and lecturers. Because of the intense stratification within higher education, conversation can be stifled.

Recognizing the very real costs to those who are acutely aware of their positionality within the hierarchy, we argue here that these difficult conversations are worth having. Without difficult conversations—whether they are about a new curricular emphasis, hiring, equity, access, an institutional stance—are necessary, and should be structured in ways (as we discuss in Chapter 3) to maximize honest, authentic, and respectful dialogue. Academics in particular often refer to higher education's "marketplace of ideas" and the value of the liberal arts to vetting ideas. What this metaphor fails to acknowledge is that the marketplace is structured in such a way as to value particular kinds of currency and products more than others (assertiveness, credentials, high status, etc.). An effective and structured set of opportunities to vet ideas—one that invites structured participation and that *specifically makes space for marginalized voices*—will be more likely to achieve a true marketplace of ideas.

CONCLUSION

In the subsequent chapters of this book, we build on this foundational set of principles to provide concrete and practical advice about how to maximize the change-work power of governance groups. Whether they are creating new policies intended to support equity, establishing a set of professional standards, or creating degree requirements, governance work, we contend, has the ability to create real, tangible improvements in our working conditions. The goal of this book is to equip readers—whether faculty working on or off the tenure track, academic or other staff—to participate effectively in this work.

APPLICATION

- Review the definition and discussion of shared governance in this chapter. Then identify how you might expand on and illustrate that definition with examples from your own experience.
- Think about a recent decision within your institution, either at the department, unit, program, or higher level (university-wide, colleges, etc.). Review the six "Characteristics of Effective and Ethical Governance Processes." Then use them to analyze the decision-making process for the situation. Were the six characteristics evident? If so, where? If not, which characteristics help explain any breakdowns or challenges within the issue you identified?
- Identify a shared governance process that you have participated in. Then analyze and evaluate the strategies that governance leaders or other decision makers used to collaborate with and involve others in the process. Think through what worked and what didn't work in the selected shared governance processes. Then list practices that you might use in future situations and those that you might change based on what you learned from your experience.

QUESTIONS FOR CONSIDERATION

1. What are the important decision-making bodies in your immediate and less-immediate institutional contexts?

2. What important documents frame, constrain, or empower those bodies in their decisions? Where are these documents located and how can you have quick access to them?

3. Who is currently in a leadership role in your immediate and less-immediate institutional contexts? How accessible are they?

4. To what extent do leaders and decision makers in your context create conditions for true shared governance to thrive? What is working well and what needs to change to create conditions for effective, equitable, and inclusive shared governance?

5. How is information communicated in your institution? How can you vet the information you need and from whom can you gather more information or get answers to your questions?

6. How transparent are shared governance processes in your work context? How might you work toward improving transparency?

WORKS CITED

American Anthropological Association. "A Statement Regarding the Violence at the US Capitol." *American Anthropological Association*, 7 Jan. 2021, www.americananthro.org/StayInformed/NewsDetail.aspx?ItemNumber=26052.

American Association of University Professors. "Statement on Government of Colleges and Universities." *AAUP*, 1966, www.aaup.org/report/statement-government-colleges-and-universities.

———. "Draft Statement on Student Participation in College and University Government." *AAUP Bulletin*, vol. 56, no. 1, Mar. 1970, pp. 33–35.

———. *Policy Documents and Reports (The Red Book)*. 11th ed. AAUP and Johns Hopkins UP, 2015.

———. "The Annual Report on the Economic Status of the Profession." *AAUP*, June 2022, www.aaup.org/file/AAUP_ARES_2021%E2%80%932022.pdf.

American Historical Association. "Ransacking Democracy: AHA Statement on the Events of 6 Jan." *American Historical Association*, 8 Jan. 2021, www.historians.org/news-and-advocacy/aha-advocacy/ransacking-democracy-statement-(january-2021).

Bok, Derek. "The Trouble with Shared Governance." *Trusteeship*, Sept.–Oct. 2013, pp. 19–23.

Bruffee, Kenneth. *Collaborative Learning: Higher Education, Interdependence, and the Authority of Knowledge*. 2nd ed. Johns Hopkins UP, 1999.

Castro, Erin L. "Addressing the Conceptual Challenges of Equity Work: A Blueprint for Getting Started." *Understanding Equity in Community College Practice (New Directions for Community Colleges 172)*. Edited by Erin L. Castro. Jossey-Bass, 2015, pp. 5–12.

Chamorro-Premuzic, Tomas. *Why Do so Many Incompetent Men Become Leaders? (And How to Fix It)*. Harvard Business Review Press, 2019.

Chin, Jean Lau. "Introduction to the Special Issue on Diversity and Leadership." *American Psychologist*, vol. 65, no. 3, April 2010, pp. 150–156. https://pubmed.ncbi.nlm.nih.gov/20350014/.

Cole, Kirsti, and Holly Hassel. *Surviving Sexism in Academia: Strategies for Feminist Leadership*. Routledge, 2017.

Conference on College Composition and Communication. "CCCC Statement on Violence at the Capitol on 6 Jan. 2021." *National Council of Teachers of English*, Jan. 2021, https://cccc.ncte.org/cccc/cccc-statement-on-violence-at-the-capitol.

Cowen, Scott. "Shared Governance Does Not Mean Shared Decision-Making." *Chronicle of Higher Education*, vol. 64, no. 40, 20 Aug. 2018, p. 1.

Gallegos, Placida. "Chapter 6: The Work of Inclusive Leadership." *Diversity at Work: The Practice of Inclusion*. Wiley, 2004.

Gilderman, Martin. "Statement of Policy." *AAUP Bulletin*, vol. 56, no. 1, Mar. 1970, p. 35.

Gindlesparger, Kathryn Johnson. "Trust on Display: The Epideictic Potential of Institutional Governance." *College English*, vol. 83, no. 2, 2021, pp. 127–46.

Guillen, Laura, et al. "Appearing Self-Confident and Getting Credit for It: Why It May Be Easier for Men Than Women to Gain Influence at Work." *Human Resource Management*, vol. 57, 2018, pp. 839–54.

Hass, Marjorie. *A Leadership Guide for Women in Higher Education*. Johns Hopkins UP, 2021.

Hassel, Holly, and Kirsti Cole, editors. *Academic Labor beyond the Classroom: Working for Our Values*. Routledge, 2019.

Hassel, Holly, et al. "TYCA White Paper on Developmental Education Reforms." *Teaching English in the Two-Year College*, vol. 42, no. 3, 2015, pp. 227–43.

Hollander, Edwin. *Inclusive Leadership: The Essential Leader-Follower Relationship*. Routledge, 2009.

Kugelmass, Judy. "Inclusive Leadership; Leadership for Inclusion." *National College for School Leadership*, Spring 2003, https://dera.ioe.ac.uk/5081/1/kugelmass-inclusive-leadership-full.pdf.

Maimon, Elaine. *Leading Academic Change: Vision, Strategy, Transformation*. Stylus, 2018.

Miller, Michael, et al. "Debate and Discourse: The Role of the Faculty Senate on the Modern American Campus." *Journal of Higher Education Theory and Practice*, vol. 16, no. 3, 2016, pp. 22–29.

Pennycook, Gordon, et al. "Dunning-Kroger Effects in Reasoning: Theoretical Implications of the Failure to Recognize Incompetence." *Psychonomic Bulletin and Review*, vol. 24, no. 6, 2017, pp. 1774–84.

Ryan, James. "Inclusive Leadership: A Review." 2005, http://citeseerx.ist.psu.edu/viewdoc/download?doi=10.1.1.548.7147&rep=rep1&type=pdf.

Sabine, George. *AAUP Policy Documents and Reports*. 11th ed. Johns Hopkins UP, 2015, p. 115, https://doi.org/10.1353/book.39933.

"Shared Governance: Changing with the Times." *Association of Governing Boards of Colleges and Universities*, www.agb.org/sites/default/files/report_2017_shared_governance.pdf.

Simplicio, Joseph. "Shared Governance: An Analysis of Power on the Modern University Campus from the Perspective of an Administrator." *Education*, vol. 126, no. 4, 2006, pp. 763–68.

Tecker, Glenn, et al. *The Will to Govern Well: Knowledge, Trust, and Nimbleness*. ASAE, The Center for Association Leadership, 2010.

Van de Graff, John, et al. *Academic Power: Patterns of Authority in Seven National Systems of Higher Education*. Praeger, 1978.

Van Esch, Chantal, et al. "How Perceived Riskiness Influences the Selection of Women and Men as Senior Leaders." *Human Resource Management*, vol. 57, 2018, pp. 915–30.

Waugh, W.L. "Issues in University Governance: More 'Professional' and Less Academic." *Annals of the American Academy of Political and Social Science*, vol. 585, 2003, pp. 84–96.

Doing Governance Work

In Chapter 2, we focused on the structures of higher education. In this chapter, we extend the discussion of key concepts like institutional literacy, inclusive leadership, and equity-mindedness by offering strategies for operationalizing change within those structures. We outline practices that increase participation and engagement, pay attention to power and privilege, and focus on changeable, high-impact efforts. In particular, we discuss shared governance within the context of and in the service of diversity, equity, and inclusion.

KEY PRINCIPLES

To frame this conversation, we begin with definitions of key terms specifically within the context of shared governance and service.

Diversity in shared governance representation means having a variety of people with different identities involved in governance processes in ways

46

DOI: 10.4324/9781003257974-3

that fully represent the social and cultural backgrounds of an institution or organization. Diversity in representation also means that people from different professional backgrounds, functional units, and employment statuses have an opportunity to participate in processes that affect their working conditions and work lives.

Equity in higher education refers to institutional, program-level, and individual practices that create equal opportunities for students, faculty, and staff regardless of their social and cultural backgrounds or statuses within an institution. Equitable practices in a workplace directly address and actively resist bias and discrimination. In shared governance, equitable practices create equal opportunities for participation in decision-making processes and ensure that both individuals and groups within an organization have equal access to fair treatment and resources (see Castro, 2015 "Addressing the Conceptual Challenges of Equity Work: A Blueprint for Getting Started" for in-depth definitional work).

Equity-minded shared governance actively acknowledges and seeks to address structural inequities and discrimination that exist within organizations, institutions, and society in general. As O'Meara, et al. note (2021), it recognizes that "Faculty workload systems are not strategically designed. There are few benchmarks or standards to acknowledge exemplary performance or to hold faculty members accountable when they do not perform" (1). Equity mindedness looks to imbue the guiding documents, structures, and practices in the institution with clear pathways toward recognition for service and governance work and standards of performance that recognize labor.

Inclusion in higher education means that students, faculty, and staff with diverse social and cultural identities are valued and supported on a campus, within learning environments, in a department or program, in a profession, and in other online and in-person spaces where they do work. Inclusion in shared governance creates conditions in which people with diverse identities and backgrounds have a sense of community, belonging, and a voice. The perspectives of individuals are valued and included as part of decision-making processes regardless of their employment statuses. Inclusivity emphasizes the "shared" aspect of governance—in other words, that governance belongs to all members of an organization and stakeholders within an institution, program, or department.

These key principles are deeply interrelated in the architecture of higher education and impact all members of the institution. They are, in ineffective governance structures, treated as lip service at best, and can be weaponized at worst. Working toward inclusive shared governance means having uncomfortable conversations and creating a space where all voices who want to participate can do so. A commitment to creating such a space can deeply and positively impact the possibility for effective shared governance. Inclusive shared governance in higher education creates equitable working conditions and opportunities for employees while also creating equitable access to higher education for students.

However, attention to diversity alone does not lead to equitable and inclusive governance. The presence in shared governance of individuals with differences in their social and cultural backgrounds does not automatically ensure equitable treatment and inclusive processes without policies and structures to ensure that governance is equitable and inclusive. Inequities in institutions and organizations frequently exist even when policies and laws are in place to require equitable treatment and prohibit discrimination. Structural inequities persist in higher education and in society because existing policies and laws are ignored, or not followed, or used to provide visible representations of diversity without actually working for positive change (see Bird, et al. 2004; O'Meara, et al., "Asked More Often" 2017, "Department Conditions" 2019). In many organizations, having a seat at the table is perceived to be enough to achieve equity goals, but sometimes being at that seat means being ignored, silenced, gaslit, or subject to micro- and macro-aggressions. Visible representation matters, but it must be buoyed with appropriate communication, treatment, compromise, respect, and space.

EFFECTIVE SHARED GOVERNANCE: THE BASICS

Develop Institutional Literacy

Colleges and universities hire based on a contract that governs employment. Committing time to reading that contract is the beginning of developing institutional literacy that will make an employee a good citizen of their organization and a potential leader (we discuss "institutional literacy" more fully in Chapter 4). The same principle applies to department or unit constitution and bylaws; the same principle applies to any organizing or governing documents in a faculty senate or union; the same principle also applies to a meeting agenda, the supporting documents, or the announcements from the president, provost, student affairs personnel, dean, and department or unit chair.

There are, of course, variations in terms of who needs to have relatively more or less extensive familiarity with their governing documents. In some colleges and universities, the faculty contract is regularly the subject of discussion. In other environments, the contract becomes a handy fallback used to react to administrative decisions. Governing documents vary—institutions might have a faculty contract, a policy manual, or a faculty handbook—some have all three. It is often the case, however, that day to day, faculty and other higher education workers may not know or remember the full details of their own contracts. This reality can be based on privilege; it can be based on an organizational lack of communication; it can be based on the fact that a website got overhauled and it is no longer available online; it can be based on the fact that the contract is under ongoing negotiation and subject to change. It is the responsibility of the leadership at the institution to make available the governing documents, but it is the also responsibility of faculty to at least know the basics of what is in them.

For faculty in union leadership, faculty council or senate members, or individuals in negotiations of some sort, it is necessary to know the contract well. Those faculty members hired in precarity may benefit directly from a healthy understanding of the documents that govern their employment. A good shorthand rule of thumb for this is: take the time to understand the workplace, and start by reading all of the documents that pertain to expected labor in the relevant position. Contractual responsibilities and labor documents change over time, so this reading is not a one-time activity. But, as a place to start, reviewing contracts and relevant labor documents helps faculty and staff to know the limits and affordances of their roles, to identify how shared governance affects someone in that role, and to eventually identify how the responsibilities as one of the stakeholders in the institution might play out.

Some possible locations or strategies for finding out more about an institution's policies governing academic employment include:

- An employment handbook on the human resources site
- A faculty or university senate set of policies
- Hiring contracts
- Union or faculty association website
- Constitutions or bylaws at the department, college, and university levels
- Cultural logics of the organization
- State- or system-level sites, including state constitutions or university system policies developed by boards

Knowing where these texts are housed and being able to locate them is the first step to identifying the role that service and governance have in a specific job description and also the expectations for participation.

Strategies for Effective Shared Governance

There are five core strategies that move shared governance work forward. These strategies will be discussed at length below and will each include an example from an individual who does shared governance work in higher education. These strategies may seem simple, but they are deeply effective.

- Making informed decisions by working across functional units
- Cultivating involvement and diverse perspectives

- Aligning governance work with expertise
- Critically and independently reading documents
- Organizing workload well and equitably

These are building blocks in a system of governance at institutions that can help structure governance processes to promote access and inclusion.

Make Informed Decisions by Working Across Functional Units

Effective shared governance frequently requires participants to work with faculty, staff, and student leaders who work outside their programs or employment units. Elected shared governance representatives can expect to work with other representatives from a variety of different departments and programs with shared disciplinary values, norms, and ways of doing work that might be different from those of their own campus or disciplinary units. Although these differences can potentially create misunderstandings and conflict, collaborating across institutional functional units and valuing the perspectives of employees who do different work strengthens decision-making processes by increasing the depth and breadth of information and viewpoints that contribute to deliberation.

However, sometimes the most crucial part of working across a campus occurs when shared governance participants need to seek guidance, feedback, and other perspectives from faculty, staff, and students who aren't directly involved in a process but who might offer valuable insights or be directly affected by a decision. This includes department and program work that requires input from other campus units (for example, academic affairs administrators, another academic department, advisors, admissions, testing services, or a scheduling office).

Questions for Determining How to Coordinate Work Across Campus Units

Here are some questions that can help shared governance groups determine how to include other stakeholders in decision-making processes or projects:

- What expertise is required for making this decision?
- To what extent do existing participants in the group have the expertise required for making an informed decision?
- Which members of the community will be most affected by the results of the decision-making process or project? To what extent do they have representation in the group?

- What knowledge and perspectives will be missing if the decision-making process (or other project) is limited to existing members of the group?
- Who do we need to invite to the discussion to make effective decisions?
- What do we need from participants outside the group (for example, informal feedback, written feedback, conversations, or active membership in the group)? How will we add them to the decision-making process in an inclusive way?
- How will we ensure that our requests for participation or feedback don't create an unnecessary workload for others?
- How will we ensure that we will use and value the diverse perspectives of others outside of the group regardless of their statuses within the institution?
- If others are joining our group, how will we create an inclusive way for them to participate, especially if the norms and procedures of their working environments are different from members of the group?

Cultivating Involvement and Diverse Perspectives

The "shared" part of shared governance works best when involvement, responsibilities, and activities include participants from diverse professional backgrounds and identities—and when leadership positions rotate among many different individuals over time. When the same people do most of the work most of the time, participating faculty can have unsustainable service workloads. More importantly, decision-making processes can become stagnant and lack new insights without the perspectives and cumulative expertise that comes to shared governance when many different faculty members have opportunities to serve in short-term positions during their careers. Cultivating the involvement of faculty members at different stages of their careers is especially crucial for academic departments and programs. If a few key individuals have most of the experience and expertise for doing governance work, then programs can experience significant disruptions if those individuals retire or move on to other positions.

The following examples illustrate just a few of the many inclusive strategies that leaders can use for cultivating involvement in shared governance:

- Place significant value on service work and contributions to shared governance in evaluation, promotion, and tenure.
- Ensure that institutional documents articulate how to assess shared governance work in equitable ways.

- Create a systematic process for helping faculty identify potential shared governance responsibilities. For example, a faculty senate can organize a list of available committees with written responsibilities, details about expected workload and time commitments, and information about how and when to apply for membership.
- Send messages to all relevant stakeholders inviting them to apply for committees and other shared governance opportunities.
- Avoid issuing invitations exclusively to people that leaders already know except when a task requires specialized expertise.
- Limit terms of service for significant leadership positions to ensure that multiple individuals can both participate and develop leadership experience.
- Develop a clear plan for shared governance mentoring to support faculty who are new to higher education. Offer similar but perhaps less formal support for faculty who have experience in higher education but are new to an institution.
- Create an orientation to shared governance through an informal meeting, written guide, or quick online training. Ensure that potential participants have access to clear information about how to participate in governance and how they can access help for learning how to do the work.
- Reduce the time commitment required for doing shared governance work. For example, limit the time that participants spend in lengthy meetings. Provide easy access to governance documents and resources online.

Align Governance Work with Expertise

Selecting governance work that is aligned with expertise and professional experience can often be the best starting point for participating in governance work and higher education service. Faculty who find ways to engage in service work that draws from their previous professional experiences can use new learning to enhance their teaching and professional development while also reducing their workload. They can then build on their previous expertise to expand their skills and eventually move to doing less familiar shared governance work. An institution, department, and program also benefit when shared governance participants bring professional knowledge and skills to service work.

For example, Holly and Joanne worked closely with student affairs staff to address problems with English placement and student retention at their previous institution. They used their expertise in writing studies to guide their activities in assessing and revising the local placement process while also learning from student affairs colleagues about advising issues and strategies for tracing retention, persistence, and degree attainment. They then engaged in a series of research projects that investigated students' transitions to college reading and writing based on their initial placement (Hassel and Giordano, "Transfer Institutions" 2009, "FYC Placement" 2011; Hassel, et al. 2015). Over a few years, they used intersections between their service work, teaching, research, and writing to learn about new ways of engaging in higher education while also contributing their knowledge to the campus. They later drew from this work for a variety of other experiences, including coordinating campus assessment activities, doing statewide committee work to revise program learning outcomes, participating in state system committees, and doing senate work that revised placement policies. This experience illustrates how aligning expertise with service work can provide opportunities for developing further expertise in doing governance work.

VIGNETTE FROM SETH KAHN, WEST CHESTER UNIVERSITY

Ernest Boyer's teacher-scholar model, and its descendant the scholarship of teaching and learning, serve a double purpose for faculty. Conventionally, the model encourages faculty to synthesize our research/creative activities and teaching in ways more sophisticated than simply teaching our results: involving students in our research-in-progress; doing-and valuing-pedagogical research; and so on. The model also offers a way to constrain what can become unwieldy, if not entirely unmanageable, demands on our attention. That is, we should be able to generate research while we're teaching, or turn data/textual analysis into teachable moments by asking our classes to help with them (and remembering to give them full credit!), or the like.

Although what I'm suggesting won't work neatly for everyone, you might be able to use the principle to focus your attention more sharply on fewer competing demands by making your research and your service (FYI: I see all service as shared governance) intersect just like Boyer encourages with teaching and research. I started to understand this years ago courtesy of my friend Kevin Mahoney. When we got tenure (on the same day), he pointed out that because of the work we were doing for our faculty union (service!), we could never produce enough scholarship to get promoted to full professor unless we researched and wrote about our union work. That would also, and maybe more importantly, make our service better because we'd be treating it with the kind of scholarly attention we couldn't when it was just another, smaller piece of our jobs.

That was 2007. As a result, starting pretty much immediately, I started writing about labor for conferences: a talk about task-creep as faculty were taking on responsibilities that Pennsylvania labor law defined as management work; another about organizing with community members beyond our institutions around issues connected to contract negotiations (I used single-payer healthcare as an example). Those kinds of projects got me some footing in the Council of Writing Program Administrators (WPAs), where I've been able to develop—among other projects—a Labor Resource Center that synthesizes research and service by providing WPAs materials they need, while operating as an archive of those materials for researchers. The turn to labor scholarship also led me to commit to contingent faculty labor equality/equity work. That work has been service—for my department/university, my union, disciplinary associations, and professional advocacy organizations (New Faculty Majority, Tenure for the Common Good). I've written about (or directly as a result of) some of that service, and that scholarly record has (sometimes) paid off in being taken more seriously on my own campus.

I want to follow up the earlier point about how broadly applicable the concept is. There are at least three factors in my favor that may not be the same for you:

- Research expectations/workload distribution: we teach 4/4, can get tenured with a few peer-reviewed articles/chapters and some conference presentations, and do a lot of service. As a result, our scholarship expectations are lower than many of yours and, probably more important, our research trajectories can be, let's call them flexible: what we publish is less important to management than that we publish. That helps to mitigate the competing demands between research you're ostensibly committed to and what you might work on as needed. It doesn't, of course, solve the problem of not wanting to let go of research that doesn't connect to any shared governance opportunities.
- Some control over service/shared governance assignments: I had no control my first two years, but as I got involved in union work and reasonably well known for doing it, I could count it as service (which the university supports, so it wasn't subversive). As my labor research record developed, and as a trusted person in the department, I could focus my department service largely on issues that were connected

to the research: for example, adjunct hiring policies, checking our bylaws against the union contract. In return, I happily did anything else the chair assigned, which leads to this recommendation: for everything you get to do because you asked, be willing to do something you don't really want to do in return. Because I'm willing to do work I don't love, I also get to do a lot I care about. It also helps (at the risk of saying the obvious) if your work is good. What most institutions evaluate is whether you're doing enough; your requests for specific assignments go a lot better if your leadership trusts you to do it well, and you have a record of engaging well.

- *I'm a cishet, white, middle-aged man with health issues that only approach "disability" in the most legalistic sense in (we hope) rare circumstances. I'm acutely aware that I don't have to deal with the demands put on marginalized faculty, and that even what I hope are good-faith efforts to absorb some of those demands are voluntary.*

If you're worried that making service and research overlap will be taken as "double dipping," that's a legitimate concern; how you address it will depend on your local policies and culture. The key is to make sure that you do enough of both that the arithmetic is easy; if you're required to publish x articles, and you have, the fact that some of them are about committee work shouldn't matter. And if you did good committee work, the fact that you also wrote about it shouldn't matter.

Service doesn't have to be a burden that deflects energy from your scholarly endeavors. You can write about your shared governance work, which makes for good writing and better shared governance work, and makes managing multiple demands on your attention easier.

Organizing Workloads

Effective shared governance and service requires more than scheduling meetings. We have observed that many of the principles that support effective teaching align with those that are effective for service, including the following:

- *Timing*—Think carefully about aligning the scheduling of meetings with the necessary time to complete tasks between the meetings, clear goals and deliverables for each meeting, a published agenda circulated in advance, and a meeting length conducive to the work that needs to be accomplished.

- *Common documents*—Effective committee work is accomplished best when there is a shared space for storing materials. Many institutions have a specified platform: Microsoft Teams, Canvas, Google Drive. There are rarely circumstances where collaborative service work can be accomplished without a dedicated space accessible on the cloud (rather than email chains and attachments).
- *Reading*—Faculty often bemoan lack of student reading compliance, but may fail to acquaint themselves with the full history and scope of tasks facing a service group. For example, making curricular recommendations or updates should be preceded by a review of current literature on the topic and a scan of recent history in that program or department of how the current curricular offerings were settled in. Reading and research are prerequisites to effective policy work, as we discuss in Chapter 4 and later in this chapter.
- *Organizing meetings*—We've all been to the faculty meeting that seemed to have no clear purpose, agenda, or end goal. Chairs or cochairs often take responsibilities for organizing meetings, but members without those formal titles can also help organize meetings by creating a Zoom link, calendar invite, or room reservation, compiling documents, or tackling a related necessary task prior to convening.
- *Conducting meetings (votes electronically)*—Many shared governance contexts rely on parliamentary procedure or some version of it (sometimes Sturgis's Guide or Robert's Rules). It can vary by institution or context as to how formal meetings may be conducted, but it is safe to say that any formal group, particularly those that are elected, should plan to use formal motions and votes in the case that decisions are made that affect other people, are committing the use of resources, or are a change from a previous practice. Records of such decisions build a historical context that can improve continuity between committee bodies and membership changeovers.
- *Follow through*—There is nothing more frustrating than attending a meeting where much of the beginning is taken up by trying to figure out what happened since last time and what was supposed to happen (and did not). This can be prevented by having clear minutes from each meeting, along with notes about "to do lists" or action items that will create accountability for members and move work forward.

CRITICAL READING FOR SHARED GOVERNANCE PARTICIPATION

In the academy, we talk a lot with students (particularly in courses focused on communication, humanities, and social sciences) about reading critically, sometimes called deep reading or rhetorical reading. The goal we have for students in cultivating this practice is to help them independently develop and derive meaning from a text. This holds as true if not more so for academic contexts—we have been at many senate meetings in which a document is summarized or a decision is handed down with reference to a new policy or statute, but no one in the room has read and understood the document besides a few people. Much as any election requires an informed electorate, service and governance requires familiarity with core documents, which can take more than a few minutes or quick glance prior to a meeting (or at the start of a meeting).

Informed decision making requires shared governance participants to read the texts that provide the rationale and corresponding evidence for decisions and institutional change, along with the exact language outlining a change. Functional shared governance also needs critically reflective participants who can examine policy work and other institutional texts to point out the implications of policy language, ensure that policies don't create or reinforce inequities, analyze both the intended and unintended outcomes of a change, make sure that policy changes aren't in conflict with other policies, identify potential problems, and propose solutions to those problems. For these reasons, a willingness to engage in critical reading is one of the most important parts of effective shared governance.

As we discuss in Chapter 2, institutional literacy is more than just getting a read on how things *seem* to be done, or what is common lore around campus about who has authority for what. It is developing an independent understanding of how the institution is structured: Where are the reporting lines? What are the jurisdictions for various functions? What is negotiable? What isn't? Initiating a new proposal at senate when the relevant people or resources aren't in the room will inevitably result in frustration and hostility. There may be grandstanding or gatekeeping. "Doing the reading" and fully understanding the implications of a given policy or proposal—or asking about genuinely unclear aspects—are appropriate for productive service work.

These strategies can work together, in healthy shared governance environments, to create functional work. Working in functional units should be the goal of all governance work—quite literally, getting it done. What does this look like?

PRACTICAL RECOMMENDATIONS FOR ROBUST AND EFFECTIVE GOVERNANCE

Do the Homework

In 2018, one author's university was revisiting the possibility of retrenchment as a way to balance a continually declining budget. In a faculty executive committee meeting, a faculty leader on campus was complaining, as some faculty do, about students in his class coming unprepared. They hadn't done the reading. The author was presenting a report (which had been sent out to the executive committee one week in advance) at this meeting that summarized retrenchment impacts on a variety of units on campus, which she and a committee had worked to compile. Halfway through the meeting, she presented the report, and that faculty leader, unironically, asked a question that was answered in the first three sentences of the report. She pointed this out. Their response, "I didn't read it." This is a simple illustration of unhealthy and nonfunctioning shared governance. So, how do institutions have healthy, robust, functional shared governance?

Take the time to understand the workplace, and start by reading all of the documents that pertain to the labor required. This is not a one-time activity. Reading information for meetings is a regular activity. Like research and teaching, service work requires preparation. Schedule time to do this work, including perhaps a calendar notification. Even if someone has their eye on the job market, even if they plan not to stay at their current institution, taking the time to understand their environment will help current and all future jobs because institutional literacies build, and participants will learn the language of labor in higher education. Learning the language means one can engage and shape it more effectively in the future.

Many institutions have policy manuals or faculty handbooks, sometimes at multiple levels. A faculty senate can have responsibility for some policies, while others might be allocated to other employment groups like staff, students, or offices like human resources and student affairs. To be effective in governance and service work, it's important for faculty to have a grasp of all the levels of the institutional policy architecture. For example, a departmental committee may want to change a curricular or personnel-related practice, but without an understanding of policies at the college or university level, may ultimately then run into roadblocks trying to bring about that change. This can feel overwhelming, but part of our emphasis on the ongoing nature of this work is that, like any good research agenda, knowledge and resources grow over time. Treating a faculty appointment like an aspect of a research agenda can only benefit an employee in the long run.

What we want to emphasize in this recommendation is the importance of consistently doing one's homework. This is not just a one-time practice with, for example, one's employment contract or union agreement. For academics, in particular, this should be an easy and familiar responsibility. Service responsibilities that are not accompanied by the dedicated time of becoming familiar with the institutional documents that shape those activities are missing the important foundation that supports meaningful change and engagement.

Listen

Krista Radcliffe originally introduced the concept of rhetorical listening in 2005, and describes and defines it as having four moves:

(1) promoting an understanding of self and other;
(2) proceeding within an accountability logic;

(3) locating identifications across commonalities and differences; and

(4) analyzing claims as well as the cultural logics within which these claims function (Radcliffe 26, cited in Marty).

Though this seems like a complicated set of steps, the underlying principle is that listening requires more than passive reception.

We want to highlight what we understand to be the most important components of rhetorical listening in the context of inclusive shared governance:

- Rhetorical listening that promotes an understanding of self and others ultimately means surfacing what priorities and values an individual or representative of a group is bringing to the table—what concerns do they have, and how are they different or similar to others in that conversation?
- Proceeding within an accountability logic means that listening is accompanied by understanding or action. This means not only listening to give space but also to hear, and potentially to act on or take steps in relation to a new understanding. It also may mean the listener needs to adjust their perspective or assumptions on the basis of truly heard perspectives.
- In shared governance groups (whether that's a department task force, a hiring and screening committee, or a faculty council), finding a shared set of values can only be achieved through active listening that helps to situate the issue or topic within the larger conversation and the dynamics of the conversers.

Listening requires active engagement, but it also, in most institutional meeting spaces, requires room to vent. For us, having led multiple organizational committees, one of the most productive ways to start a meeting is to take five minutes to let people talk. A simple, "how are things going?" can make space for the rest of the work that needs to be done, but it can also give effective leaders a touchstone for how their folks are doing, and alert them to issues that are on the horizon (and potentially directly related to the work they are doing in the committee, etc.). Though it can feel inefficient, the value of listening to people's complaints or concerns outweighs the inefficiency that can result. Sometimes called "venting," we endorse a constructive opportunity with dedicated time to surface concerns, issues, and questions. Venting releases frustration. It is a pressure valve. It makes people feel heard.

Space to do this kind of community-building work (within a specific amount of time) has different functions. For example, governance and service require all those who are involved in the work to understand its parameters and how it works. "Venting" is sometimes just an opportunity to understand what people don't know—and sometimes legitimate issues may be raised having to do with processes or roles that would otherwise go unstated. At the same time, it's important not to leave an issue at the "venting" stage, at risk of spiraling into an unproductive path that stays at the level of complaining without an accompanying plan for addressing the issues (see Chapter 7 on emotional and affective labor).

Likewise, structured feedback can take place in multiple ways. The first five minutes of a meeting, for example, or an anonymous feedback form or poll through an online tool can let people feel like their priorities are being documented and provide valuable information to leaders in such groups about what the groups' needs are. Feedback in this way can also perform the service of helping leaders to "check their expectations." It may be easy to assume that those in one's immediate circle are reflective of a larger group, but this is often false and exclusionary. Assuming one's immediate circle reflects the larger group leaves out marginalized and multi-marginalized voices, and silences them. Making issues and concerns visible in informal (and sometimes anonymous) ways ensures that those perspectives that are held but not verbalized are reflected in the decision-making process.

Compromise with Goodwill and Good Faith

At a recent inaugural meeting of a large governance body that one of the coauthors participated in, the senate leadership resisted making adjustments to the meeting format (or even querying participants about their preference) because of their personally held beliefs in in-person meetings, even during the COVID-19 pandemic. Despite strong encouragement from group members to query the larger body about their preferences, the senate president insisted on imposing their own preference about format (in-person) until the pressure to survey became too great. Despite the results (that three quarters of the senators wanted a remote-only meeting), the president insisted on a hybrid model, which resulted in multiple technology and dialogic challenges, along with high frustrations on the part of both those attending in person and those online. We use this as an example of good-faith compromise to suggest that those in leadership positions need not only to demonstrate the *appearance* of listening, but also actually listen and act in accordance with the larger group preference even if it's not what they want, especially when not doing so interferes with the ability of the group to do its work.

Anyone who spends enough time in higher education leadership will discover that engineered chaos (in this example technology and dialogic challenges) can be purposeful. It is easy to pretend that voices were heard (but not very well because Zoom cut in and out, oh dear!) and move forward on the decision or policy in the way you intended to begin with. This is bad-faith acting. It's making a show of goodwill to silence anyone who might object or disagree while also physically silencing them. This move is particularly relevant in the ongoing new models of decision making during the pandemic. At worst, folks who are high risk are excluded by the mere format of the meeting and are therefore left out of decisions that directly impact them.

Good-faith actions in an organization's structures require every single stakeholder to understand this simple principle: the goal is not to win, the **goal** is to **compromise**. Some stakeholders approach even the most minor of negotiations (or points of information) with the desire to win because they think they know what is best (and, in the case of some administrators in US higher education, they have been trained from the premise that faculty are the problem; see Hassel and Cole, 2020). But by maintaining your own expectation of compromise through goodwill and good faith, you can begin at least to expose such hostility as ineffective and, at best, to shift the culture away from such aggressions. And while compromise is the goal, and the most that can be expected, in some cases it is particularly necessary to hold your ground.

Strategically Know When to Stick to Convictions

Shared governance usually requires compromise, but what if something larger is at stake? What if at-risk student populations are bearing an undue burden? What if marginalized faculty members are being harassed? What if a policy is preventing someone from graduating or getting promoted, but it is outdated and long overdue for revision? What if administrative hiring priorities are out of alignment with college or department needs? These are just some of the possible myriad of situations in which nimbleness is required, but so too might be sticking to convictions and fighting for what is necessary. Depending on an academic worker's role and status in an institution, there can be risks involved in advocacy. Institutions are built to resist change. In the more than 80 years of scholarship focused on organizational and institutional change, one fact remains: resistance to change is a persistent and inevitable consequence of organizational change initiatives (Agócs 1997). Some of this resistance can be managed and overcome by using these change strategies, including doing the homework and understanding the structures and stakeholders. Being strategic and reasoned, building allies, and making good use of guiding documents are key strategies to bring about change in the face of resistance.

Make Invisible Labor Visible

It is, in the special language of institutions, no accident that invisible labor is kept invisible. Most of the people doing invisible labor are at least in part marginalized, underpaid, undervalued, underresourced, and overworked. Institutions are built to resist change, but they are also built on exploitation. Sometimes exploitation is so firmly built into the system that it is simply rendered invisible. Part of good governance, good communication, and an equitable and inclusive institution is rendering those exploitations visible.

61

To make the invisible visible, part of the labor that shared governance must do is documented and transparent tracking not only of policies, decision-making practices, debates, and conversations, but also of time spent doing different duties, with adequate and ample acknowledgment of every person involved in the work. Understanding what is done, by whom, and for what particular ends and advantages is a key aspect of organizational integrity that is frequently unmentioned. In the face of ineffective and highly bureaucratized systems, adequately presenting and acknowledging labor is important. For example, O'Meara et al. outline the practice of using a "service dashboard" for tracking and making visible at a department level the commitments that department members have across more than just that site, to accurately represent service responsibilities that may be outside of the visibility of one's immediate colleagues.

Invisible labor particularly impacts faculty of color and LGBTQIA+ faculty, as well as multi-marginalized faculty. In her 2021 *IHE* article, Kimberly A. Truong writes, "Faculty of color have continued to engage in disproportionate amounts of invisible labor in higher education, especially when it comes to supporting justice, equity, diversity and inclusion (JEDI) efforts on college campuses." A proposed solution to this inequity is to put into policy language (see Chapter 4) an acknowledgment and recognition of the invisible labor that is done and, in Truong's case, to articulate that labor in terms of credits taught. These are not fast fixes; historian Heather Cox Richardson puts it, "Building things takes slow, hard work" and stands in contrast to the ways that destroying things can be fast and decisive.

DEALING WITH ADMINISTRATION

Building things is a cross-organizational project, which is why we address the role and engagement of administration (however that might be structured within a campus or institution) in this chapter on doing governance work. There is no shortage of *Chronicle of Higher Education* and *Inside Higher Ed* stories about higher education administration and administrators stepping "out of their lane," or engaging in overreach of their authority (see Kiley 2013; Zahneis; Moody, "Faculty Votes" 2022, "Maine Chancellor" 2022; Spearie 2022). This can range from individual administrators failing to abide by the respective magisteria of faculty, staff, administration, and student governance bodies; criminal charges and scandals (Stripling 2019), or board/system-level groups engaging in activist reframing of university/college missions or practices (Kaufman-Osborn 2017; Fischer 2022). But as Marjorie Hass reminds us, talking about "the administration" as a "catchall term for the people who have the power to make decisions" or as a "nameless and faceless wall of 'no'" (9) is a stereotype to resist because it is an unhelpful proxy that can frustrate dialogue. By naming who has the power and authority—rather than conceptualizing a boardroom full of anonymous suits—it is more possible to move change forward and work in collaboration. That being said, there is also no shortage of uninformed faculty groups or individual leaders who have not adequately prepared to address a key issue that may involve a different point of view with their administration or key administrators. Preparatory and rhetorical incompetence each contributes to governance failures.

What many faculty senates sometimes get wrong is the assumption that service and governance are about personal relationships rather than collegial and professional relationships. What many faculty get wrong is the assumption, or fallback, that service and governance are about becoming part of a powerful (boys') club. For example, one of our interim deans regularly golfs with "the guys" (department chairs), except that over half of the department chairs are women, and they do not get invited to golf. Another of us regularly attended faculty representative meetings where some members would brag about going out with the system president for drinks the evening before the actual meeting. But sexism is not always the motivating factor in these personal relationships. Sometimes it is just about power. One of our former faculty senate presidents would casually announce that he had the university president's personal phone number in his mobile phone and that they would occasionally text each other to get hamburgers. It is possible that this was presented in the spirit of having a good relationship with administration to make a positive impact on how the senate functioned, but instead, it lost the senate president credibility with his faculty because it looked like he was attempting to curry favor with administration in lieu of a productive professional relationship whose primary goal is to represent and act as liaison for the needs of the groups he represented.

Likewise, faculty senate bodies or representatives may assume that governance is about using rhetorical persuasive techniques (or coercive pressure from those in authority or seemingly unchangeable structures or processes) to bring about change. For example, we have observed situations in which proposals are brought forward and then objections are systematically rejected, or concerns raised from people with perspectives outside the initial circle are dismissed. Those with concerns may be told their concerns are not relevant to the present issue or not important. Persuasion to a point of view is different from using feedback to revise and improve a proposal or policy. All three of us are trained as compositionists and rhetoricians. Persuasion is one of the key components of rhetorical theory. Persuasion based in coercion, dismissal, or microaggressions is not only ineffective for the health of the governance body, it is ultimately a waste of everyone's time (see Hurley, et al., 2017; Hillin, 2017). Ultimately, healthy organizations build communication and negotiation structures in the best interest of their key stakeholders: the students.

Additionally, faculty may assume they have less autonomy or choice in a given policy landscape than they actually do. Faculty governance bodies can actually exert quite a bit of influence (even if the stated jurisdiction is within particular parameters). For example, a recent policy revision was put forward at one of our universities regarding free speech, the student code of conduct, and freedom of expression, particularly around funding for speakers and student groups, as well as so-called "intellectual diversity." Initially placed on the consent agenda because the policy language revisions (which were significant) were framed as necessitated by a change to state-level policy (which was itself informed by national groups like the Koch foundation working to reshape higher education values). It would be easy to assume that the move to "bring policy in line with new guidelines" or current practice means that the senate has no agency in how to respond to these changes.

However, bringing the item off the consent agenda (in part because the edits themselves had been made by a student affairs administrator, charged with the changes regardless of their own personal views on or support of the policy change), allowed for the policy language to be discussed, if only what level of support the faculty senate itself had for that policy. The policy changes were presented as "mandatory" but what many faculty senate groups don't seem to realize is that mandates are mandatory in the sense that they can be imposed—but that governance groups do not have to endorse or approve those, and, in fact, can make lots of noise about them. It requires, however, potentially creating conflict, or allowing the senate to be viewed as obstructionist, even if the end goal is registering the dissent of the governance group in the imposed policy change.

The reality is, however, that we have to work with administration and indeed, as Susan Ramlo writes in *Innovative Higher Education* (2021), "Collaboration among faculty, staff, and administrators allows for improved, inclusive decision making and problem solving" (791). It is the case though that in many institutions, administrations do not have to deal with faculty and are able to make decisions unilaterally that must then be resisted and pushed back against. Preparation in these environments is key, as is demanding a seat at the table with allies who understand the value of all stakeholders being included. How do you find and build allyships? Ask questions and watch who answers them and how they are answered. Faculty with limited time, energy, and space in their workload have to make critical decisions about how to allocate their time. In the next section, we offer some strategies for meaningful change-making that addresses the issue of consultation theater and allows for collaborative and productive governance work.

STRATEGIES FOR BRINGING ABOUT CHANGE WITH THE SUPPORT OF ADMINISTRATION

Too often, the strategies that faculty governance bodies and groups rely on are continuous attempts to offer well-constructed or persuasive arguments; however, these are inadequate and insufficient tools to bring about change, if only because they may fail to recognize the real material, bureaucratic, or contextual factors that influence the extent to which any decision maker can act on a per-suasive argument. Likewise, they have structures above and beyond their own milieux that also require a justification and whose priorities and logic may oper-ate very differently.

Bowen and Tobin (2015) argue: "Simplistic as it may sound, we believe that shared governance should be viewed not so much in terms of who owns what, but as embracing a commitment to a genuine sharing of perspectives—to the avoid-ance of constituency-based thinking" (A22). This may be simplistic, particularly in contexts where administrators and faculty groups (or boards and specific insti-tutions or faculty groups) have a hostile and adversarial relationship. The 2014 American Association of University Professors (AAUP) statement on "Faculty Communication with Governing Boards: Best Practices," for example, asserts that "Every standing committee of the governing board, including the executive committee, should include a faculty representative" and that "Direct commu-nication between the faculty and the governing board should occur through a liaison or conference committee consisting only of faculty members and trustees and meeting regularly to discuss topics of mutual interest" but also acknowledges that just "one-fourth of surveyed institutions (27 percent) included faculty repre-sentatives as members of the governing board. In 14 percent of the institutions, the head of the faculty senate was a member of the board" (Tiede). The point here is that when it comes to negotiating on issues that are of shared interest between multiple constituencies and in asymmetrical power relationships, some creativity can be required to identify the best possible paths toward shared deci-sion making.

Governance groups can deploy a range of strategies, depending on the circum-stance, effort, or topic:

Demonstrate and Align with Needs and Priorities

So often, faculty governance groups (whether at the department, college, uni-versity, or system level), assume that persuasive reasoning, or logic, or research-supported appeals to an ethical obligation for change or action will be sufficient to motivate decision makers to act on their request. In actuality, decision makers have a much larger decision landscape than just the persuasiveness of any single argument. A department chair has multiple faculty, student, and staff constitu-ents who are making requests and who have needs. The university or college president has hundreds of considerations across the campus to keep in mind when granting, refusing, or making decisions on request.

This is why it is absolutely essential to approach any policy or practical action request with evidence, and with a clear understanding of how the request **aligns with the needs** of the larger body, while maintaining the understanding that **compromise** will happen. Evidence can mean demonstrating how a request aligns with a strategic plan, with bylaws, with budget priorities, or with best

65

practices. The important thing to remember is that administrators (of whatever type) answer to powers above them, and to the multiple other stakeholders below them who are making similar requests. At the campus- or system-wide level, this is even more true. For example, public institutions are subject to state-level, legislative, or political policies, and private institutions are intensely involved, and dependent upon, alumni groups or trustees.

Find the Table and Find a Seat

A common misstep among governance groups is to fail to understand the nature and location of "the table." That is, we often hear the phrase that participants need to be at the table, but there's insufficient consideration of where the table is and whether it is the right table. For example, (and as we discuss below in principles of governance), a faculty member in a department might assume that an injustice or oversight is the fault of a department chair or a committee, but not fully recognize that the decision-making authority for that issue is actually held at the dean level or above. A committee may believe that a new policy on curriculum can be implemented by the department but fail to understand that the process requires a college and university-level curricular approval as well, along with participation from the registrar. Before we act, we must do our research, we must ask questions, and we must understand the location, shape, and availability of the table. Consider the following example:

> A faculty senator wants to change the university-wide grading scheme which allows only for whole grades (A, B, C, etc.) and not pluses or minuses. He sketches out a proposal to bring to the senate and opens discussion, believing that because faculty assign grades, the appropriate table is faculty senate. What the senator fails to understand is that the table is much wider: grades are part of a system which involves the information technology department, student affairs, university, college, and department policy, and in some cases, the student senate. GPAs are used for scholarships, financial aid eligibility, academic standing, and other issues under the purview of the Registrar and the registration and records office. Individual departments, programs, and colleges—of which there are a hundred on campus—would be significantly affected by any proposed change. The proposal fails to gain traction in the senate and is instead referred to a committee. The faculty senator is dismayed, believing that the process has failed.

In this small, low-stakes example, the faculty member has misunderstood the landscape, and is at the wrong table because the homework was not done. The faculty member did not take the opportunity to listen or understand the stakeholders, and they did not engage in governance processes in good faith. Having thoughts and opinions is a good thing, but knowing how and to whom to communicate about those thoughts and opinions and finding out the history of the issue are a key component to finding the appropriate shared governance table.

Faculty involved in governance must also find their seat at the table. This can take time, effort, and a reliance upon an organization that may at times seem to be or simply is overtly hostile. Stepping in and out of roles as elected, volunteering for different low-stakes and higher-stakes positions, and easing into leadership are key aspects of finding the table and taking a seat.

Engage in Real Networking

"Networking" has become a cringy word in faculty circles, and for a good reason. Networking is, when done badly, exclusionary, and includes things mentioned above like the golfing bro-club, beers with the university president, and hamburgers with administrators. This is not real networking; it is cronyism. According to Melé, real networking is ethical and, in some scholarship, referred to as "virtuous" (2009). Ethical networking requires, "(1) acting with good faith, sharing honest goals, and participating in licit activities; (2) sharing information, knowledge, and resources with reciprocity and even with gratuity; (3) serving with justice in asymmetrical power relationships; and (4) exercising a positive ethical influence within the network" (Melé 487). But, of course, there are different types of relationships and different structures of relationships in any organizational structure. Melé and other organizational ethicists argue that these relationships have four attributes: status, strength, multiplexity, and asymmetry. Cronyism stops at status and sometimes toys with strength, but it tends to ignore multiplexity and asymmetry, and this is where the true impact can be felt for diverse and marginalized individuals. If folks in leadership merely seek status and power, they ignore the multiplexity and asymmetry of their networks to the detriment of diversity.

Work Through Discomfort

Though the academy prizes the marketplace of ideas and the idea of academic debate or argument, there is a surprising level of conflict avoidance when it comes to people and decisions (rather than ideas or data). This means that being uncomfortable will sometimes be necessary to moving change forward. At times, governance discussions may involve conflict that then will suggest that questions being asked of an authority are a kind of unnecessary conflict or form of hostility. As we discuss in the practical strategies offered in this section, doing homework and listening are key parts of setting the stage for conversations, and careful consideration of a balance between compromise and convictions can provide guidance for how to handle deliberation and dialogue (we discuss this in more detail in Chapter 7).

CONSIDERATIONS OF GOVERNANCE

The following five considerations drive effective shared governance and build on the recommendations, principles, and strategies discussed above. Each requires a basic lay of the land at the specific institution to enact them in meaningful ways.

67

Assessing Jurisdiction

A critical component of effective governance is accurately assessing the conditions of jurisdiction—in the context of faculty governance, this is equivalent to staying in your lane (but also knowing where the lane is and where it goes). For example, curriculum decisions are, in nearly every institution of higher education, the purview of the faculty (see, for example, the Higher Learning Commission's "Criteria for Accreditation: Core Components," or any of the other national accreditors who spell out the minimum expectations for accrediting colleges and universities).[1] For the most part, faculty can assume that issues related to the curriculum, including approving and discontinuing programs, changing standards or catalog information about programs, changing course prerequisites or names, will be the responsibility of the appropriate faculty committee. Likewise, the American Association of University Professors' "Statement on Government of Colleges and Universities" similarly affirms that "The faculty has primary responsibility for such fundamental areas as curriculum, subject matter and methods of instruction, research, faculty status, and those aspects of student life which relate to the educational process" (AAUP, 2015). That being said, there are a diverse array of ways that curriculum oversight can be structured and operate within any given institution.

For two-year colleges, this may be a multidisciplinary unit that is charged with review and approval of new courses, while research-intensive universities with graduate programs will have graduate faculty and department-specific groups as the first stage of curricular review of change. Though faculty have primary responsibility for academic programs, there are often subsequent stages of approval and review by other academic leaders at different levels, for example, university-level committees for new courses or course changes and a university system board or board of trustees at the last phase of approval. Effective faculty service and governance starts with understanding the nature and scope of jurisdiction on any given issue.

Knowing Which Structures and Processes Are Changeable

One of the most common issues we have seen with faculty governance and service related to finding the table and taking a seat is a failure to recognize which parts of any given structure or process are changeable within the authority of a group and which are not. In short, any document that is under the purview of the faculty that describes a structure or process is likely changeable, and it can be used to restructure a group's operations or change a process. If the process of approving a policy in the department or senate seems onerous, then typically processes are spelled out in bylaws or a constitution, which are both changeable documents that require the approval of the governing group. If the membership in a department committee is exclusionary or limited, then typically one can turn to the bylaws or constitution of that committee and adjust it with a vote of the group. What many faculty do not seem to realize is that just because something has always been done in a certain way doesn't mean that with new energy or department dynamics those ways of doing things cannot be changed.

Accounting for Preparation and Time

Likewise, for large-scale change, faculty can underestimate the time, energy, communication, and feedback cycles that are necessary for bringing about structural and process changes. Because changing the way things have been done can feel uncomfortable, scary, or stressful for institutions and the people in them, it is essential to build in multiple stages of a change-work process. For example, starting with a subcommittee or group within a larger elected group means that the changes emerge from a group with the legitimacy to make those changes. By this we mean legitimacy in the political sense of the word—ad hoc groups and temporary task forces may make requests or try to change things, but they ultimately are not imbued with the actual authority to make those changes, which is a typical roadblock for change work. Circling out from groups with the authority and responsibility for the work is essential.

Multiple cycles of feedback ensure that the larger body not only gains a growing understanding and awareness of the work that is taking place, but the group doing the work can benefit from the cycles of feedback and perspectives that such conversations surface. Presenting fully finished work to a larger group for a vote, for example, is a failure to recognize that people from different positionalities within the organizations, with varied past experiences and with diverse identities will bring perspectives that absolutely have to be accounted for in policy language because *policy language applies to everyone*. Multiple cycles of feedback invite more people into the process, and they improve the overall final product. What also has to be recognized is that this kind of work requires time, labor, and energy, which often feel in short supply. But investing the time at the front end of any cycle of change can eliminate crisis, conflict, and backlash that result from poor communication and a failure to engage stakeholders.

Creating Cultures of Participation

One of the largest sources of frustrations that faculty who are leading governance work, particularly that type of work that is advocating for policy or practice changes, is a perceived lack of engagement by colleagues. The solution to disengagement has to be multipronged. A common misstep, for example, is to ask for a specific kind of feedback or review at a single stage. What this fails to account for is that people are extremely busy, have multiple competing priorities at any given time, and have different ways of engaging. Without multiple engagement opportunities and modes, faculty leaders will be frustrated by what they perceive as a lack of engagement.

What does this look like? It means preparing documents for dissemination in multiple ways—through email, summarized at scheduled meetings, for example,

69

or if appropriate depicted visually. Likewise, inviting feedback in multiple ways maximizes the amount and quality of engagement. For example, at a revision stage, leaders can invite email comments, while also holding one or two listening sessions, while also setting up a feedback form. Making the results of the feedback available to stakeholders (through a spreadsheet or document) is another way to increase transparency and enhance the quality of the feedback. (When people can see what has already been communicated, they are less likely to rehash something that has already been addressed.) Providing a summary of the ongoing feedback that has been received or the levels of contact with affected groups is another way to make the feedback and engagement process visible. The effect of this is a greater level of overall confidence that an inclusive process has been undertaken, even if individual faculty have not made themselves a part of the work.

Ensuring Equity and Representation

At the core of any effective governance work is having people at the table, doing the work, who are affected by the outcomes. As with the grade change example earlier, what the faculty member initiating the proposal failed to account for is that many people are affected by this issue: registration and records staff, financial aid, students in different programs, faculty in different programs, faculty whose programs are governed by external and specialized accreditation bodies, etc. Decisions, for example, about graduate students or about adjunct faculty that include no representation from those groups will ultimately fail because they will not be able to have a fully accurate understanding of the issues under discussion.

CASE STUDY: GIVING RELEVANT STAKEHOLDERS REPRESENTATION

A large academic program had more than 150 instructors with less than one third of those positions on the tenure track. Tenured faculty were concerned about working conditions and equity issues for full-time contingent and part-time adjunct faculty. The department organized a task force to investigate adjunct labor issues in the department with representation from different disciplinary areas of study. However, institutional human resources guidelines prevented part-time and non-tenure-line instructors from serving on committees without additional compensation, and the department didn't dedicate any funds to the task force. As a result, adjunct instructors had no representation, and the task force was unable to accurately assess adjunct issues and make recommendations for change.

APPLICATION EXERCISES

- Applying the principles of doing effective shared governance makes good work look easy. In the case study above, what workarounds might the department leadership have used based on the "Questions for Determining How to Coordinate Work Across Campus Units," earlier in the chapter? You might also select a similar example of shared governance work in your own institution.
- Review the "Considerations of Governance." Which of these concepts work effectively in the shared governance processes used in your institution or program? Which parts of the process might work more effectively? What strategies might you use for changing shared governance processes?
- Select a shared governance policy or other change that is currently under review in your work context. Identify the individuals and groups who are most affected by the change. Evaluate whether relevant individuals have been given a seat at the table and then determine how the process for developing and implementing the change might become more equitable and inclusive.
- Create a timeline of meetings in your governance group. Think about the preparation that members in that group might need. Use this timeline to create a pre-meeting, during meeting, and post-meeting schedule that includes notifications, calendar settings, communication of documents and agenda, and reports.

QUESTIONS FOR CONSIDERATION

- Who are the stakeholders in your organizational leadership? How and in what ways are they accessible to shared governance participants?

- What strategies have you effectively used to engage in shared governance work? How do you adapt your shared governance strategies to the particular constraints of differing situations and decision-making processes?
- What challenges or obstacles have you experienced in shared governance and higher education service work? What strategies might you use to address similar challenges in the future?
- What principle or strategy might you employ in your current governance role to effect a small-scale change and productively work within a group?
- To what extent is labor visible within your institutional or program context? What changes might your institution or program make to make labor more equitable and more visible?
- Where (if anywhere) do you already have a seat at the shared governance table? If you don't have a seat in the spaces where you would like to participate, what strategies might you use to engage in shared governance work and have a voice in decision-making processes? If you already have a seat at the table, what strategies might you use to help others participate and have a voice?

NOTE

1 The accreditation criterion under "Teaching and Learning: Quality, Resources, and Support" clearly spells out the responsibility of qualified faculty for the ongoing maintenance and assessment of the curriculum: "The institution has sufficient numbers and continuity of faculty members to carry out both the classroom and the non-classroom roles of faculty, including oversight of the curriculum and expectations for student performance, assessment of student learning, and establishment of academic credentials for instructional staff."

WORKS CITED

Agócs, Carol. "Institutionalized Resistance to Organizational Change: Denial, Inaction and Repression." *Journal of Business Ethics*, vol. 16, no. 9, 1997, pp. 917–31, www. jstor.org/stable/25072959.

Aguilar-Smith, Stephanie, and Leslie D. Gonzales. "A Study of Community College Faculty Work Expectations: Generous Educators and Their Managed Generosity." *Community College Journal of Research and Practice*, vol. 45, no. 3, 2021, pp. 184–204.

American Association of University Professors. "Faculty Communication with Governing Boards: Best Practices." *Academe*, vol. 100, July–Aug. 2014, pp. 57–61.

————. "Statement on Government of Colleges and Universities." www.aaup.org/report/statement-government-colleges-and-universities.

Ashburn-Nardo, Leslie, et al. "Who Is Responsible for Confronting Prejudice: The Role of Perceived and Conferred Authority." *Journal of Business and Psychology*, vol. 35, 2019, pp. 799–811.

Babcock, Maria Recalde, et al. "Gender Differences in Accepting and Receiving Requests for Tasks with Low Promotability." *American Economic Review*, vol. 107, no. 3, 2017, pp. 714–47.

Bird, Sharon, et al. "Creating Status of Women Reports: Institutional Housekeeping as 'Women's Work." *NWSA Journal*, vol. 16, no. 1, Spring 2004, pp. 194–206.

Bowen, William G., and Eugene Tobin. "Toward a Shared Vision of Shared Governance." *Chronicle of Higher Education*, vol. 16, no. 8, 16 Jan. 2015, p. 1.

Chamorro-Premuzic, Tomas. "Why Do so Many Incompetent Men Become Leaders?" *Harvard Business Review*, 22 Aug. 2013, https://hbr.org/2013/08/why-do-so-many-incompetent-men.

Cox Richardson, Heather. "Letters from an American." 2021, https://heathercoxrichardson.substack.com/p/october-21-2021.

Curcio, Andrea, and Mary Lynch. "Addressing Social Loafing on Faculty Committees." *Journal of Legal Education*, vol. 67, no. 1, Autumn 2017, pp. 242–62.

Fischer, Karin. "A Playbook for Knocking Down Higher Ed." *Chronicle of Higher Education*, 18 Oct. 2022, https://www-chronicle-com./article/a-playbook-for-knocking-down-higher-ed.

Hass, Marjorie. *A Leadership Guide for Women in Higher Education*. Johns Hopkins UP, 2021.

Hassel, Holly, and Joanne Giordano. "Transfer Institutions, Transfer of Knowledge: The Development of Rhetorical Adaptability and Underprepared Writers." *Teaching English in the Two-Year College*, vol. 37, no. 1, 2009, pp. 24–40.

Hassel, Holly and Kirsti Cole, editors. Academic Labor beyond the Classroom: Working for our Values. Classroom. Routledge, 2019.

————. "FYC Placement at Open-Admission, Two-Year Campuses: Changing Campus Culture, Institutional Practice, and Student Success." *Open Words: Access and English Studies*, vol. 5, no. 2, Fall 2011, pp. 29–59.

Hassel, Holly, et al. "The Imperative of Pedagogical and Professional Development to Support the Retention of Underprepared Students at Open-Access Institutions." *Retention, Persistence, and Writing Programs.* Edited by Todd Ruecker, et al. Utah State UP, 2017, pp. 74–92.

Higher Learning Commission. "Criteria for Accreditation: Number: CRRT.B.10.010." *Higher Learning Commission,* www.hlcommission.org/Policies/criteria-and-core-components.html.

Hillin, Sara. "We Are All Needed: Feminist Rhetorical Strategies for Building Trust Among Colleagues." *Surviving Sexism in Academia Strategies for Feminist Leadership.* Edited by Kirsti Cole and Holly Hassel. Routledge, 2017.

Hurley, Elise Verzosa, et al. "Rhetorics of Interruption: Navigating Sexism in the Academy." *Surviving Sexism in Academia Strategies for Feminist Leadership.* Edited by Kirsti Cole and Holly Hassel. Routledge, 2017.

Kaufman-Osborn, Timothy. "The Downfall of Shared Governance at Wisconsin." *Academe,* Jan.–Feb. 2017, www.aaup.org/article/downfall-shared-governance-wisconsin#.Ywv59XbMJPY.

Kiley, Kevin. "Voting with No Confidence." *Inside Higher Ed,* 23 Apr. 2013, www.insidehighered.com/news/2013/04/23/votes-no-confidence-proliferate-their-impact-seems-minimal.

Marty, Debian. "Rhetorical Listening." *The Review of Communication,* vol. 8, no. 1, Jan. 2008, pp. 74–77.

Melé, Domènec. "The Practice of Networking: An Ethical Approach." *Journal of Business Ethics,* vol. 90, 2009, pp. 487–503.

Moody, Josh. "Faculty Votes No Confidence in Sonoma State President." *Inside Higher Ed,* 11 May 2022, www.insidehighered.com/news/2022/05/11/faculty-votes-no-confidence-sonoma-state-president.

———. "Maine Chancellor Seeks to Rebuild Trust." *InsideHigher Ed,* 18 May 2022, www.insidehighered.com/news/2022/05/18/after-several-no-confidence-votes-maine-chancellor-regroups.

Oluo, Iljeoma. *Mediocre: The Dangerous Legacy of White Male America.* Seal Press, 2020.

O'Meara, KerryAnn, et al. "Asked More Often: Gender Differences in Faculty Workload in Research Universities and the Work Interactions That Shape Them." *American Educational Research Journal,* vol. 54, no. 6, Dec. 2017. pp. 1154–86.

———. "Department Conditions and Practices Associated with Faculty Workload Satisfaction and Perceptions of Equity." *The Journal of Higher Education,* vol. 90, no. 5, 2019, pp. 744–72.

———. "Equity-Minded Faculty Workloads: What We Can and Should Do Now." *American Council of Education,* 2021, www.acenet.edu/Documents/Equity-Minded-Faculty-Workloads.pdf.

Ramlo, Susan. "Universities and the COVID-19 Pandemic: Comparing Views About How to Address the Financial Impact." *Innovative Higher Education*, vol. 46, 2021, pp. 777–92.

Ratcliffe, Krista. *Rhetorical Listening: Identification, Gender, Whiteness*. Southern Illinois UP, 2005.

Robert, Henry M. III, et al. *Robert's Rules of Order, Newly Revised*. 12th ed. Public Affairs, 2020.

Spearie, Steven. "Voting UIS Faculty Members Express 'No Confidence' in Provost." *State Journal Register*, 28 Apr. 2022, www.sj-r.com/story/news/education/2022/04/28/uis-faculty-express-no-confidence-provost-and-vice-chancellor/9565197002/.

Stripling, Jack. "At Michigan State, a Disruptive Presidency That Few Could Muster the Will to End." *Chronicle of Higher Education*, 17 Jan. 2019, www.chronicle.com/article/at-michigan-state-a-disruptive-presidency-that-few-could-muster-the-will-to-end/.

Sturgis, Alice. *The Standard Code of Parliamentary Procedure*. 4th ed. McGraw Hill, 2000.

Tiede, Hans-Joerg. "The 2022 AAUP Survey of Tenure Practices." *American Association of University Professors*, 2022, www.aaup.org/file/2022_AAUP_Survey_of_Tenure_Practices.pdf.

Truong, K. A. "Making the Invisible Visible: Acknowledging Faculty of Color Invisible Labor." *InsideHigherEd*. 27 May 2021. https://www.insidehighered.com/advice/2021/05/28/why-and-how-colleges-should-acknowledge-invisible-labor-faculty-color-opinion#:~.

Zahneis, Megan. "What's Behind the Surge of No-Confidence Votes." *The Chronicle of Higher Education*, 18 May 2022, www.chronicle.com/article/whats-behind-the-surge-in-no-confidence-votes.

Chapter 4

Developing Effective, Equitable, and Transparent Policies

GUIDING QUESTIONS

1. What is a policy? And what "counts" as policy in your institutional structure?
2. How are policies, procedures, and governing documents different?
3. What are the key principles that help support policy development or revision processes?
4. What strategies are most effective in moving developing policies forward? What prevents effective policy work?
5. What practices help shared governance participants write effective and transparent policies?
6. What strategies are effective in creating or supporting effective diversity, equity, and inclusion in policy development or revision work?

Higher education policies guide and drive institutions, but they are also created by members of that institution with specific, changing, and ongoing contexts that may include extra-institutional stakeholders. Strategies for creating equitable policies within an institution, department, program, or disciplinary organization are complex, varied, and situated within local contexts. When procedures at institutions are well understood by shared governance participants and other stakeholders, processes for developing, implementing, maintaining, and revising policies provide a pathway and a shared understanding for effective service and other institutional work. Effective, carefully designed policies create a framework for shared values, transparent decision making, accountable leadership, and functional collaboration within and across units in higher education.

This chapter emphasizes policy development work as an inclusive and recursive process that accounts for the needs and voices of diverse stakeholders. Policies look

DOI: 10.4324/9781003257974-4

different at different places, but they have common functions: bylaws, constitutions, handbooks—all texts that provide governance and guidance. To better understand them though, workers in higher education must cultivate institutional literacy. There are no ivory towers left from which to ignore higher education workplaces or to fail at maintaining equitable working and learning conditions for faculty, staff, and students.

VIGNETTE: SHEILA AMIN GUTIÉRREZ DE PIÑERES, UNIVERSITY OF CENTRAL FLORIDA

At my first university, a flagship, I was only one of a few faculty of color in the college and as a result was placed on every college committee that dealt with resources. My service was mainly within the college. While it could have been seen as a burden, I chose to take advantage of the opportunity to engage with full professors and learn about the college, including college politics. The key is to make sure the committees have a purpose, and you feel you are learning from the experience. When placed on a committee I used my voice and provided my opinion. If you are not comfortable sharing your voice, then it is better to decline service.

My second university, highly research intensive, had a mature and defined faculty senate model of shared governance which encouraged participation and balanced workload. Because processes and procedures were clear, it was much easier to make an impact. Frustration was minimized because roles and responsibilities were well defined. The faculty senate had representation from across the university and engaged in constructive dialogue. You could see from beginning to end how change occurred and decisions were made.

My third university, a small liberal arts college, operated as a faculty of the whole. While faculty of the whole ensures all voices are present it does not guarantee all voices are comfortable. Small colleges often operate with unwritten rules which lead to power imbalances. As I learned, oral history is more often than not defined by the orator. We worked hard to add clarity and logic to the governance process, including lines of accountability. The outcome was an environment where faculty felt ownership over the academic side and an understanding of their influence in the nonacademic areas.

My current university has a faculty senate and a union. To compound matters the university grew rapidly and the governance structure did not mature with the growth. Ownership and lines of authority are not as clear as they could be, which creates a sense of frustration. Here it will be interesting to see the coming evolution of faculty governance, if nothing else in response to the budget model.

As Dr. Pineres's vignette suggests, an institutionally literate understanding of your policy architecture is essential to developing effective, equitable, and transparent policies; they vary significantly between institution types. Only by understanding the framework of a particular policy issue will it be possible to identify needs and make recommended changes. But it's more than that. Seeing themselves as a member of the institution at which they are employed, regardless of hiring status, makes it possible for higher education workers to engage in the framework and architecture of the institution. In underresourced positions, this engagement can feel particularly tricky because faculty who are paid (poorly) to come to campus or log in to teach one class and leave have no motivation to be invested in their institutional organization. It is incumbent upon permanent faculty to fight to include, promote, and work to create the conditions of security that allow all faculty members and staff to feel safe to be involved. The danger, writ broadly, is the continued divesting of permanent faculty positions, which guts faculty participation in governance processes.

Policy, when written inclusively and with justice in mind, can create and support an environment of positive change work. One example from the Minnesota State system, which is a unionized environment, is how faculty within a union environment could advocate for and maintain just working conditions for all faculty. Within this system, the adjunct hiring policy is a good example of a nonexploitative policy. While it is common knowledge that part of the dismantling of faculty rights is a continual decline of permanent positions in favor of part-time positions, this particular policy attempts to safeguard both full-time employment and temporary employees. In the Minnstate system, adjunct appointments may only be authorized:

1. "To meet temporary staffing needs due to enrollment increases for which normal full funding is not provided.
2. To meet temporary staffing needs when faculty are reassigned to other duties or who are on sabbatical, phased retirement or the annuitant employment program, or on other leaves of absence.
3. To teach courses requiring special expertise and/or to meet special programmatic needs of departments where such expertise and needs cannot otherwise be provided by the faculty within the department" (IFO Master Agreement 58–59).

The nature of these three conditions is equitable and they are meant to make clear what temporary staffing can be. This contract language does not allow for a reliance on non-tenure-track positions. While demonstrating a union commitment to support all faculty, this policy is also clear about how and when temporary faculty can and should be employed. This means that even when questions or critiques are posed, there are policy and union documents that allow employees to do something about structural exploitation of faculty labor. What it takes is leveraging the policy and doing something about, in this case, inequitable working conditions. Well-written policy like this is why faculty involvement in shared governance matters. To understand how to leverage such a policy, however, faculty must understand the policy architecture at their institutions.

POLICY ARCHITECTURE

How do higher education workers find the blueprint for an institution's policy architecture? The first step is to build and apply institutional literacy, which means identifying where policies and guidance for faculty, staff, and administrator roles within the institution live. For example, the faculty and student handbook are good places to start, along with any documents such as senate policies or a policy manual. A human resources website will offer resources on employee rights and services. Accessing and understanding the policy architecture of a higher education workplace takes time and investment, but it can be considered part of a work portfolio just like learning how to advise undergraduate students, figure out how to make copies, use the library, or find proper forms for graduation. In a more traditional job market experience, candidates likely meet several faculty members who have been at the institution for a long time—these people can serve as a resource. Talking to them (with the appropriate grain of salt) to get a feel for how the university works can provide a starting point for engaging in service and shared governance work in a new workplace.

All institutions, regardless of whether they are unionized or in "right-to-work" states, have policies. They have to. There are rules that govern student, faculty, staff, and administrative behavior and activities in every workplace environment, and higher education is no exception. Institutions also have legal mandates to maintain written policies that govern a range of issues, including implementation of the Americans with Disabilities Act, the Family Educational Rights and Privacy Act, and Title IX. The policy architecture of an institution reveals much about its values, processes, and working conditions. How is policy decided? Who decides? Is it reviewed? When, by whom, how often? As they begin to understand existing policy, shared governance participants also start to discover how to develop policies that are effective, equitable, and transparent. Learning what is already in place also helps with the review, revision, and development of policies.

UNDERSTANDING THE LANDSCAPE OF POLICY NEEDS

What strategies are most effective in moving policies forward? In this section, we outline the important components of policy work in higher education, with self-assessment questions that can guide a policy planning and development process. Three research and knowledge components are essential for moving policy work forward:

79

First, Identify and Understand Institutional Policy Architecture

What and who influences what a faculty member can do, say, and/or write? This question requires taking stock of where policies live and how they are structured. For example, policies that operate at a program or department level are often subsumed under broader college policies or under a different office like the provost (academic affairs), a faculty senate, human resources, or other campus offices. More broadly, policies can be influenced by larger system policies—for example, if a campus is part of a multicampus institution, or is part of a public university or two-year college system that is subject to the system's regulations. Further, there are policies that are influenced by a state legislature or other state-level governance. For example, states like Texas, Florida, and California have in the last few years implemented mandates around placement testing, curriculum for first-year students, and developmental education reform (Whinnery and Pompelia, 2019; Bailey, et al., 2015). Colleges that are under the auspices of a faith-based group may have requirements influenced by the sponsoring faith. Tribal colleges, for example, may have structures and policies set by a tribal authority and unique student body considerations (Mangan, 2022; Davis, 2022; Ellen Sorensen, 2022). See the State-Specific Resources Guide at the end of this book for some suggested places to begin locating system- or state-level policy structures.

Second, Understand the System

Policy architecture is nearly always part of a larger system, whether it is a board of regents or trustees or a system office. A key step of policy development or revision is understanding where policies live—that is, not necessarily their literal location such as a webpage or handbook but where they are situated within the policy architecture. In essence, policies have addresses on the map of the institution's hierarchy, and those addresses shape how changes to them can take place. A policy governing family leave for faculty, for example, is shaped by the Family and Medical Leave Act (at the federal level). At a public institution, however, it may also be influenced by a state-level human resource office that could govern all public employees (or make exceptions for positions like faculty, which may fall under special exemptions). Likewise, different campuses within a system may have special dispensation to offer employees benefits that are not offered at others, even within the same system. It is this location that those interested in improving or altering the policy landscape need an accurate understanding of to effectuate change.

Third, Understand the Policy Landscape

In addition to architecture and system, the policy landscape we refer to here is less about the neighborhood where the policy lives and more about the neighbors. That is, who has a say in how that policy works, who has jurisdiction over changes, or in how it is implemented? For example, policies on general education

80

requirements may be influenced by many contexts but, in the end, the content of the curriculum is the purview of faculty and every higher education accrediting body mandates that jurisdiction. This is because a body of faculty is the group with credentials and expertise to make determinations about student learning and student outcomes. This is true as well of, for example, requirements for a major or graduate program. Some areas have murkier boundaries, for example, delivery modes or schedule of courses; even though these affect faculty, administrative decision makers have made cases for their jurisdiction in meeting students' needs through new modes or models. And during the COVID-19 pandemic, policy writing has sometimes had to be rushed and "on the fly," with sea changes to process and technology tools (see Workman, et al. 2021).

CASE STUDY: GENERAL EDUCATION POLICY PROCESS

Though nearly every university and college in the country has some kind of general education foundation, there are infinite incarnations, outcomes, categories depending on context: student population transfer articulation agreements, different degree program requirements, etc. Though institutions can defer to some of the national leadership on general education (for example, the American Association of Colleges and Universities initiative, Liberal Education America's Promise, or the General Education Maps and Markers project), institutions are often working from a patchwork set of resources and restrictions that can range from system-level policies to state-mandated distribution categories). Policy architecture can look like that shown in Figure 4.1.

A policy-making process that fails to account for the relevant factors will run into several predictable roadblocks and result in frustration. In thinking about the illustration in Figure 4.1:

- A faculty committee or representative body might try to initiate a new program but run up against state-level transfer articulation agreements or policies that require particular categories be adhered to.
- The administration or academic affairs leadership may want to implement a new DEI (diversity, equity, and inclusion) course requirement for all students but run up against limits in faculty expertise and capacity.
- A multidisciplinary group of faculty leading general education reform undertakes a year of planning and proposal writing, only to discover the curricular authority for implementing the proposals is held by the faculty senate or another group, requiring significant bridge-building and retreading of work already completed.

In other words, understanding policy architecture and contexts is essential to moving any successful governance and service effort forward.

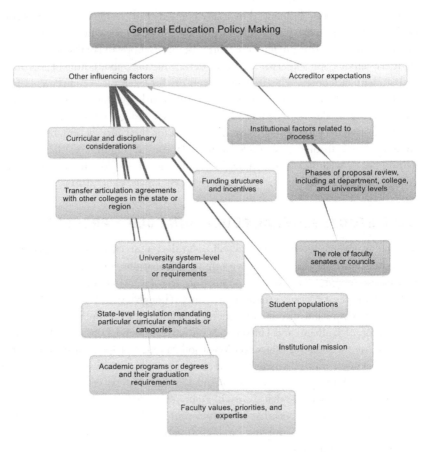

Figure 4.1 Considerations for a general education policy process.

POLICY DEVELOPMENT PROCESSES

In this section, we offer strategies for developing policy documents and practices, along with examples and questions that help readers apply concepts to their own policy development processes. The goal in this section of the book is to help readers understand the policy apparatus of their institutional context, partly to identify whether it is effective and how the process might be improved. Each process has some strengths and weaknesses (or benefits to particular groups and to the outcome), and those who are participating in governance work that includes policy development must have a robust and critical understanding of the policy development processes in their local context.

Assessing the Need for Change

Effective and inclusive policy development processes often begin with an assessment of how policies need to be created or revised to reflect institutional changes, challenges, new priorities, and gaps in existing policies. An initial policy assessment process depends heavily on the nature of the policy and local circumstances. Examples of initial assessment activities for the policy planning phase include:

- A careful and critical analysis of the existing relevant policies (if any)
- Feedback from institutional stakeholders who are most affected by the current policy or lack of a policy
- Facilitated discussions within the relevant shared governance group about potential ways to change a policy or create a new one
- Consulting with institutional administrators and legal teams
- Reviewing relevant state system policies

To illustrate, as the coleader of a strategic planning effort, Dr. Molly Secor describes the importance of building confidence and dialogue into a multipronged policy development process.

VIGNETTE FROM MOLLY SECOR, MONTANA STATE UNIVERSITY

To begin this process, the university administration nominated a core team of university personnel to form the Strategic Planning Committee (SPC). Initially, members of the committee included administrators, faculty, students, staff, and outside community members. Upon realizing that many of the initial committee members were selected because of official positions of power on campus (e.g., faculty senate president, vice-president for research, large donor alumni), we requested to expand the membership to include more broad representation and involvement of stakeholders who did not have official positions of power to ensure that all voices were heard in the process, including those often excluded from decision-making conversations. Diversifying representation on the committee created more equity in access to power and decision-making issues affecting the entire campus. In addition, purposeful selection of committee members that was representative versus true democratic representation allowed for more meaningful collaboration among committee members. The participating members were committed to the process and given time to study the complex issues and make decisions, not just make recommendations.

Accountability was also a focus of the approach the SPC used in the planning process. From the beginning, the SPC leadership emphasized that the committee had ownership in developing solutions to the problems and challenges identified, not just identifying and reporting them. It was clearly communicated that the strategic planning process involved both setting priorities and determining actions to achieve the priority goals that were set. As such, the committee was empowered to identify and thoughtfully consider solutions to problems that involved input from the diverse campus stakeholders included in the committee membership. The SPC members were committed to demonstrating accountability to the stakeholders who were involved in the process by clearly connecting feedback received to priorities they set and the proposed action to achieve the strategic goals. The committee maintained a website to document the strategic planning process and provided regular updates to the university administration, faculty, staff, and students to share survey results, feedback received, and the work of the committee throughout the process to maintain transparency and accountability to the stakeholders.

The SPC was also committed to being a voice of connection to the administration because many students, staff, and faculty may not feel comfortable directly sharing feedback with administrators. The strategic planning process involved anonymous surveys, listening sessions, open forums, and meetings with all departments across campus to provide an opportunity for university stakeholders to provide feedback on the strategic plan vision. Providing this safe space for feedback to be shared with university administration was important to ensure open communication. Further, maintaining communication with the administration was important to ensuring that the proposed priorities, goals, and actions would be implemented in collaboration with the administration. As the final decision makers on campus, any work from the SPC could not move forward without the support of the administration. The SPC committee assured accountability to the stakeholders by providing this feedback to administration and following up on identified challenges and potential solutions.

Overall, the strategies we used did provide diverse perspectives in the strategic planning process. However, there were certainly perspectives that were missed because of the approaches used. For example, listening sessions required time away from work duties that may not have been available to some stakeholders and online surveys required access to computers.

Another challenge was a climate of distrust toward administration that impacted trust in the strategic planning process. While the SPC viewed the communication with administration as a strength to the process, some stakeholders instead incorrectly assumed this led to administrative interference with the process. Despite these challenges, the process stayed true to the intention to provide equity in the strategic planning process while maintaining accountability to the stakeholders the strategic plan would serve.

As Secor notes, accountability, transparency, and leveraging positions toward inclusion can be a powerful way to improve campus environments through policy work. Without the group's assessment of need and research, this equity action would not have been possible.

Doing Research

Many policy development processes benefit from informal or formal research to ensure that policy changes are effective, equitable, legally sound, and compliant with other policies. For significant policy changes, skipping the research part of the process can result in problematic policies or difficulties with getting a policy through a shared governance voting process. Research is especially important for policies that impact student success, pathways toward a degree, retention, and access to higher education resources—or that potentially create equity issues for faculty and staff. Faculty and other shared governance participants can draw from the research strengths they develop in other areas of their work to engage in effective policy research.

The research phase of policy development might involve an individual or small team within a larger committee or shared governance group who collects, organizes, and shares data with other shared governance participants. The questions that research processes answer depend on the specific policy changes, but they typically answer some of these questions: Do we need to make a policy change at all? If so, why? What specifically needs to change? What are the most effective ways to make a change? How might the change impact faculty, staff, and students?

Most policy research activities require participants to collect, read, and analyze secondary sources, including:

- Identifying and working with employees who have relevant expertise and access to existing evidence required for making policy changes
- Identifying and analyzing relevant state laws, federal laws, and state system policies
- Identifying and analyzing internal institutional and program-level policies that might have an impact on policy changes

- Finding and examining relevant institutional research, disaggregated by student, faculty, or staff groups
- Collecting examples of successful policies on the same topic within the state system and at institutions nationally with a similar mission
- Finding published relevant studies on the issue

Policies that are likely to have a significant impact on institutional stakeholders sometimes benefit from informal primary research, which can include surveys, focus groups, and interviews with stakeholders. When research is used only within a committee, assigned researchers for a policy development process can simply share their research with others who are working on policy changes. For research that is used to explain and support policy changes, the researchers typically prepare a report on their findings to include with a rationale that shared governance participants can read before taking a vote. Effective data collection can be structured as part of a plan to assess policy changes (which we discuss in Chapter 6).

Developing a Rationale

Policy language changes do not stand alone. They need to be contextualized, maintain transparency, and provide exigency for stakeholders. An effective rationale answers some of these questions: What is the rationale for the new policy or policy change? What evidence helps support the need for change? What stakeholder needs does the change appeal to? Does the body considering the request have agency in the adoption of the policy or not? What are the implications of the policy change for the group considering it?

Policy Revisions

Audience-focused policy revisions are accompanied by a rationale for changes, including annotated versions of policies that have been changed to clearly demonstrate the difference between the original version and the revised version. This is sometimes referred to as a "red-line" version in which the changes are marked with bold, italicized, and/or underlined text. Effective communication about policy changes will also include either a rationale before the document or the use of marginal comments that explain the reasoning for the change and the implications. It may also be accompanied by a separate document outlining the changes and what alternatives were considered by a smaller policy-writing or representative group prior to bringing it before a larger body.

New Policy Development

A rationale will likely look slightly different if a policy is being created nearly entirely from scratch. A prologue that establishes the exigency for the policy provides necessary context, whereas an annotated version of such a document should make clear which aspects of the policy were, for example, negotiated prior to presentation to a new group of readers.

A carefully constructed rationale can accomplish a reduction in rehashing previously decided aspects of a policy document and makes visible the conversations and vetting that have taken place at each stage of a shared governance process. While a rationale may not eliminate the need for deliberation, which is an important component of shared governance, it can document the perspectives that have been considered and integrated or discarded and keep subsequent discussions focused on the relevant aspects to that body.

CASE STUDY: COMPARISON OF MULTIPLE POLICY DEVELOPMENT PROCESSES

Example A: A Midwest state university's shared governance structure includes three senates: a faculty senate, a staff senate, and a student government association. An umbrella group—the Senate Coordinating Council—outlines and manages policy development. In this model, policies can be proposed and forwarded by any senator, so long as the policy passes through the bureaucratic checkpoints. The pathways are logical, benchmarked, and named, for example:

- Proposal form completed
- Review by legal counsel
- Disseminated to governing bodies
- Reviewed and approved (or not) with feedback, timeline established for resubmission (six months)
- Forwarded through a specific hierarchy for approval (initiator, coordinating council, governance bodies, executive leadership, etc.)

However, this approach also uses a relatively byzantine, regimented, and nonqualitative or regular way of managing policy. This policy development process has several challenges, including:

- The only qualitative (versus compliance) assessment of the policy revision proposal takes place on the floor of the governing body, meaning that senate discussion time can be scattershot, dominated by only those with an investment in that specific policy, and result in particular kinds of debate or wordsmithing on the floor.
- Only policies that are forwarded by an interested stakeholder/senator then undergo review and discussion (compared with a structured annual review of parts of a policy manual or governing handbook), which creates inequities in what is prioritized.

- Emphasis on compliance with other policies means that all policy reaches the floor for discussion, should it be compatible with existing policy; on the other hand, frivolous or special-interest requests may subsequently be forwarded for discussion even if they are not supported or relevant to even a small minority of representatives. This also means that a preliminary vetting of policy that might be better handled in a small subcommittee or standing senate committee takes up chunks of discussion time in a much larger body, which can lead to frustration and disengagement by electors.

Example B: A multicampus public community college provides another example. This structure includes an institution-wide senate that has three governing bodies as one voting body, while also being separated into councils representing each of the stakeholder groups: a faculty council, a staff council, a student government body. Policies relevant to the individual groups within the larger senate are addressed within those bodies, then moved to the larger senate for review and approval.

Unlike in Example A, policy changes can be initiated by senators, but are first routed through a standing committee of the full senate (for example, Professional Standards, or Academic Policy), each of which has jurisdiction over a group of the institutional policies. When changes are mandated (such as federal rules–driven changes, or changes required by the larger university system in the state), the relevant senate's standing committees take up the initial phase of review before forwarding it to the executive group, which prepares the agenda for the full senate meeting. Votes on issues affecting only one of the consistent groups (for example, faculty, staff, or students), are handled within councils, while issues affecting multiple constituency groups are taken up in the combined senate. If debate or concern on the floor of the meeting is too significant, it is relatively easy to return the policy issue back to the standing committee or council that is responsible for the policy issue. This approach has the following strengths:

- Lines of authority for different policy issues are clearly defined, with jurisdictional oversight established.
- There are clear channels that spell out who is responsible for what, and a recognition that different stakeholder groups may have distinct issues and interests that are best undertaken within their relevant constituency groups.
- Standing committees of the larger senate (for example, professional standards, academic policy) include representatives from each of the three constituency groups, allowing for a multiperspective vetting of issues that are relevant to all groups.

- Minimal senate meeting time is taken up by on-the-spot vetting or word-smithing because much of the labor takes place outside of whole-senate meetings

Some concerns or weaknesses with this second approach may be that there is more of a bureaucratic apparatus that could dissuade constituents from taking up issues of concern if they feel they do not sufficiently understand the policy-making process. Standing committees could also be viewed (or actually function) as gatekeepers, meaning some issues could be prevented from reaching the floor for discussion if they are deferred by the standing committee.

Each policy development process has benefits and drawbacks. As higher education workers become further involved in governance processes, the benefits and problems with particular policy development processes often become evident. Nelson and Blakeman's vignette in Chapter 6 addresses tools for assessing and making changes to governance structures themselves.

WRITING POLICY

A *term of art* is "a word or phrase that has a precise, specialized meaning within a particular field or profession" (Definition from Oxford Languages). Policy language can be some of the most challenging to write. Good policy has the features of universal design (UD) and the plain language scholarship from the field of technical and professional communication. UD centers on seven principles, among which are "Simple and Intuitive Use: Use of the design is easy to understand, regardless of the user's experience, knowledge, language skills, or current concentration level," and principle 4, "Perceptible Information: The design communicates necessary information effectively to the user, regardless of ambient conditions or the user's sensory abilities" (Center for Excellence in Universal Design). These principles and the guidelines that follow them mirror the "robust plain-language strategies" (Dreher, 2021) recommended by Technical Communication scholars (Schriver,1997; Willerton, 2015). Robust plain language "prioritize[s] users' needs through effective content, style, and design, and by involving users themselves" (Dreher). Policy language binds many diverse constituents to specific conduct in multiple contexts and must account for all those constituents and contexts. Policy across contexts is also shaped by the purpose, conventions, and related policies in the rhetorical situation of that particular policy.

In the field of rhetoric, composition, and writing studies (RCWS), we define a rhetorical situation as "the circumstances that bring texts into existence. The concept emphasizes that writing is a social activity, produced by people in particular situations for particular goals, refers to the circumstances that bring texts into existence" (Jory). The purpose of this section is to discuss the rhetorical needs of policy writing within shared governance settings in higher education.

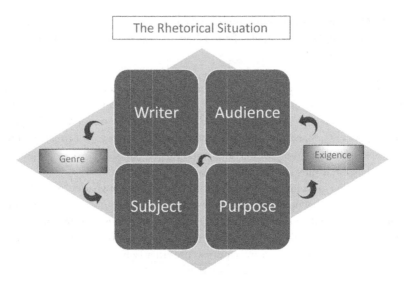

Figure 4.2 Illustration of rhetorical situation.

In other words, what circumstances bring policy texts into existence? State-level policies (either at a legislative or board level) can shape and constrain what is possible at the university, college, or department level. However, smart policy writing requires attunement to the current policy architecture while maximizing flexibility that will work for a variety of circumstances.

Anyone who has been on a faculty senate or governing committee knows that the process of writing policy (not just the language of the policy itself) can make or break whether a policy is able to secure the support of a voting majority. Thinking carefully about how to approach policy writing involves making determinations about audience, purpose, and genre, as well as how the contributors to policy (or documents with influence over working conditions) are developed. For example, policy documents are highly constrained by the existing policy infrastructure and may be required to follow certain formats, use intratextual references to other policies within the body of the policy handbook or collection, and might impact existing long-standing policies that must also be reviewed. See the "additional resources" links at the end of this chapter for multiple examples of policy and procedure-writing documents provided at a range of universities and colleges.

Other documents may serve, for example, as guides or procedures, and can take on more of the genre conventions of a report or resource. It is important to assess the rhetorical landscape and constraints in making determinations about how to approach a text. Once these aspects are determined, they will then influence who needs to be at the table, based on the consequences for stakeholders and constituents, and who is affected by the documents.

This relates to Chapter 3 in which we discuss representation and parity as contrasted with stakeholder and equity—that is, an approach that uses a same and one-to-one correlation between a larger body and a smaller body only works in situations in which every single piece of the larger body is equally affected by the outcome. Thinking carefully about who is affected (and who has to live with the consequences of the decision) is crucial. Relatedly, equity in membership must follow a similar line of thinking. While everyone might have a stake in the outcome, some groups have a larger stake than others and their needs should be reflected in a more robust way than those who are affected in a limited way.

Understand the Rhetorical Function and Genre of Policy Writing

Policies as a genre tend to be clear, formal, and (if they are well written) accessible to a range of readers. It is important to remember that policies are documents that are rarely browsed at one's leisure or read from start to finish in a sequence. Policies are used on an as-needed basis—and sometimes in the midst of a crisis or conflict—to guide next steps, rule on behaviors, confirm procedures, or provide structure to institutional or program processes. People skim policies, even when they need them. Write policies that enable an audience to scan a document or quickly skim read to access information. Policies that conform to the following conventions are more likely to be effective than those that do not.

Write Policies So They Are Helpful

Policy for policy's sake is bad policy. Helpful policies help members of an institution both understand existing institutional guidelines and implement changes. A helpful policy includes the following information: why the policy exists, who it affects, its major conditions and restrictions, when and under what circumstances it applies, and how it is to be carried out.

Write in Plain Language

Policies should be understood by all university or college constituents, including students, their parents, community members, as well as faculty, staff, and administration. The Center for Plain Language (CPL) offers this definition: "A communication is in plain language if its wording, structure, and design are so clear that the intended readers can easily find what they need, understand what they find, and use that information" (2019). The CPL offers five steps, each with substeps, to communicate in plain language. As Jones, et al. 2012 found in their study on plain language (PL), "In a variety of settings, PL has been shown to improve text comprehension of readers with varying levels of familiarity with document content" (335) (see Appendix B for the details of the five steps).

Focus on Essential Information Required for Understanding and Implementing the Policy

Policies cannot anticipate all situations, nor can the people writing them. The policy itself doesn't need to contain all the details related to a policy and how it might be implemented throughout an institution. Details can be laid out in FAQs or resources on the site where the policy is housed.

Write in General and Clear Language

Use language that is commonplace in your organization or at your institution. People, places, titles, locations, offices, and employment positions should be described in general (and if possible, contractual) language because those parts of an institution typically change over time. Using someone's name or office location will require frequent policy updates. When describing processes or references to actionable steps within the policy be specific. For example, instead of using "contact the appropriate committee," identify the committee: "contact the Chair of the Senate Diversity and Equity Committee."

Write the Policy to Support Transparency

In the first chapter, we offered the following definition for transparency in shared governance: "visibility of the rationale, thinking, and information that is considered as part of institutional decision making to the greatest extent possible within the context of policy." Policy writers can make rationale visible by clearly stating the purpose of the policy and providing concise reasons for policy changes. A rationale or explanation for exigency also helps policy users understand what situations the policy might apply to. Transparent policies also make institutional processes and procedures clear for all members of an institutional community.

Define Key Terms

Because readers use policies quickly and in interpretive ways, clearly define specialized terms used throughout the policy. Terms that are likely to have different meanings to different users because of their positions, professional expertise, or experience in the institution are particularly likely candidates for confusion, along with terms required to comply with legal mandates. In addition, terms that are specific to the topic or have a specialized meaning that is critical to understand the policy also require defining.

Be Attentive to Words that Hold Significance

Because individual word-level decisions in a policy can have significant interpretive weight (and because policies sometimes govern sensitive or intense issues like faculty evaluation, student academic standing, or bullying), it is especially important to carefully select and assess the language choices in a policy. For example, policy writing directives consistently caution against using *should* or *shall*, instead recommending *must*. *Should* holds a connotation which suggests that something may be optional or a choice on the part of the individual. *Shall* has more than one meaning and can refer to future tense.

Format Policies According to Institutional Standards

Most institutions have a university policy template or formatting guidelines, or an individual on campus who can make recommendations. Using institutional formatting creates writing that administrators will recognize as "policy."

SEEKING FEEDBACK AND BUY-IN FOR PROPOSED CHANGES

A key component of an inclusive and equitable policy development process is to circulate that policy for feedback and approval from all relevant members of an institution or program. Creating a transparent development process with opportunities for feedback is the core of what good shared governance does, though the feedback process can seem tedious and even potentially ignorable because one-stop discussion among decision makers can seem more efficient. However, the negotiation around and approval of policy is fundamental to the shared governance process.

To do this work, there must be effective processes in place, not just processes that exist for the sake of saying that they exist. Thinking about policy as architecture is a useful metaphor because architecture is not only about place, but about process—about moving through a space with ease. The processes around policy, policy development, and policy assessment must exist, be discoverable, and be usable for constituents working in the shared governance spaces. They must then have a clear and accessible public-facing home so that they can be used in the organization. We discuss practices for seeking feedback more fully in Chapter 6.

APPLICATION

- Identify the policy documents that outline the policy development processes for your institution or program. Analyze, evaluate, and discuss them with colleagues. What parts of the policy development process effectively work to meet the needs of institutional stakeholders? Which parts created barriers to effective shared governance? Which parts of the process might be improved?

- A faculty senate committee was reviewing and revising requirements for an office hours policy. After developing a policy draft, the senate committee that submitted it realized that the current policy language made assumptions about office hours taking place in an office, effectively excluding contingent faculty who did not have consistent office space and online-only instructors who held virtual office hours. Imagine this exact scenario in your institutional context. What policy development steps would be necessary to avoid missteps with the process and how could they have been undertaken in your institution?
- Find a campus policy that is in the current review cycle at your institution. Apply the Center for Plain Language "Five Steps to Plain Language" from Appendix B to that policy to see what kind of revisions might serve the campus community more fully.

QUESTIONS FOR CONSIDERATION

1. Think about your institutional context: what are or have been barriers to including the voices of stakeholders in policy development and related decision-making processes, especially individuals or groups that have been marginalized and left out of policy-making processes? What strategies have been used to overcome those barriers?
2. Who has the primary responsibility within your institution for drafting guiding or binding documents, depending on the context? What training do they have in writing? What steps for feedback processes are in place for the drafting and finalizing process?
3. What experiences have you had in moving change ahead within your institution (either in policy or practice)? What made it successful or unsuccessful?

WORKS CITED

American Association of Colleges and Universities. "Essential Learning Outcomes." www.aacu.org/trending-topics/essential-learning-outcomes.

Bailey, Thomas R., et al. *Redesigning America's Community Colleges: A Clearer Path to Student Success*. Harvard UP, 2015.

Center for Excellence in Universal Design. "The 7 Principles." *Center for Excellence in Universal Design*, https://universaldesign.ie/What-is-Universal-Design/The-7-Principles/.

Center for Plain Language. "Five Steps to Plain Language." *Center for Plain Language*, https://centerforplainlanguage.org/learning-training/five-steps-plain-language/.

Davis, Jaime. "Increasing Student Engagement in Shared Governance: Identifying and Reducing the Barriers." *Tribal College Journal*, vol. 34, no. 1, Fall 2022, https://tribalcollegejournal.org/increasing-student-engagement-in-shared-governance-identifying-and-reducing-the-barriers/.

Dreher, Kira. "Engaging Plain Language in the Technical Communication Classroom." *Effective Teaching of Technical Communication: Theory, Practice, and Application*, Edited by Michael Klein. The WAC Clearinghouse, UP of Colorado, 2021, pp. 45–66.

Ellen Sorensen, Barbara. "Reflecting Strength and Unity Shared Governance at Tribal Colleges." *Tribal College Journal*, vol. 34, no. 1, Fall 2022, pp. 20–26.

Governance Unit. *Write Policy*. UP of Wollongong Australia, 2015, https://documents.uow.edu.au/about/policy/write/index.html.

Higher Learning Commission. "Criteria for Accreditation: Number: CRRT.B.10.010." *Higher Learning Commission*, www.hlcommission.org/Policies/criteria-and-core-components.html.

IFO Master Agreement. 2021–2023, https://static1.squarespace.com/static/59304e9ad2b85773b3fbdf63/t/63d95220ff47317b355992f9/1675186722330/Final+2021-2023+IFO+Contract.pdf.

Jones, Natasha, et al. "Plain Language in Environmental Policy Documents: An Assessment of Reader Comprehension and Perceptions." *Journal of Technical Writing and Communication*, vol. 42, no. 2, 2012, pp. 331–71.

Jory, Justin. "Elements of the Rhetorical Situation." https://pressbooks.pub/openenglishatslcc/chapter/the-rhetorical-situation/#what.

Mangan, Katherine. "Race on Campus: How a Tribal College Grew from 9 to 55 Nations." *Chronicle of Higher Education*, 1 Feb. 2022, www.chronicle.com/newsletter/race-on-campus/2022-02-01?.

Office of Policy and Efficiency. *User Guide to Writing Policies*. UP of Colorado, www.cu.edu/sites/default/files/APSwritingguide.pdf.

Schriver, K. A. *Dynamics of Document Design: Creating Texts for Readers*. Wiley, 1997.

University Policy and Standards Program. *Guidance for Writing Policy: Drafting University Policies or Standards*. Oregon State UP, 2021, https://policy.oregonstate.edu/resources/guidance-writing-policy.

Whinnery, Erin, and Sarah Pompelia. *Common Elements of Developmental Education Policies*. Commission of the States, 2019.

Willerton, R. *Plain Language and Ethical Action: A Dialogic Approach to Technical Content in the 21st Century*. Routledge, 2015.

Workman, Erin, et al. "Drafting Pandemic Policy: Writing and Sudden Institutional Change." *Journal of Business and Technical Communication*, vol. 35, no. 1, 2021, pp. 141–46.

Chapter 5

Engaging in Shared Governance Work to Support Educational Opportunities

GUIDING QUESTIONS

1. What are common challenges in implementing institutional changes that support equity, diversity, and inclusion? How might these challenges be resolved?
2. How do policies and shared governance practices affect students' ability to go to college, stay in college, and work toward attaining a degree?
3. What common types of policies affect students' educational opportunities and sense of belonging in college?
4. How can institutions and programs adapt their practices based on the needs and challenges of the student communities that they serve?
5. What can shared governance participants do to ensure that policies and other shared governance decisions are implemented in an equitable and inclusive way for students while also maintaining an equitable workload for faculty and staff?
6. What considerations do shared governance leaders need to account for when including students in shared governance processes? What strategies can institutions use to make decision-making processes transparent and inclusive for students?

DOI: 10.4324/9781003257974-5

HIGHER EDUCATION AND EQUITABLE OPPORTUNITIES

Equity service and governance work in postsecondary education focuses on equal opportunities for participants, fair treatment, equal access to resources, and fair processes within an institution or in higher education in general. Equity work can and must address inequities for faculty and staff based on their social and cultural identities and/or their statuses within an institution. However, some of the most essential and challenging equity work that takes place at colleges and universities aims at improving access to higher education and the benefits of a postsecondary credential. Whether one works at a selective private liberal arts college, an elite Ivy League, or an open-admissions community college, campuses have an obligation to support equitable outcomes for students from diverse cultural, racial, social, linguistic, and educational backgrounds. Student-centered equity work can force participants to challenge their own beliefs and assumptions about the purpose of higher education and the systems that have been created over generations to privilege some students based on their while perpetuating disadvantages, bias, and discrimination against other students—including potential students who aren't given an opportunity to enroll in college in the first place. Engaging in this work often requires shared governance participants to rethink their assumptions about who does and doesn't belong in college (McNair et al., "Building the Racial Equity" 2016) and then center governance and service work on creating equitable conditions that support all students in learning and participating in campus life. Equity work is the responsibility of anyone who has a leadership or shared governance role in higher education (Kezar, et al. 2021).

The term *educational opportunity gap* describes the differences between students who have adequate access to financial and social resources to support their pathways toward a degree (or other attainment of their own educational goals) and students who lack those privileges, which reduces the opportunities that they receive on their pathways toward going to college, staying in college, and receiving a degree (see for example Sawhill. 2013; Jenkins, et al. 2018; Bailey, et al. 2015). College students experience inequities that reduce their educational opportunities based on intersecting parts of their social and cultural identities, which include (but are not limited to) their race, language(s), ability status, socioeconomic status, gender identity, sexuality, ethnicity, age, and residency status. Students can also arrive at college with dramatically different educational experiences that are connected to resources in the communities where they live and how public education is locally funded. The concept of an *opportunity* places responsibility on postsecondary institutions and programs to address structural inequities in society and in higher education that limit access to educational resources for some student communities.

One of the first steps in participating in student-centered institutional change work is acknowledging that colleges and universities (and their employees), academic disciplines, and professional organizations often create and maintain structural inequities that prevent some students from attending college, returning from one semester to the next, and working toward receiving a degree. McNair, Ford, and Smith (2016) note that sustainable change for racial justice requires recognition of how systems maintain inequities: "To address racial equity within higher education, we must first understand and acknowledge that higher education institutions are part of a larger community ecosystem that must dismantle the deeply embedded belief in the hierarchy of human value that fuels systemic and structural racism" (64). They argue that "Sustainable change will only come from shared and collective action—starting with changing individual mindsets through truth and racial healing that can lead to transformation" (64). This type of individual and collective change is at the heart of equity-minded, student-centered governance work.

For example, many students at community colleges and other open-admissions institutions face barriers to learning and developing a sense of belonging in college because of social injustices and a lack of equal opportunities (Castro 2015). These learners experienced unequal access to educational and financial resources before enrolling in college, and many continue to experience those inequities throughout their time at postsecondary institutions (see Karp and Bork 2012; Xu, et al. 2019; Griffin 2018; Barnett, et al. 2022; Fink, et al. 2022). In contrast, students with more access to financial, educational, and social resources do not experience those same challenges, which means that institutions with selective admissions standards face very different equity challenges in comparison to community colleges and other open-admissions institutions (O'Banion and Culp 2020; Castro 2015; Sullivan 2008), historically black colleges and universities (Wing 2022), tribal colleges (Crazy Bull et al. 2020), and institutions serving the Hispanic community (Garcia 2019), or even less-selective public regional universities. Effective service and shared governance in all these contexts are necessary to reimagine and restructure higher education in ways that increase access and success for the broadest range of students.

Bensimon, et al. (2015) argue that "An equity-minded approach [to higher education" raises consciousness of the need to consider equity in connection with historical and political understandings of stratification." They define "equity-minded individuals" as those who "are aware of the sociohistorical context of exclusionary practices and racism in higher education and the impact of power asymmetries on opportunities and outcomes, particularly for African Americans and Latinas/os." For the purposes of this chapter, we define equity-minded, student-centered governance and service work as collaborative change work that seeks to reduce structural inequities that create barriers to higher education for some students, faculty, and staff.

TYPES OF EQUITY-MINDED SHARED GOVERNANCE AND SERVICE WORK

In general, equity-minded shared governance and service that strives to improve educational opportunities focuses on work related to helping students go to college, stay in college, become successful in their courses, develop a sense that they belong in college, and complete a degree in a timely way. Educational opportunity work includes (but isn't limited to) the following areas of shared governance and service.

Developing or revising policies to close opportunity gaps: Effective policy work can help institutions ensure that students have equitable access to educational opportunities and support as they work toward receiving a college degree. Examples of relevant policies that affect educational opportunities include admissions, academic standing, placement into core writing or math courses, teaching practices (e.g., office/student hours, curricular requirements, late work and absences, etc.), and degree and program requirements.

Improving higher education access: This work focuses on developing, revising, or participating in programs that increase college access and enrollment for students who have traditionally been excluded from postsecondary education in general or from all or part of the local institution. Access work can also aim to increase access to programs within an institution that have low representation or participation from some student communities. Examples of relevant work include changing admissions standards, working on recruiting practices, engaging in work to reduce the cost of college attendance, and revising placement processes into core courses that can be bottlenecks for student progress.

Improving retention: Effective retention work helps students persist from one semester to the next and stay in college from year to year as they work toward attaining a degree (Tinto 1993). The focus of a retention program or initiative can be institutional, for example, retaining students to the institution and to higher education) or program-level (e.g., improving course completion rates or retaining students within a major). Retention work can focus on all students or particular student communities with low persistence or course completion rates (see Center for Community College Student Engagement 2022; Scrivener, et al. 2015).

Increasing student success: Participating in work that improves students' general academic success or discipline-specific success can take place within an academic department or program but also frequently happens through collaborations with student affairs or other campus functional units. The

100

definition of student success is context specific, and the academic needs of students depend on admissions policies that determine who can enroll at the institution in the first place. A few examples of the many possibilities for student success initiatives include new student orientations, first-year seminars, bridge programs, international student programs, early alert processes, and peer mentoring programs.

Strengthening or creating pathways toward a degree: Activities and programs that improve educational pathways often aim to reduce students' cost of attendance and remove barriers to degree completion through curricular structures, advising, and sometimes faculty development work that help students identify programs of study and stay on a timely pathway toward a degree. Guided Pathways (Bailey, et al. 2015) is a model that is increasingly used at community colleges to develop an institution-wide program with the goal of closing equity gaps by helping students choose a program of study and work toward completing an associate degree through a focused set of courses taken over the first two college years. Math Pathways (Complete College America) is another national model that aligns gateway courses in mathematics (and sometimes high school coursework) with students' programs of study. Examples of more informal educational pathways work include streamlining requirements for a major or a degree, aligning curricular offerings with student needs, developing enrollment management or scheduling strategies to reduce barriers to timely degree completion, and developing online and hybrid programs for students who are place bound or employed full time.

Improving transfer success: This type of institutional and department-level or program-level work related to educational pathways supports student transfer, removes barriers to transfer, limits unnecessary credits and time toward degree completion for transfer students, and helps community college students and others with associate degrees work toward attaining a bachelor's degree after transferring. Some programs also focus on helping transfer students develop a sense of belonging at the new institution. This work can take place at system or state levels to coordinate curriculum issues and eliminate transfer barriers as students move between campuses within and between states.

Creating a sense of belonging in college: This type of work creates or improves inclusive conditions for learning and student participation in the institution, helping students feel respected, valued, and connected to members of the campus community. Although some change work connected to student belonging focuses on teaching practices and/or curriculum development, service work that fosters a sense of belonging in college often helps build or contribute to support systems that help students stay in college through engagement beyond the classroom (Bentrim and Henning 2022; Nunn 2021). Examples of work that supports a sense of belonging in college include mentoring student leaders, advising clubs, creating campus activities, and providing educational and service opportunities for students outside the classroom. Belonging-focused equity work can also include diversity, equity, inclusion, and social justice activities that directly address problems and issues that cause some students to feel like they don't belong in college based on one or more intersecting parts of their social and cultural identities.

Providing access to resources: Governance and service work can also focus on helping students have access to the resources that enable them to stay in college or develop a support network. Some work focuses on creating material resources, for example, increasing access to technology, participating in scholarship fund-raising, developing a food pantry program, or revising policies to allocate funding to student-centered campus or online resources. Other resource-focused work involves an ongoing investment in time and labor in addition to financial resources, for example, creating a multicultural or LGBTQ+ resource center, developing a student leadership program, or establishing a STEM mentoring program aimed at underrepresented student populations.

Much of the student-centered work described in this chapter can take place through compensated positions and an employee's contractual responsibilities. However, effectively engaging in this work requires administrators, faculty, and staff to collaborate across institutional units in ways that often require participation from employees who do the work through service. Institutions can also implement student-centered equity work as a service requirement without offering compensation in a way that adds layers of work on top of a faculty or staff member's existing contractual obligations. In other words, what is part of someone's compensated job responsibilities to support students at one institution or in just one part of an institution can be service work at a different institution or for a different employee at the same institution. In working toward creating equitable institutions and programs, it's important to acknowledge distinctions between service, professional development, and contractual obligations.

ACCOUNTING FOR LOCALLY SITUATED NEEDS AND DIFFERENCES

All higher education work related to social justice, diversity, equity, and inclusion is inherently local. Higher education institutions and programs or units within those institutions experience locally situated student opportunity gaps and equity issues. The following table outlines some differences between institutions that shape challenges and opportunities for engaging in student-centered, equity-minded shared governance and service work:

Table 5.1 How Institutional Contexts Shape Educational Equity Work

Admissions requirements and practices	Standards for which students can and can't enter into the educational space and the processes used to include or exclude students from an entire institution or an individual degree program
Selectivity	The extent to which institutions and programs create and maintain a gatekeeping function that excludes some students from programs of study while including others
Institutional missions	The role of an institution within a community, state system, and/or region, including the student communities that an institution is (and isn't) designed to serve
Program missions	The role of a program within an institution, the preparation or gatekeeping function that it serves for career preparation, and the student communities that the program is designed to serve
Student communities	The social and cultural characteristics of the student communities that enroll at the institution based on recruitment practices, marketing, tradition, local communities, available programs, and other factors connected to enrollment patterns
Affordability	The cost of college attendance and the resources available (or missing) that enable students to enroll in college and progress toward a degree
Hiring practices	Priorities for hiring faculty, staff, and administrators and the professional backgrounds and skills that those hiring practices privilege (which may or may not be aligned with participation in equity-minded, student-centered work)
Graduate student participation	The role of graduate students in shared governance and their dual role as both students and instructors; program emphases that encourage and/or discourage their participation in shared governance process; the resources and opportunities that graduate students have access to for their own educational goals
Shared governance structures	The processes used for doing student-centered policy and program development work; which voices are privileged and which are ignored; the role of shared governance in creating educational opportunities and/or reinforcing equity gaps; the level of commitment to prioritizing and working toward achieving equity goals
Compensation and professional credit for equity work	Whether people are paid for their work or expected to do it as service; whether equity work counts toward tenure and promotion and/or leads to professional advancement within the institution

(Continued)

103

Table 5.1 Continued

| Institutional and program values | How an institution, department, or program values student-centered equity work and allocates related resources; whether some employees are expected to do the work based on their cultural and social identities while others are exempt; whether many people participate in equity work in a collaborative way or whether only a few individuals value the work |

Faculty, staff, and administrators who engage in student-centered equity work need to frame their efforts within these context-specific issues and other local factors. Part of participating in equity work is acknowledging the positionality and social privileges of participants (including one's self) and how they shape the challenges and opportunities that institutions and programs experience. For example, community colleges, tribal colleges, historically Black colleges and universities, and Hispanic-serving institutions experience especially complex equity issues because a majority of students at many of those institutions have experienced previous educational inequities based on their social class, race, linguistic background, age, and other intersecting parts of their identities before they enroll in college. Selective institutions by definition exclude some students from higher education and may have fewer students who experience inequities on their pathways toward a degree, but all institutions have student-centered equity issues that require ongoing service and shared governance work.

PRINCIPLES FOR EQUITY-MINDED AND STUDENT-CENTERED LEADERSHIP

In their book, *Equity by Design*, Mirko Chardin and Katie Novak (2020) provide an equity audit that educators at all levels can use to "objectively examine what the data says about the experience of marginalized groups in your classroom" (41). The audit also works as a starting point for assessing how practices and programs outside of a course create inequities for students and initiating difficult conversations about equity within shared governance:

- Which groups have been historically and/or are currently being marginalized in your [educational] setting?
- What does it mean to acknowledge that a group has been and/or is currently being marginalized in your setting?

104

- How do both quantitative and qualitative forms of data support this? How have we, as educators, contributed to this?
- How have our beliefs and actions contributed to this?

These questions can also be used to examine the extent to which faculty and staff who are engaging in student-centered governance and service work have also been marginalized or excluded by the processes and practices of an institution.

The following principles provide an overview of how shared governance participants can engage in equity-minded work that improves educational outcomes for students while also maintaining a sustainable workload for employees who do that work. Each principle includes a set of questions that shared governance participants can use to assess and reflect on strategies for implementing student-centered changes at their institutions.

Focus on How Locally Situated Practices Impact Students' Educational Opportunities

Because structural inequities are embedded in the culture of higher education, the work of improving educational equity can be overwhelming and literally never ending. Shared governance participants can start the work by focusing on changes that potentially have the most impact on students' educational opportunities in their own local contexts (in contrast to borrowing ideas from other institutions without first determining a local need for implementing those changes). The following questions provide a starting point for thinking about student-centered work:

- Who is allowed to participate in higher education at the institution or in the program? Who is given opportunities? Who is excluded? What are the stated and unstated reasons for choices about who can and can't participate in higher education in your context?
- In your institution, how do students' prior educational experiences impact their pathways toward a degree? Where and when in their pathways toward a degree might shared governance practices and processes improve their success and retention in college?
- How does social privilege in your institution or program shape attitudes toward student learning and participation in higher education? How might institutional change work address how social privilege gives some students access to educational resources that other students do not receive?
- How do issues related to race, socioeconomic status, gender, sexuality, language, and other parts of students' social and cultural identities affect students' sense of belonging in college at your institution? What institutional changes might help students develop a sense of belonging and respect for their diverse identities that helps them stay in college and receive a degree?

- To what extent do existing policies and practices account for the ways in which some students experience inequities because of intersecting parts of their social and cultural identities? What changes might the institution make to reduce structural inequities that create barriers to a college degree for some students based on their social and cultural identities?

In other words, equity-based policy work requires critically analyzing how things work and the presumed "rightness" of those practices and value. As Williams, et al. (2021) observe, meeting the needs as "the pool of college attendees continues to diversity" requires "making deliberate connections to different aspects of their cultural backgrounds," advocating for both a "cultural affirming" approach to campus climate improvements and outlining recommendations for "culturally engaging campus environments" (752).

Include All Relevant Members of the Campus Community Whose Work Intersects with Student Experiences

Shared governance decision-making processes that center on students' experiences in college, their sense of belonging, and their pathways toward a degree often require faculty and other decision makers to work across multiple offices and programs within an institution. In particular, all employees who have points of contact with students and direct experience with helping them navigate higher education challenges need structured opportunities to participate in developing and assessing policies, programs, and initiatives for students. Processes for developing new initiatives or revising existing policies become more equitable for both employees and students when everyone whose work is affected by a decision has a direct role in the process.

For example, a curricular change that happens at the department level often needs consultation with advisors who work directly with students as they select courses, determine whether to drop a course, and make decisions about their programs of study. Revising a policy that sets standards for academic standing may require input from faculty who teach courses, advisors who explain processes to students and support them when they aren't in good standing, academic affairs specialists who understand issues related to retention, administrators who know how academic standing is addressed at the state system level, financial aid specialists, staff who deal with transfer, and staff and faculty committee members involved in student appeals processes. Decision making might also need to include employees with knowledge about how academic standing affects student opportunities and experiences, for example, an athletic director, student government advisor, and federally funded TRIO program staff. Consider the following questions to help determine the stakeholders who are best able to contribute change work around policies and programs:

- Which employees have knowledge of and experience with existing relevant policies and programs? How and where in the shared governance process do those employees need to provide input to ensure that the results improve educational opportunities?
- For an existing policy or program that needs revision, where are the points of contact for students? Which employees have the knowledge of student experiences required for making effective decisions?
- Which employees have the most direct experience and knowledge about how the policy or initiative will impact students?
- Which offices or individual employees have the knowledge, skills, and resources required for assessing how the change impacts equity and inclusion in higher education for students?
- What is the process of implementing the proposed policy change or initiative from start to finish? Which faculty, staff, administrators, and students are already involved in that process? Which relevant institutional members will be involved when the change is implemented?
- What change work to support students is already taking place outside of shared governance processes? What steps will shared governance leaders take to provide relevant employees and students with opportunities to participate actively in the process and in equitable ways?

As we discuss in previous chapters, part of service and governance that has the goal of effecting change means not just knowing what table to be at but where the table is and who needs to be at the table in order to effectively move work forward.

Account for the Varied Types of Labor that Create Student-Centered Institutional Change

Faculty and staff can engage in work to support educational opportunities through contractual responsibilities (i.e., work attached to their position descriptions), service that counts toward tenure and promotion, reassigned time (i.e., release from one or more courses), contractual overloads, summer stipends, and grant stipends (funded from sources outside the institution). However, some employees participate in work for students through uncompensated work that doesn't count toward tenure or promotion—for example, through uncompensated committee assignments, leadership roles, responsibilities assigned by an administrator, or work that employees take on as an expectation based on their social or cultural identities. An essential part of doing equitable change work for students is to recognize that the labor required for doing the work is often distributed unequally within an institution in ways that can create an overwhelming workload for some employees while having minimal or no impact on others. Because the results of equity work can be high stakes for some students, faculty and staff can feel obligated to participate even when the conditions for their participation require uncompensated labor.

Consider these questions for determining the mechanics of labor associated with service and governance change work for equity:

- Which institutional employees will be responsible for implementing the change? *Identify both the functional units or programs and the individuals or position types within those programs.*
- Is the work part of an employee's existing contractual obligations? If not, how will they receive compensation and/or time to do the work?
- What is the existing workload for the employees who will need to implement the change and sustain it after implementation? What impact will the change have on their workload and working conditions?
- How will participants ensure that labor for implementing the change is fairly distributed and accounts for varying levels of compensation (if applicable) for participants, including faculty, staff, and students who might be participating on a voluntary basis?
- Which student leaders or groups (if any) will need to participate? How will they receive compensation for their time and labor?
- If the work is uncompensated for faculty or staff, how will it count toward evaluation, tenure (or job security for non-tenure-line employees), and promotion? If it won't count for those purposes, what changes need to happen to ensure that student-centered work is valued by the institution and counts toward evaluation, tenure, and promotion?
- How will the process account for the varied types of labor and status of participants in the process?
- How will those who lead the process ensure that employees can say no to participating in labor-intensive parts of the project (regardless of potential consequences for students) if they aren't compensated for their work or given time to do it within their existing job responsibilities?

Institutions or institutional units that have relied upon the uncompensated generosity of nontenure and tenure-line employees or by adding responsibilities to, for example, salaried staff with an already full plate of responsibilities will likely need to reevaluate this practice if the goal is to support substantive change.

VIGNETTE FROM DAVID M. GRANT, UNIVERSITY OF NORTHERN IOWA

Our University Writing Committee was disbanded during a structural reorganization of the university and that left a great deal of work with no person tasked to carry it out. Before the UWC was disbanded, I also had a course release, so the austerity measures were imposed gradually, with warning, but still without the necessary dedication to the labor. To adjust to this new organizational impetus, I changed my talk and approach using a servant-leadership approach.

Rather than serving faculty and attempting change through the overt levers of power (the UWC reported to the faculty senate), I focused my messaging on students' needs and how I was in a position to serve those faculty, administrators, and staff members who were tasked with student support. At each moment, I reminded faculty and administrators that we serve students first. For example, I began to ask what other faculty wanted to read from students rather than what they felt students ought to write. A physicist said he loved to read sci-fi and began to offer science fiction prompts in his teaching so students could practice writing in physics rather than for physics. I also presented with a theater colleague on using annotations as a writing/thinking practice, thus also building on the research-writing connection.

Finally, I took advantage of the structural reorganization's general education revision to attend the University of Minnesota's Writing-Enriched Curriculum (WEC) workshop and presented the WEC model to the general education revision committee. This led to the inclusion of process in the final outcomes for all writing classes, and the director of our Center for Excellence in Teaching and Learning to gather a group of faculty for WEC's second workshop. Again, even though the actors here involve faculty, staff, and administration, it is all guided by an approach that focuses on the need for students to practice writing in more diverse forms than a research paper (confirmed by our National Survey of Student Engagement data and course program reports).

Grant's vignette offers insights on repurposing existing structures to support students' literacy development. In the face of reductions, Grant's approach builds connections and cross-campus networks for the purpose of strengthening students' literacy development.

Assess, Revise, and Create Policies to Support Educational Opportunities and Student-Centered Equity

Policies that are entrenched in an institution and that are rarely critically assessed can reinforce educational inequities and create barriers to degree attainment. Institutions and programs can systematically review policies to determine their impact on students. Examples of policies that impact students' educational opportunities include:

- Policies that affect who can go to college (admissions, placement, prerequisite policies)
- Policies that affect who can stay in college (academic standing, probation, expulsion, academic warnings, etc.)
- Policies that shape progress toward a degree (degree requirements, transfer, placement, curriculum, graduation standards, etc.)
- Policies that set teaching standards for an institution, department, or program (late work, absences, modalities for office/student hours, number of required assignments, etc.)
- Policies that ensure compliance with equity-focused laws (for example, Title IX, the Americans with Disabilities Act, Family Educational Rights and Privacy Act, and state laws)

In considering student-centered equity policies, the following questions can help create a map for change work:

- Are there federal or state system regulations that dictate how the policy must be worded and/or implemented?
- To what extent is the policy aligned with the equity values, mission, and goals of the institution, department, or program? What message does this policy communicate to students and employees about whether the institution or program values or does not value educational equity and opportunities?
- To what extent does the policy create, reinforce, and/or maintain practices that reduce students' access to educational opportunities?
- What are the implications for implementing the policy? How is it used? Where and how does it create systematic practices within the institution that affect students and employees?
- What does this policy imply about who can and cannot participate in higher education and work toward attaining a degree or other postsecondary credential?
- Who benefits from the policy? Which students and/or employees receive benefits, privileges, and/or access to resources because of this policy?

- Which student and employee communities are or might be harmed by the policy? What educational barriers does the policy create for some or all students? Are those barriers connected to educational equity?

Chapters 3 and 4 offer principles and strategies for navigating these issues around compromises and convictions.

Develop and Implement Assessment Plans that Disaggregate Data

Institutional change work that effectively improves students' educational opportunities requires carefully planned and ongoing assessment to determine whether changes actually achieve their stated equity goals. Equity-minded assessment, data collection, and analysis requires institutions and shared governance groups to disaggregate data (McNair et al. 2016) and avoid assuming that data about overall student successes apply to all student communities. For example, an initiative that focuses on student success outcomes in a course or program needs to assess both current practices and the impact of changes on all relevant student groups. Depending on the context, this might mean breaking data down by race, gender, course placement, Pell grant recipients, linguistic background, first-generation status, returning adult learners, and/or full-time and part-time students, etc. Drawing conclusions about the success of a program or change based on overall student success rates or experiences can hide inequities that persist for students from historically and contemporarily underrepresented and excluded groups in higher education. Participants in a student-centered change process also might need to broaden their perspectives on what types of data to collect (for example, moving beyond basic information on course grades to retention rates or qualitative data about student experiences).

The following questions are important for assessing initiatives, programs, and policy changes that affect students' success in college and their pathways toward a degree.

- Which student communities are important to identify and trace throughout the change and implementation process? How are those student communities identified in existing data? How might further disaggregation of data help monitor the impact of changes on students and help to determine whether the change achieves intended equity goals?
- How might the institution or program collect qualitative data about the experiences of students and employees in implementing the change?
- Who will interpret the data? How can participants ensure that data interpretation both accurately reflects the change and eliminates potential bias that might reinforce inequities for some student communities?

Chapter 6 describes specific strategies for developing plans for assessing institutional and program changes, including work that impacts students' educational opportunities.

Assess the Impact of Changes on Faculty and Staff Workload

Decision-making processes—including those aimed at improving equity and inclusion for students—can be implemented in inequitable ways if they produce or reinforce workload issues for the employees who are responsible for bringing about the planned changes. For example, curricular reforms aimed at student success and retention can create workload challenges for adjunct instructors if they are expected to transform how they teach without adequate time, compensation, and resources. Initiatives for students from historically marginalized communities in higher education replicate structural inequities when the faculty and staff who identify as belonging to those communities are expected to do disproportionate labor to support students and/or implement change in relation to other employees. For major student-centered initiatives that require substantial labor to implement, the planning process needs to include a thorough assessment of participants in the implementation process and a careful, critical review of the labor and resources required for carrying out the changes, especially for staff who may lack a structured way to participate in shared governance within the institution (we discuss such approaches in great detail in Chapter 6). This planning includes accounting for the time and labor of any students who will need to participate in making successful changes.

The following questions provide examples of equity issues to consider when balancing the need for student-centered change with the working conditions and workload of staff and faculty who are responsible for implementing a change.

- What is the existing workload for the employees who will need to implement the change and sustain it after implementation? What impact will the change have on their workload and working conditions? How might the change affect their existing responsibilities for supporting students?
- Which employees will have the most direct contact with students in the implementation process? What resources will they need to provide support to students?
- What steps will the institution take to ensure that the change won't have a disparate impact on employees from historically and contemporarily underrepresented or marginalized groups?
- What steps will the institution take to ensure that the employees and students involved in the change process have adequate resources, compensation, and time for doing the work required for creating and maintaining the change?
- What compromises might need to happen to balance the equity needs of students with those of faculty and staff?

INCLUDING STUDENTS IN SHARED GOVERNANCE PROCESSES

Involving students in shared governance processes is an important but often difficult endeavor. Perhaps the most compelling reason to include student voices in institutional change work is that shared governance processes are truly shared only when they include all stakeholders, and students are the institutional community members who are most affected by student-focused policies and initiatives. As a recent study from Nir and Musial (2021) found that "the overwhelming majority of students have not spent time in civic spaces," and in pre-study assessments observed that "students did not trust governance processes or political elites" (50). With the exception perhaps of Ivy League or other elite institutions, most college students will not have experience interacting with professors and administrators. In this section, we outline some of the common challenges to including students in shared governance processes and devise strategies for overcoming those challenges in an intentional way.

First, meaningful participation can require a time commitment that is difficult for students to make when balancing school, work, family obligations, and social activities. Second, faculty and staff normally participate in governance as part of their compensated work, and asking students to become involved in a process on a volunteer basis can exploit their labor. Third, students who are committed to governance participation (for example, elected student leaders) might not represent the needs and interests of differing student populations or the student body as a whole. This can be fostered by institutional culture, as Patrick (2022) observes that many campuses characterize student leadership as "leadership practice instead of leadership in practice" (4). Other established research has confirmed the relationship between participation in student government and increased satisfaction with the institution and growth in leadership skills (Kuh and Lund 1994).

The following strategies can help faculty, staff, and administrators create inclusive pathways for students to participate in governance processes.

Prioritize Where, When, and How Students Need to Participate in Institutional Processes

For example, in situations where it is difficult to find student representatives for committees and other governance work, focus on groups that do work that has the highest level of impact on students' sense of belonging in college and their abilities to make progress toward receiving a degree. As Patrick (2022) notes, to create truly meaningful opportunities for student leadership, "structural avenues need to be created that allow students to meet other education stakeholders on a fair playing field" (18). Governance leaders can strategically plan for policy making and program development work in a way that allows students to provide feedback selectively at key points in the process where student voices matter the most.

113

Compensate Student Participants for Their Time and Labor

Providing students with funding to participate in shared governance processes ensures that their work takes place in an equitable way that doesn't exploit their labor in the name of achieving perceptions of inclusivity. Participation in campus organizations is linked to preparation for life beyond college (Seymour and Lopez 2015). However, student leadership opportunities can perpetuate inequities when they are only available to students with financial stability and social privileges. Compensation for participation enables students from a more diverse range of social backgrounds to participate in leadership opportunities and shared governance. (Similarly, programs and institutions can compensate adjunct faculty for their participation.) Depending on the context, compensation can take place through hourly wages for small commitments and through tuition waivers and stipends for leadership roles and time-consuming activities. Internships with course credit can be another alternative but can also perpetuate inequities and reduce participation opportunities if students have to pay for that credit.

Provide Equitable Access to Voting and Feedback

In groups where students are included as representatives, give them voting rights that are equal to other members of the committee. However, you may need to account for a lower participation level from students who are balancing leadership roles with coursework, paid employment, and other responsibilities. For example, committees might give students a vote when they are present and, if appropriate, not count their presence or absence toward a required voting quorum when it's difficult to have consistent student participation. Alternatively, allow for student members to vote electronically outside of scheduled meetings or to give a proxy vote to another student representative.

Create Meaningful Opportunities for Authentic Participation

In arguing for graduate student participation in shared governance processes, Aguilar-Smith and Crossing (2021) note that "seats matter little if the people who occupy feel disempowered from using them. And often feelings of disempowerment stem from actual disempowerment." Offer students equal opportunities to participate in committee work, time to speak during meetings, and provide input into decision-making processes. Having a graduate student representative who is truly an elected representative (rather than 'tapped' by a chair or other leader) from the body of people they represent is an important way to build confidence for the student representative because they are advocating for others and responsible to others.

Provide Direct and Assigned Mentoring

Use participation processes that acknowledge students' role as learners and enhance their educational opportunities by providing mentors who can guide them through leadership processes, support their learning, help them navigate the culture of higher education, and help them work toward achieving their individual goals for participating in governance work. This can and should be done in a formal way such that the student has a clear sense of which member of the committee or group they are serving on can be relied upon to answer questions and check in on their understanding. Golden and Schwartz (1994), for example, document how there can be stressors associated with participation in student government, including balancing the role with their academic responsibilities, intragroup conflict, or campus controversies. Formal mentoring can help students navigate these stressful aspects of governance work.

Develop Participation Structures that Initiate Graduate Students into Higher Education Service and Governance Work

When appropriate for the mission of the governance group, provide graduate students with mentoring and leadership opportunities that help them develop the professional skills and strategies required for successfully transitioning to careers in academia or leadership roles in careers outside of higher education. Commonly, graduate students tend to be offered ad hoc opportunities such as serving on search committees or rely on graduate student only opportunities for service such as graduate student organizations. However, the experiences of graduate students in institutions that have such programs are important to an overall understanding of most of the issues within a department—for example, curriculum, instructional needs, and student support services, as graduate students in some programs do a significant amount of teaching (and often independently as the instructor of record) and therefore have close contact with undergraduate students. Look for opportunities to integrate graduate students and graduate teaching assistants into important conversations about departmental culture, priorities, and resources.

Avoid Assuming that Elected Student Leaders Represent All Students

Some student groups aren't invested in equity-minded practices and inclusivity, and they may even actively seek goals that are inequitable for some students. Shared governance groups often need to work with elected student leaders, but participants should work toward ensuring that other relevant student voices are included in decision-making processes. Experienced faculty and staff can mentor elected student leaders in developing equitable and inclusive processes for seeking feedback, inviting representation from a diverse range of students in student governance processes, and collaborating with other student groups.

Engage in Regular Cross-Governance Group Meetings and Discussions About Priorities

Work toward creating an institutional culture that supports collaboration across different student-centered groups. Create governance structures that support students in coordinating efforts across different groups to establish priorities and equitably allocate resources. This kind of governance work may require a written plan that creates a transparent structure for determining how and when student-centered governance groups work together to achieve common institutional goals.

APPLICATION

- Identify the policies in your institution or program that affect students' educational opportunities. Analyze the relationship between those policies and the student communities that your institution or program serves. Determine which policies (if any) might need to be revised to align them with the needs of students and the mission of the institution or program.
- Using the guiding questions in any of the subsections in this chapter, choose a policy, practice, or program and assess how it may create inequities for students. Then initiate conversations about equity within the processes and structures of your institution or program.
- Select a student-centered institutional practice (for example, a policy, initiative, or way of doing things). Analyze the shared governance processes used for making decisions related to the work connected with that practice. Determine whether shared governance participants who are included in decision making represent an inclusive range of perspectives, especially staff and faculty who have direct contact with students and (when appropriate) students.

Also evaluate whether decision-making processes place an inequitable or uncompensated workload on some participants. Develop a plan for revising the practice with a focus on equity, inclusion, and informed decision making.

- Examine the practices and processes used for including students in shared governance work (if any) in your institution. Assess the extent to which those practices are equitable and inclusive for students—and whether they are effective in providing student perspectives in decision-making processes. Identify strategies that might create more inclusive and equitable opportunities for students to participate in shared governance.

QUESTIONS FOR CONSIDERATION

1. What policies at your institution create equitable and inclusive educational opportunities for students and/or help them develop a sense of belonging in college? Which policies reduce educational opportunities and/or students' sense of belonging?

2. What strategies might your institution or program use to bring about lasting change that supports equity and inclusion for students who are historically and contemporarily excluded from higher education?

3. How might your institution assess existing structures and identify barriers to student success and retention, especially for students from historically and currently marginalized and minoritized communities?

4. What strategies might your program or institution use as part of shared governance to increase educational opportunities? What might need to change about your shared governance processes

to account for student communities that may have been excluded or harmed by current practices?

5. What strategies might your program or institution use to ensure that student-centered work doesn't create inequitable workloads or working conditions for the staff or faculty responsible for implementing initiatives and policy changes?

6. What practices might you use to include the perspectives of faculty, staff, and students who are most affected by changes in decision-making processes?

WORKS CITED

Aguilar-Smith, Stephanie, and Adrianna Crossing. "Allowed in the Room But Not at the Table." *Inside Higher Ed*, 2 Mar. 2021, www.insidehighered.com/views/2021/03/02/graduate-students-should-have-more-voice-shared-governance-opinion.

Bailey, Thomas R., et al. 2015. *Redesigning America's Community Colleges: A Clearer Path to Student Success*. Harvard UP.

Barnett, Elisabeth, et al. "The Role of Higher Education in High School Math Reform." *Community College Research Center*, Feb. 2022, https://ccrc.tc.columbia.edu/media/k2/attachments/higher-education-high-school-math-reform.pdf.

Bensimon, Estela Mara, et al. "Five Principles for Enacting Equity by Design." *American Association of Colleges and Universities*, vol. 19, 2015.

Bentrim, Erin M., and Gavin W. Hennig, editors. *The Impact of a Sense of Belonging in College: Implications for Student Persistence, Retention, and Success*. Stylus, 2022.

Castro, Erin L. *Understanding Equity in Community College Practice*. New Directions for Community Colleges 172. Jossey-Bass, 2015.

Center for Community College Student Engagement. "Listen to Me: Community College Students Tell Us What Helps Them Persist." *Center for Community College Student Engagement*, 2022, www.cccsse.org/SR22.

Chardin, Mirko, and Katie R. Novak. *Equity by Design: Delivering on the Power and Promise of UDL*. Corwin, 2020.

Complete College America. "Math Pathways." *Complete College America*, n.d., https://completecollege.org/strategy/math-pathways/.

Crazy Bull, Cheryl, et al. "Tribal Colleges and Universities: Building Nations, Revitalizing Identity." *Change: The Magazine of Higher Learning*, vol. 52, no. 1, 2020, pp. 23–29.

Fink, John, et al. "An Opportunity to Expand College Access? Rethinking Dual Enrollment Eligibility Policies Post-Pandemic." *Community College Research Center*, 30 Aug. 2022, https://ccrc.tc.columbia.edu/easyblog/rethinking-dual-enrollment-eligibility-policies-post-pandemic.html.

Garcia, Gina Ann. *Becoming Hispanic Serving Institutions: Opportunities for Colleges and Universities*. Johns Hopkins UP, 2019.

Golden, Dennis, and Harriet Schwartz. "Building an Ethical and Effective Relationship with Student Government Leaders." *New Directions for Student Services*, vol. 66, Summer 1994, pp. 19–30.

Griffin, Sarah. "English Transition Courses in Context: Preparing Students for College Success." *Community College Research Center*, CCRC Research Brief, Nov. 2018, https://ccrc.tc.columbia.edu/media/k2/attachments/english-transition-courses-preparing-students.pdf.

Jenkins, Davis, et al. "What We Are Learning About Guided Pathways." *Community College Research Center*, Apr. 2018, https://ccrc.tc.columbia.edu/media/k2/attachments/guided-pathways-part-1-theory-practice.pdf.

Karp, Melinda, and Rachel Bork. *They Never Told Me What to Expect, so I Didn't Know What to Do: Defining and Clarifying the Role of a Community College Student*. CCRC Working Paper No. 47, July 2012, https://ccrc.tc.columbia.edu/media/k2/attachments/defining-clarifying-role-college-student.pdf.

Kezar, Adrianna, et al. *Shared Equity Leadership: Making Equity Everyone's Work*. American Council on Education, 2021.

Kuh, George, and Jon Lund. "What Students Gain from Participating in Student Government." *New Directions for Student Services*, vol. 66, Summer 1994, pp. 5–17.

McNair, Tia Brown, et al. *Becoming a Student-Ready College: A New Culture of Leadership for Student Success*. Jossey-Bass, 2016.

———. "Building the Racial Equity Ecosystem for Sustainable Change." *Change: The Magazine of Higher Learning*, vol. 52, no. 2, 2020, pp. 63–67.

———. *From Equity Talk to Equity Walk: Expanding Practitioner Knowledge for Racial Justice in Higher Education*. Jossey-Bass, 2020.

Nir, Esther, and Jennifer Musial. "Engaging Politically Disenfranchised Students in Governance." *Journal of the Scholarship of Teaching and Learning*, vol. 21, no. 2, June 2021, pp. 43–57.

Nunn, Lisa M. *College Belonging: How First-Year and First-Generation Students Navigate Campus Life*. Rutgers UP, 2021.

O'Banion, Terry, and Marguerite Culp. *Student Success in Community College: What Really Works?* Rowman and Littlefield, 2020.

Patrick, Justin. "Student Leadership and Student Government." *Research in Educational Administration and Leadership*, vol. 7, no. 1, Mar. 2022, pp. 1–37.

Sawhill, Isabel. "Higher Education and the Opportunity Gap." *Brookings*, 2013, www. brookings.edu/research/higher-education-and-the-opportunity-gap/.

Scrivener, Susan, et al. "Doubling Graduation Rates: Three-Year Effects of CUNY's Accelerated Study in Associate Programs (ASAP) for Developmental Education Students." *MDRC*, Feb. 2015, www.mdrc.org/sites/default/files/doubling_graduation_rates_fr.pdf.

Seymour, Sean, and Shane Lopez. "'Big Six' College Experiences Linked to Life Preparedness." *Gallup*, 8 Apr. 2015, https://news.gallup.com/poll/182306/big-six-college-experiences-linked-life-preparedness.aspx.

Sullivan, Patrick. "Measuring 'Success' at Open Admissions Institutions: Thinking Carefully About This Complex Question." *College English*, vol. 70, no. 6, July 2008, pp. 618–32.

Tinto, Vincent. *Leaving College: Rethinking the Causes and Cures of Student Attrition*. 2nd ed. U of Chicago P, 1993.

Williams, Krystal, et al. "Centering Blackness: An Examination of Culturally-Affirming Pedagogy and Practices Enacted by HBCU Administrators and Faculty Members." *Innovative Higher Education*, vol. 46, 2021, pp. 733–57.

Wing, Kelisa. *Historically Black Colleges and Universities*. Racial Justice in America. Excellence in Achievement Series. Cherry Lake Publishing, 2022.

Xu, Di, et al. *College Acceleration for All? Mapping Racial/Ethnic Gaps in Advanced Placement and Dual Enrollment Participation*. CCRC Working Paper No. 113, Community College Research Center Teachers College, Columbia UP, Oct. 2019.

Chapter 6

Strategies for Implementing and Assessing Change

GUIDING QUESTIONS

1. What can shared governance participants do to ensure that policies and other shared governance decisions are implemented in an ethical, inclusive, and equitable way?
2. What strategies help shared governance participants assess the impact of initiatives and policy changes on faculty, staff, and students?
3. What practices help faculty, staff, and administrators assess policy changes over time?
4. How might shared governance participants adapt assessment strategies based on the nature of a policy and how it is used within an institution or organization?
5. What strategies can decision makers use for collecting feedback in an inclusive way while also determining an endpoint for feedback?
6. How can shared governance participants address challenges with collecting institutional data required for assessing the impact of changes on faculty, students, and staff?

The social relations that are important to sustaining oppression include the division of labour, decision-making power and procedures, and cultural forms of interacting and communicating. Addressing oppression requires that we take note of, first, how social groups are positioned in relation to each other, second which social groups enjoy non-material goods such as respect, power, and opportunity and, third, how the enjoyment of these goods is sustained by particular social relations (Young, Justice 16). In doing so, what becomes exceedingly clear is that social inequality is structural in the sense that it is reproduced by social processes 'that tend to privilege some more than others' (Young).

DOI: 10.4324/9781003257974-6

Unlike rules that either allow or bar all individuals within a particular category from engaging in a specified activity (e.g. 'No Blacks need apply'), social processes create tendencies, through incentives and disincentives that affect social groups without necessarily directing the behaviour of each and every individual.

(Eisenberg, 11)

ASSESSING IMPLEMENTED CHANGES WITH A FOCUS ON ETHICS

Political philosopher Iris Marion Young, in *Justice and the Politics of Difference* (1990) outlined critical components of her philosophical theory of justice, resisting what she describes as a distributive paradigm of justice and calling for a justice that eliminates oppression and domination, explaining "The concept of social justice includes all aspects of institutional rules and relations insofar as they are subject to potential collective decision. The concepts of domination and oppression, rather than the concept of distribution should be the starting point for a conception of social justice" (Young, *Justice* 16). Eisenberg, a scholar of Young's work, explains that social relations are critical to understanding how oppression and are reproduced:

. . . what becomes exceedingly clear is that social inequality is structural in the sense that it is reproduced by social processes 'that tend to privilege some more than others'. (Young, 2001 2). Unlike rules that either allow or bar all individuals within a particular category from engaging in a specified activity (e.g. 'No Blacks need apply'), social processes create tendencies, through incentives and disincentives that affect social groups without necessarily directing the behaviour of each and every individual.

(Eisenberg, 2006)

We highlight the philosophy of Iris Young in this chapter because of its compatibility with the practices for equitable and inclusive processes for implementing change in an institution, department, program, or professional organization.

Embedded throughout this book is the guiding concept of ethical approaches to shared governance. Without clear ethical foci for decision-making processes, determined by efforts around equity and inclusion, important voices might be lost. Policies and initiatives may be implemented in ways that create, reinforce, or maintain inequities for students and employees. Institutions of higher education are notoriously labeled as liberal but are, in reality, slow-moving, cautious, and largely conservative. In other words, they are mired in a clinging to traditions or "the way things have been" whether on the individual level (Dunican, et al. 2019), within specific disciplines (Lane 86) or the broader institutional level (see Diamond 2006). For this reason, significant institutional or organizational changes of any type can be difficult to implement in ethical ways.

Understanding the history of an institution, a degree program, a policy, or a process provides useful context for conversations, but institutions can't function in an ethical and equitable way through adherence to the practices and policies of the past. Effective, ethical, and inclusive governance processes reflect the current challenges of institutions and the people they serve. Higher education in the United States is experiencing a great deal of upheaval, and meeting the needs of the students, faculty, staff, and communities in which our institutions reside is a deeply ethical act that can require difficult conversations. As policies are created, or amended, over time, transparent assessment of policies and their implementation is crucial for ensuring that policies are changed, developed, and implemented in ethical ways, not only internally for the organization but externally for the communities that the institution serves. Assessment is also crucial for meeting legal obligations, accreditation requirements, state and federal mandates, and professional standards. In this chapter, we discuss the ways in which shared governance participants can monitor and assess the potential impacts of policy changes, receive feedback, and achieve buy-in throughout the process for implementing change, and develop robust and useful assessment practices.

DEVELOPING AN ASSESSMENT PLAN FOR IMPLEMENTING CHANGE

Integrating a transparent assessment process into policy revisions, new initiatives, and other institutional changes lays a foundation for equitable, transparent, and effective shared governance. Developing an assessment plan with a timeline as part of a policy or initiative development process creates a structure that allows an institution or program to determine whether the change has achieved its stated goals and whether it is implemented in an ethical, effective, and inclusive way. Assessing the effectiveness of change work is a good practice regardless of the kind of policy or program, but assessment processes are essential for changes that are likely to have a significant impact on students and/or employees (for example, policies that impact students' academic standing, a complete revision of general education requirements, family and medical leave policies, budget process, staff job titling and classifications, or new methods for evaluating staff performance). In particular, ethical implementation requires careful and systematic monitoring when a change might affect students' educational trajectories or the workload and working conditions of staff and contingent faculty.

Clear assessment processes with carefully planned activities and assessment measures can be a particularly useful tool for moving policy changes, institutional restructuring, and new initiatives forward and addressing the concerns of stakeholders. First, an assessment process builds accountability for the impact of

123

a change into its implementation, which can increase buy-in and support from people who are most affected by the change and who may be responsible for all or parts of its implementation. Second, written assessment plans also provide relevant members of a higher education community with a transparent way of knowing when and how the institution or program will determine whether the change achieves its goals. Third, a plan can also help decision makers monitor whether a change creates barriers or negative consequences for students, inequities for staff and faculty, or workload challenges for employees charged with implementing the change. Finally, assessment plans can identify systematic methods for policy makers and implementation leaders to seek feedback and information about the successes and challenges of implementing the policy change, especially when staff or faculty who are responsible for the labor of implementation didn't make the change or the policy. Carefully planned assessment offers a mechanism through which—if the change has failed or has negative effects—a course correction can be implemented and people will have a voice in making adjustments.

Strategies for creating a fully developed assessment plan for an institutional, program, or organizational change include the following:

- Identify how and where participants will collect, organize, and store data used to support the rationale for the change, monitor its implementation, and assess the results.
- Create a timeline for assessing each component of the implementation process, including a specified time for revisiting the change to make adjustments (if needed).
- Set benchmarks for determining whether the change has achieved its stated goals (which may require initial data collection and assessment to develop for long-term projects).
- Identify the institutional research, assessment reports, and other relevant data that are already available within the institution for informing decision making and creating a starting point for monitoring the impact of the change.
- Establish the varied measures and pieces of data that will be used for monitoring varied stages of the implementation process and assessing the change.
- Plan for how assessment data will be collected (for example, who will do the work, when they will do it, and how they will receive compensation or reassigned time for their labor).
- Develop methods for collecting feedback from faculty, staff, and/or students who are involved in the implementation process and/or impacted by the change (for example, an anonymous survey, feedback form, focus groups, or scheduled check in with relevant campus groups).

- Name the methods for reporting on the results of the assessment process in an accountable and transparent way, including reporting methods, the groups or individuals who will do the reporting, and how the results will be disseminated.
- State the processes that will be used for making adjustments to the implementation process if results of the assessment work identify challenges, problems, or inequities.

The preceding list describes assessment planning strategies that are important to consider whenever an institution or organization is working on significant changes. However, the components of an effective assessment plan typically reflect the scope of a project, its purpose, and its potential impact on students, staff, and faculty. Plans for assessing policy implementation processes can be as simple as a short "to do" list for minor policy changes or a fully developed, multipage document for institutional change work that alters an institution or an organization (for example, the overhaul of an associate degree, changes to the structure of colleges or departments within an institution, or a new way of classifying and compensating staff). An ethical development process for major institutional or organizational changes typically includes opportunities for relevant stakeholders to read and provide feedback on a written assessment plan, which can help decision makers receive feedback on the measures and processes that they plan to use to bring about a significant change. Opportunities for feedback can increase buy-in, identify potential problems from the perspective of people who will be responsible for implementing the change, and create a more ethical implementation process.

In most cases, colleges and universities have existing assessment practices, institutional research resources, and policy review processes that can be adapted or leveraged for assessing and implementing policy changes. It's rare to start an assessment process from scratch for standard policy changes and revisions to routine higher education practices. For example, accreditation depends on a multiple measures approach to systematically collecting both quantitative and qualitative data for evaluating institutional practices (see, for example, the Higher Learning Commission's policy "Criteria for Accreditation"). The starting benchmark data and planned processes required for assessing a change might already be available through work completed for accreditation or other evaluation processes, such as program reviews and annual institutional research collected to meet state system requirements. Often assessment processes and institutional research practices already exist across different administrative units, but they might be part of institutional practices that typical faculty and staff members are unaware of until they become involved in leadership or governance. Even experienced shared governance participants may not know about available data collection processes for institutional units that are different from their own and that are outside the scope of their previous policy work.

125

New initiatives that completely change multiple parts of an institution may require a substantial and organized effort to organize available data and collect new information. For example, the Guided Pathways model (see Bailey, et al. 2015, *Redesigning America's Community Colleges*, "What We Know"; Dedman 2021; Jenkins, et al. 2021; McNair and Bonneville 2021) that is increasingly used at community colleges to shape students' programs of study requires intensive preparation and participation from faculty, administrators, and advisors to implement change over a long period of time. Those types of initiatives require multiple pieces of data collected over a timeline by many different units within the institution, including information that might not be available through existing assessment and institutional research processes.

In some cases, faculty and staff need to change policies or institutional practices that seem set in stone and immovable, but opportunities then arise for implementing change across a broad series of initiatives (for example, hiring a new administrator, an accreditation visit, state system changes to staff classifications, a self-study, or a curriculum revision to name a few). These opportunities for change benefit from a clear plan for assessing how implementation impacts members of the institution or program, especially when a change requires faculty and staff to change not only collective practices for their units but also parts of their work lives. As they develop and guide policy changes, shared governance participants benefit from paying close attention to the extent to which assessment is a check-the-box-and-move-on activity at an institution and whether the culture of assessment also needs to change. Using assessment data to gauge progress, create a foundation for change, and make institutional processes more transparent to faculty and staff can fundamentally change the nature of shared governance on a campus or in a department.

Assessment can be a rich and engaging experience for individuals who live, work, and learn on a campus or in a virtual higher education space if the resulting data is used for specific purposes that create a more ethical, equitable, or inclusive teaching, learning, and working environment. But this often requires stakeholders to shift their thinking away from traditional assessment practices that are connected to annual review or accreditation requirements. While policy changes may not seem like the stuff that intellectual breakthroughs are made of, understanding the policy architecture of an institution and engaging actively in policy change processes can directly impact the lived experiences of faculty, staff, students, and higher education community members.

ASSESSING CHANGE IN INCREMENTAL AND FORMATIVE WAYS

Any policy change with the potential to have a high-stakes impact on students, faculty, staff, or the institution needs to have an implementation plan that allows for incremental data collection feedback in the early stages of implementation and at varied points in a process before formal assessment results are available. For the purposes of this chapter, *assessment* means collecting data for the purpose of monitoring and evaluating a change. Effective assessment results in data that is formative, usable, and presents key shared governance participants with accurate and necessary information to help make decisions, improve circumstances, and inform future paths. For that reason, assessing a change typically needs to happen incrementally through processes that reflect the change itself, the people doing the work, and the institutional structures that are (or aren't) available to support implementation of the change.

Formative assessment is a strategy for assessing change through small steps and then responding or intervening when assessment data shows that an implementation process needs adjustments. It is a term that comes out of education and describes work that teachers engage in constantly: "Formative assessment provides information that teachers can use to focus or redirect instruction; it also provides information that students can use to assess their own and each other's learning" (Cizek, et al. 2019; see also Bennett 2011, for additional definitional work on formative assessment). In shared governance and service work, formative assessment is typically used for projects that have a pilot or another process for implementing a small, temporary, or limited change before determining whether it becomes a permanent practice and/or scales up to affect a larger part of an institution or program. However, incremental and small-scale assessment measures can also be used for other types of changes to receive feedback and information about whether a change is being implemented in an effective and/or ethical way.

When used in inclusive ways that involve multiple stakeholders, formative assessment steps in an implementation process create opportunities for everyone involved with or impacted by a change to have access to data that can inform their decisions and practices before the institution or organization has finished collecting data and reporting on it in a formal way. In contrast, *summative assessment* refers to the processes for collecting, analyzing, and reporting on the results of a change at the end stages of an implementation process. Summative assessment is important for creating accountability and generating data that an institution, program, or organization can use for assessing the overall results of a change. But when a high impact change only uses summative assessment and final reporting, decision makers and people implementing the change often lack the data required for making adjustments as problems arise.

Assessing the implementation of a policy change can be either a short-term activity for a relatively low-stakes change (such as increased parking fees or a change in committee structure) to long-term data collection over a period of semesters or even years for high-stakes changes that have a significant impact (for example, curricular changes that alter students' pathways toward a degree or the requirements for promotion that affect employees' career pathways). The length of a policy assessment process depends on the nature of the policy, its actual and potential impact on students and employees, and whether the change is linked to accountability (for example, for accreditation, equity initiatives, legal requirements, or state system mandates).

CASE STUDY: FORMATIVE ASSESSMENT BEFORE SCALING UP A PILOT INITIATIVE

Two of the coauthors spent several years working with colleagues and administrators to revise the placement practices and processes for a state-wide open-access institution. Although placement shared governance work typically involves Math, English, ESL, and/or developmental education faculty, placement practices frequently set prerequisites for many disciplines across an entire institution, and the results can have a significant impact on faculty, students, and academic affairs staff. Over time, the entire placement project required collaboration between the Math and English departments, the provost's office, local campus associate deans and student affairs leaders, advisors, testing services staff, and admissions specialists. Implementation of the initial project pilot started on a small campus, and a local assessment project showed that a new multiple measures placement process increased first-year academic standing and success for students. However, that initial data was insufficient for making arguments for doing statewide implementation or for drawing conclusions about how the change affected the employees involved in the process. The project took several years of incremental implementation with related data collection using a variety of different measures before the project could be scaled up across the entire institution. Small pieces of data systematically collected over multiple semesters showed that the project successfully achieved its equity goals and increased the number of students who placed directly into credit-bearing coursework (see Eubanks, 2017 for some of the challenges of aligning assessment measures with data needs; and Horst and Prendergast, 2020 for an assessment taxonomy of skills).

However, the formal collection process was insufficient for monitoring the effects of the change on the staff and local advising processes. Different campuses had different realities and practices that were shaped by their student populations, campus sizes, available staffing, and existing student affairs processes. Additional summative assessment data from individual campuses revealed challenges, successes, and barriers to implementation that local faculty and staff, along with institutional leaders needed to address before and during the process of scaling up placement changes across the entire state. Informal feedback from faculty and staff along with placement data and success results permitted project participants to monitor implementation and make adjustments that reflected locally situated needs. Because parts of the change were mandated by the state system, the institution also needed to do institutional research and write documents that reported on the summative results of the project. But the varied assessment measures used by multiple participants in multiple locations became the information that was most useful in achieving buy-in from institutional stakeholders and monitoring the effectiveness of the project. This case study illustrates that formative assessment leads to summative assessment but is largely more usable for practitioners on the ground because it's timely, active, and allows participants to transparently engage in their own reflection work and use it to adjust course if needed.

ALIGNING ASSESSMENT WITH POLICY PURPOSES AND STAKEHOLDERS

Any policy change with the potential to have a high-stakes impact on students, faculty, staff, or the institution needs to have an assessment plan and strategies that are aligned with the purpose of the change and that involve the stakeholders affected by the policy. The type of policy shapes decisions about assessment processes and the individuals or groups who need to participate. Some general categories in which policies and their assessments can fall include:

Academic and curricular policies—Examples include department, committee, program, or senate bylaws; curriculum development, review, and program requirements; placement and prerequisites; program review; program discontinuance; assessment of student learning; accreditation compliance; concurrent and dual enrollment course requirements; and the academic calendar. Academic policies require faculty participation (including adjunct and contingent instructors), but many of these policies need participation from academic affairs leaders, advisors, a registrar's office, and academic staff who have firsthand knowledge of how a policy change impacts students. Careful consideration of adjunct and/or graduate instructor perspectives is especially important when they are the primary instructors who work directly with undergraduate students in a program. When policy development and assessment of an academic or curricular change happens only through administrative leaders, tenure-line faculty,

129

and/or elected shared governance leaders without the perspectives of relevant academic staff and instructors, implementing the change and ensuring equitable results can become difficult when a complete picture of what happens during implementation requires the perspectives of employees who have been excluded from the process.

Employment policies for faculty—Examples include retention, tenure, merit evaluation, and promotion (including positions that are outside of a tenure system or off the tenure track); faculty handbook or other guidelines; contingent and adjunct employment; and other contractual requirements. Faculty policies benefit from assessment participation from full-time faculty in every relevant department and program (and not just those involved in shared governance). With the exception of tenure and promotion policies that are specific to tenure-line faculty, perspectives from full-time contingent and adjunct faculty are also essential in assessing a policy change, especially when policies affect their working conditions, workload, or compensation. Administrators and human resources staff with knowledge about employment practices and regulations almost always need to provide feedback before and during the process of changing and implementing employment policies.

Other employment policies—These policies govern institutional practices that apply to all employees or to every employee within an employment category (e.g., full time or part time and exempt or nonexempt). Examples include equitable and inclusive hiring, vacation and sick leave, retirement and early retirement, overloads, overtime for hourly and nonexempt employees, work hours for nonexempt staff, and reduction in workforce. When policies affect all employees, the implementation process needs to account for varied ways for employees from every part of an institution to provide feedback that will help monitor the successes and challenges of the change. However, levels of involvement and types of feedback for employment policies need to reflect the varied responsibilities that some employees have for implementing a process. For example, human resources administrators and staff and people who oversee budget processes need structured and ongoing ways to provide feedback on processes that they are directly involved in implementing (in contrast to other employees who are affected by a change but don't deal with it as part of their workloads).

Institutional policies for all employees—These widely varied policies maintain the stated standards and guidelines that provide an institution with organized structures, processes, and expectations for creating a transparent working environment. Examples include policy development, shared governance, mandatory training, behavioral intervention, budgets and expenditure, benefits, internal audits, security, travel reimbursement, use of facilities, motor vehicles, public safety and emergency management, mandatory training, community relations, parking, employee conduct, grievances, and conflicts of interest. Like employment policies, changes to these institutional policies benefit from opportunities for all stakeholders to give feedback while providing more structured and ongoing ways for employees to provide feedback when implementation is part of their position responsibilities and workloads.

Student-focused policies—Examples of student policies include academic standing, probation, suspension, and return after probation; admissions; student conduct; role of student representatives in shared governance; bylaws for student groups and student-centered programs; student employment; alcohol and drug use; and student complaints. All student-focused policies require ongoing feedback and perspectives from the academic staff and other employees who are directly involved in an implementation process. Policy development and assessment processes also need to account for how to include student perspectives in an effective and ethical way. Faculty also need to provide feedback when student-centered policies intersect with their service responsibilities (for example, their roles on a student appeals or admissions committee).

Staff policies—These policies outline institutional guidelines and structures for staff who work outside of tenure-line positions, often including administrators (especially those in middle level positions). Examples include staff evaluation processes, reporting, promotion, professional development, policies, and bylaws for staff organizations. The structure of staff policies and the employees that they cover usually depend on institutional shared governance structures and/or state system practices. Depending on how an institution structures and classifies employment positions, there might be unified guidelines for most staff or varied sets of policies that affect particular groups of staff (for example, administrators, classified staff, academic staff, or administrative staff). Full-time contingent and/or part-time adjunct instructors might be included in some or all of the policies that apply to staff, or they might work under some or most policies that apply to tenure-line instructors (with the exception of tenure and promotion). An institution also might have policies that are governed by different ways that employees are classified within a state system (for example, coordinators and directors with particular types of oversight for other employees). Faculty and staff who participate in shared governance work typically need to draw from existing institutional documents to identify which staff stakeholders are affected by policy changes. Higher education professionals who move to new institutional contexts often need to adjust their understanding of stakeholders for staff policies to reflect practices at the new institution.

131

Institutional policies for compliance with legal requirements—These policies draw from both federal and state law but might also include state system implementation mandates that describe how to implement legal requirements. Examples include the Clery Act, Family Educational Rights and Privacy Act, Title IX, Americans with Disabilities Act (ADA), Fair Labor Standards Act, affirmative action; implementation of state antidiscrimination or employment laws; family and medical leave; mandatory reporting; use of public resources; open records; and permitted or prohibited weapons on campus. Policies connected to legal mandates may have language and requirements that come directly from the state system or the law itself, and the development of and implementation of changes to those policies typically require a legal review. Shared governance participants can monitor how policy changes with implications are implemented, but typically assessment work focuses on ensuring that employees understand and comply with legal requirements—and not on the guidelines of policy itself, which can often be changed only through legislative action, by governing boards, or state system leaders that operate outside of shared governance.

Each of these categories of policies and their stakeholders share similar affordances and constraints, but they also each require different types of implementation and assessment strategies that account for the stakeholders with whom and for whom the assessment of the policy matters.

IDENTIFYING RELEVANT ASSESSMENT MEASURES AND TOOLS

As we discuss briefly in Chapter 3, institutions and programs can use multiple tools for assessing a policy change or a new initiative. Most institutional or program change work benefits from at least two stages of assessment with accompanying measures and tools: (1) initial data collection to inform the policy development process and (2) informal or formal data collection during or after the policy implementation process to determine whether the change has achieved its intended goals. In addition to providing information about how a policy might be changed, initial data collection before a policy is implemented provides a baseline benchmark for subsequent assessment work. For many policies (especially those connected to student success outcomes and employee equity issues), it's difficult to determine whether policy changes have achieved their intended goals without a starting point for assessing practices before the change.

The measures and tools used for initial data collection are sometimes the same as those used to assess a change in summative or formative ways, but they can also be different because institutional and program changes generate new types of data. The change itself can generate information that previously was unavailable for decision-making processes. For example, if an institution creates a new degree, the initial data collection process can focus on the need for a change and information about similar programs at other institutions. However, baseline data about the program isn't available for assessment purposes because the program doesn't exist until after the change is implemented.

The examples in Table 6.1 illustrate how diverse types of policy assessments are shaped by the nature of policies and how they are used within an institution before and during the process of implementing changes.

Table 6.1 Policy overview

Type of policy	Examples of data collected before a change	Examples of data used to assess implementation
Program-level curricular policies	Disaggregated student success outcomes; relevant policies and standards from disciplinary professional organizations; program completion rates for students disaggregated by different groups; transfer equivalents and curricular requirements for similar institutions in the state or region; transfer data for students completing a program	Disaggregated student success outcomes; information about impact of changes on students' degree pathways; assessment of policy changes in relation to disciplinary standards; experiences of faculty and students in courses affected by the change
Hiring practices	Information from legal counsel about relevant employment laws, state laws, and state system policies; institutional data about demographics of faculty and staff in relation to the student communities the institution serves; information about available search advocate or hiring training; information about relevant state laws and/or state system requirements; informal or formally collected feedback from recently hired faculty	Legal review of policy changes before implementation; data about employee demographics collected over time in relation to goals of the policy change; qualitative data about the experiences of newly hired employees and participants in the search process
Faculty evaluation	Surveys of faculty and administrators; data about how faculty evaluations are used within departments and programs to inform decisions and compensation; information about faculty evaluation processes at institutions with similar missions; professional standards from higher education groups	Surveys of faculty and administrators about the change; assessment of policy changes in relation to professional standards; institutional research about changes to faculty outcomes based on the evaluation process

(Continued)

133

Table 6.1 Continued

Type of policy	Examples of data collected before a change	Examples of data used to assess implementation
Faculty appeals and grievances	Information about relevant employment laws, state laws, and state system policies; data about when and how frequently appeals and grievance processes are used; informally or formally collected information about the experiences of faculty and staff involved in appeals and grievance processes	Legal review of policy changes before implementation; surveys of faculty and staff involved in processes; institutional research about the impact of policy changes on processes

MAINTAINING A LEGAL AND ETHICAL IMPLEMENTATION PROCESS

All institutions are legally accountable to multiple agencies at federal, state, and local levels. The higher education environment is one that is complex in terms of legal issues because there are laws that relate to such things as financial aid, admissions, licensures, privacy, and nondiscrimination. The most common legal issues in higher education pertain to discrimination, accessibility, and free speech, and institutional work related to these issues typically has corresponding offices or officers such as Title IX, the ADA, Affirmative Action, and the Legal Counsel. One benefit of a good shared governance environment is that there are administrators whose job it is to know what those various compliance and accreditation directives are. Working closely with them is essential for ethical and legally compliant policy implementation. These can include employees of an office of human resources, of equity and diversity, of faculty affairs, student affairs, or an office of institutional research. Some institutions may also have a specific position on a senate or council with recordkeeping responsibilities. This might be an elected office (for example, a senate secretary) or a staff position with responsibility for clerical and communication tasks. A large institution can have faculty or administrative staff positions charged with managing policy compliance and records maintenance. Such a person or institutional unit will know the history of policies, as well as methods for implementing and assessing changes in an ethical and legally compliant way. In an era when education is under more scrutiny than ever in the United States, accounting for legal issues in policy change is a necessary first step for transparency not only for the university or college community but also for the public.

Legal issues in higher education not only include policies but the nature of the existence of higher education itself. Since the 1970s, there has been debate over the relative independence or not of public higher education, as well as whether a university or college should be treated as an industry, with students as consumers. As always, public vs. private sector issues matter in these discussions but point to the necessity of well-reasoned, clear, and transparent policy review and revision. The impacts of policy, then, cannot be understated—having a blueprint for how decisions are made within your university policy architecture is paramount to the function of a good institution because there is always something in writing that can be referred to as a potential source of mediation should the need arise.

IDENTIFYING FEEDBACK BENCHMARKS

As we discuss in Chapter 3, cultivating involvement and creating a culture of engagement are both important parts of successful policy development and revision work within institutional governance. Those sections provide ideas about how to use multiple methods and modes of gathering input from affected groups that is used to inform policy development and assess the results after implementing a change. Diverse representation in shared governance processes promotes diverse representations of feedback. With equitable representation comes reasonable expectations for a process of review. In this section we offer benchmarks for assessing when and how shared governance leaders have reached the feedback saturation point, and when and how to decide when to stop gathering feedback as part of an assessment process. An endless feedback loop will create a protracted process and ultimately benefit no one. These benchmarks and related timelines can also function as a way to determine when issues under review will come under review again in the future.

Benchmark 1: When More Feedback Isn't Equitable or Inclusive

A clear timeline for how feedback will be received and used in a shared governance process establishes how to receive timely input from relevant stakeholders, both in collecting input on a potential change and assessing its implementation. Adhering to a stated timeline for input is usually more inclusive than altering deadlines in a way that gives some people more opportunities to participate than others. If a timeline is extended multiple times, this may shut out equitable opportunities to weigh in on documents or proposals, particularly because the majority of faculty are on semester or nine-month contracts. A timeline exists so that the stakeholders in the outcomes can participate in the shared governance process and maintain their investment. For example, if major changes are made at the last stage of a process by someone with significant power and authority, the process itself can become inequitable because it doesn't represent the needs of all the stakeholders. This is particularly true if a person with an unfair opportunity for input has no direct consequences as a result of the action item.

At the senate or department level, this means that a final version of a revised policy document should largely resemble what was previously viewed by stakeholder groups unless it is subsequently recirculated after revision. A clear timeline for circulation includes ample time to circulate the policy for feedback while also constraining parties who may not be involved at the actual institution or individuals who want to impact the policy for reasons that are not always aboveboard (e.g., they might be motivated by self-interest or want to drown out the need for equitable revisions).

Benchmark 2: When a Multiphase Timeline Has Passed

When shared governance leaders have in good faith offered multiple, public opportunities for groups or individuals to give input on a proposal, then it is reasonable to call a halt to further feedback in the interest of moving items forward for a vote. Similarly, a timeline for assessing a change after implementation needs to include a stopping point for collecting feedback for the purpose of making decisions and drawing conclusions about the impact of a change. As we encouraged earlier, a structured and planned sequence of feedback opportunities should be made available to those who are ultimately affected by the outcome of a decision; however, it is perfectly reasonable to maintain a planned end to feedback gathering, even if some stakeholders may have missed the window.

Benchmark 3: When Additional Feedback Is an Ongoing Effort to Derail an Action Item Despite Lack of Support For It

Sometimes, calls for delays or further deliberation are reasonable efforts to ensure the best quality final product, one that can have the maximum level of buy-in and meet the needs of the most people. However, if requests to provide more feedback or give changes are a persistent demand for the same issue to be addressed when it has already been given due consideration, then it's more productive to move work forward without additional feedback. For example, in a senate or department context, a policy discussion can get bogged down in the specifics of a word choice that holds a great deal of meaning to perhaps one insistent member of the group. Calling a vote on the proposed amendment and moving on (rather than continued discussion of the single instance in an attempt to please or capitulate to the blockader) is likely appropriate in order to move forward.

Benchmark 4: When the Same People Loudly and Insistently Dominate the Feedback Process

Somewhat similarly, synchronous meetings (whether virtual or in-person) can become the staging ground for a few voices to dominate a conversation, and participants may insist on continuing to state and restate their views, even when the majority do not support the objection or concern. It's reasonable in such cases to take steps to test the will of the majority (taking a straw poll or formal vote) about the concern and move on if the results show that the concern is not widely shared. A good way to ensure equitable buy-in is to provide multiple opportunities for submitting anonymous, written feedback, and to make that feedback openly available for all constituents.

CHALLENGES WITH COLLECTING ACCURATE AND ETHICAL ASSESSMENT DATA

Effective shared governance assessment activities often require participants to work within institutional structures and processes for collecting data that informs decision making and/or determining whether a policy change or initiative has achieved its intended outcomes. Participants can face challenges in ensuring that data is collected and interpreted in an ethical and effective way. The following list provides examples of how shared governance leaders can be strategic in resolving challenges with collecting or accessing data that is important for high-stakes decisions (for example, initiatives that require disaggregated data about student retention or progress toward a degree, issues with legal implications, or work toward reducing gender or racial barriers in campus leadership).

Unethical Processes Can Be Used to Block Data Collection

Sometimes people in positions of power make it difficult or impossible to collect the data required to assess the need for a change or monitor the outcomes of an initiative, especially when they perceive that revealing data might have negative professional consequences for them. Shared governance participants can sometimes appeal to accreditations or accreditation standards, state system officials, or even the press (Baer offers a succinct synthesized overview of the relationship between assessment, accountability, and accreditation).

Faculty or Staff With Relevant Expertise Aren't Allowed to Participate

Ethical and effective data collection for assessment purposes sometimes requires specialized expertise that draws from research experience or advanced knowledge of an issue. Sometimes institutional stakeholders who have already done relevant research are shut out of assessment processes for a variety of reasons, including faculty discounting staff expertise or decision makers not recognizing their own lack of knowledge or skills that others possess. Shared governance leaders need to ensure that people within the institution who have the expertise required for informing a decision-making process have an opportunity to participate in identifying existing data and determining how to collect new information.

137

Participants Try to Manipulate Data to Support Something Different from What the Results Actually Show

Because shared governance processes are closely connected to power structures within higher education, some people want to interpret data and curate the results to achieve their own purposes, which are different from the common good of an institution or program. Shared governance leaders can reduce the potential for data manipulation by taking a multipronged approach to using data for decision making that includes carefully planning assessment measures, asking relevant experts to review proposed data collection processes, getting people who are external to the shared governance processes to review data for accuracy, and seeking feedback on how the results are interpreted.

Some People Can't Understand the Data Required for a Particular Task and Have Difficulty Providing It (Even if They Have It)

The process for collecting data within an institution often requires shared governance participants to work with an institutional research office, various campus functional units, and/or administrators who have access to databases and other data sources that faculty and staff can't access. Shared governance leaders may need to ask institutional employees to collect data that is different from what they are normally used to accessing for other parts of their jobs. In these cases, it's useful to have a written plan with clear assessment measures, along with a rationale for why the data collection is important and an explanation of how it will be used. Sometimes faculty or staff need to bring administrators into the conversation to support the use of time and resources for collecting and organizing assessment data.

The People With That Data Might Misunderstand What They Can and Can't Share

Employees who have access to the necessary data for a decision-making process may be reluctant to share it, especially when data collection for other purposes may require a different set of permissions. For example, information gathered for research purposes requires institutional review board approval, whereas data used for internal assessment purposes does not. Disaggregated data about overall student outcomes doesn't need the same privacy permissions as information that identifies individual students. Shared governance participants can address these issues through clear shared governance documents that outline the processes for collecting institutional data as well as collaborative work with administrators and relevant heads of campus functional units.

138

Some assessment challenges can't be overcome when the people who have ownership for data or who control the processes are in high positions of power within an institution. At other times, the institution doesn't have the workforce or time to gather data even if it would be useful for informing decision-making processes. Sometimes the labor required for data collection may place an inequitable workload on staff. Shared governance leaders and other stakeholders benefit from a realistic approach to collecting data that acknowledges the possibilities and limitations of doing shared governance assessment work within an institutional context and available time and resources.

CASE STUDY: EXAMPLE OF A LONG-TERM POLICY REVIEW CYCLE

At Minnesota State University, Mankato, the policy process is clear and embedded in shared governance. This example is one that shows a process that is equitable if followed and engaged. MSU has a Policy Consultation and Approval Committee that includes representatives across administration, the faculty union, the staff union, and the student government. Comprised of 14 people, this committee is charged to:

- "Solicit recommendations from the University community for policies that may need review or development;
- Establish priorities among the policies that are recommended for review;
- Issue a public list of policies that will be reviewed or developed during the academic year;
- Coordinate the work of the individuals who develop policy drafts;
- Ensure a broad-based and comprehensive review of the policy drafts."

Every year, between 10 and 12 new and existing policies are subject to an informal and formal review. Anyone reviewing a policy on the university website can submit a comment about the policy, and those comments are taken into consideration by the committee and presented for formal review to the university community before they are put into effect. They are also available to be viewed on the website. The policy website clearly details what the policies are, who they affect, and how they will be reviewed, implemented, and maintained.

Minnesota State University, Mankato University Policy	
Policy Name: Gender Neutral Restrooms	**Effective Date of Last Revision** New Policy
Custodian of Policy: Vice President for Finance and Administration	**Date of Last Review** New Policy
Date of Adoption August 1, 2015	**Date of Next Review** September 2021

Policy

Campus facility renovation and new construction projects of sufficient scope will include at a minimum one single stall gender neutral restroom.

Procedures

Facilities Management will ensure gender neutral restrooms are included during the planning and implementation of construction and renovation projects.

Rationale

Minnesota State University, Mankato is committed to achieving equal opportunity and access, and full participation for all students, staff, faculty and visitors. Individuals who are gender non-conforming, transgender, have opposite gender assistants or caregivers, or who are on campus with opposite gender children should have a conveniently located restroom that accommodates all genders.

Figure 6.1 Minnesota State University Gender Neutral Policy under review 2021–2022.

The policy is available as a PDF in a table of policies under review. To post a comment, users are directed to a Microsoft form in which they select the relevant policy from a drop-down menu and leave a comment. Comments are collected and included in the policy review table on the website. Comments may or may not affect the actual policy, but all comments are included in subsequent discussions with the various constituents and stakeholders. In the case of a policy such as this, comments range from supportive to those that parrot conservative talking points. Since this policy has existed since 2015, frequently the committee will take on suggestions like this one, "In addition to the required restroom, signage indicating its existence and location should be posted at every NON-gender neutral restroom in the vicinity. 'A single-stall, gender-neutral restroom is located on level two of this building, near the elevator.'" Such suggestions support the equitable use of this policy.

Sometimes, the structures of governance themselves can require ongoing assessment and adjustment. For example, a proliferation of committees or continued struggle to fill vacancies or positions within governance can signal that the structure of governance no longer matches the realities of the institutional needs, architecture, or staffing. This vignette by Nelson and Blakeman illustrates a systematic assessment approach.

VIGNETTE: NERISSA NELSON AND KATHRYN BLAKEMAN, UNIVERSITY OF WISCONSIN-STEVENS POINT

What are the major barriers to effective service and governance in higher education, particularly those factors that are within the control of those bodies?

In 2015, our institution, the University of Wisconsin-Stevens Point, a regional midwest public university with three campuses and a student body of 8,135, constituted a new governance structure—the Common Council. This council consists of representation from faculty, academic staff, and university staff, as the main governance body, and a plethora of 34 committees (almost 400 committee seats) reporting to it. The new structure was created to be more inclusive, but as it turned out, the number of committees and seats, as well as the processes put in place to fill those seats, created a serious problem.

More than one third of all employees on our campus are asked to do governance work (our total employee count as of spring 2022 was 1,100, down from previous years as a result of budget and staff cuts). Many faculty and staff do not put forth their names during the call for nominations in our governance election cycle, typically leaving about half of those seats unfilled. The Common Council Office (the secretary and chair) then scramble to fill the open seats by appointment. Many committees remain short of members, and some committees do not meet a quorum to conduct business.

Aside from the obvious—too many committees for the size of our campus—what are the barriers to participate in shared governance on our campus? In pursuit of answers, one of our existing committees conducted a survey, and another working group conducted a campus-wide workload study.

Findings from these efforts revealed some of the reasons we already suspected:

Staff cuts have led to increased workload.
Constitution diversification rules turn away interested participants.
Faculty and staff do not see the connection between governance and
    how it applies to their position or to campus.
Meeting schedules conflict with other work obligations.

To illustrate a couple of these points, our constitution has specific diversification requirements for every committee. These requirements include that every committee is comprised of members from a certain employment category, constituency (campus unit/department/school), and the number of committee members is based on the size of a college/school/department/unit. We have experienced instances where people have expressed interest in serving on our Common Council when we have vacant seats not filled after an election, but we often have to turn these people down because the open seats do not match their respective employment category or constituency. Our self-imposed rules and requirements contribute to seats remaining unfilled.

Another example is our meeting schedule. Many of our governance meetings occur in the afternoon between 2:00 and 5:00 p.m. These meeting times have been set for more than two decades and are often in direct conflict with classes, labs, and other job duties (as well as family responsibilities such as school and daycare pick up), yet no one has sat down to figure out a better schedule that may accommodate more people at a better time.

To address this, we are constituting a working group to start conducting a systematic review of the number of governance committees and processes. Our hope is that by the end of the academic year we have a set of recommendations for short-term fixes (such as changing our meeting schedule times) that can be implemented right away, and for long-term structural actions, and constitutional changes (such as revisiting the number of committees, their scope, and their purpose), that will eventually alleviate some of the problems we have right now.

We have created these barriers ourselves by making participation in governance harder than it should be. University personnel levels shift, strategic directions change, curriculum and general education requirements alter, and governance structures and policies should adapt to these changes. The goal is to determine what work is most important and valuable, and what is needed to support that work. Faculty and staff need to feel their time and energy is in service to policy, not process.

APPLICATION

- Using the strategies from this chapter, outline an assessment plan for a policy or procedure that is under review at the program, department, college, or institutional level.

- Select an existing policy or practice in your work context that needs revision or review. Identify the assessment measures and strategies that shared governance participants in your institution or professional organization might use for assessing the impact of the existing policy and determining whether the policy or practice needs to be revised.
- Identify barriers or challenges that have made it difficult to assess the impact of policy changes and/or new initiatives in your work context. List strategies that you might use for overcoming those barriers and collecting the data required for ensuring that changes are implemented in effective, equitable, and inclusive ways.
- Reflect on previously used feedback practices in your shared governance contexts. Assess what worked and what didn't work in helping the institution or organization collect useful and inclusive feedback. Identify one or more changes to make to improve feedback practices.

QUESTIONS FOR CONSIDERATION

1. What practices (if any) are used in your shared governance context to assess the impact of policy changes and new initiatives on students, faculty, and staff? What overall changes to assessment practices might provide decision makers with effective data for making informed decisions and monitoring the impact of changes?

2. How might the institution or program use multiple assessment measures to collect effective data about the impact of the change? What are the most important parts of the project to assess? What measures would be most effective for the purpose of the proposed change?

3. What new resources and potential funding are required for effectively assessing the change?

4. For proposed initiatives and policy changes, what data is already available to inform decision-making processes? What additional data is needed for monitoring the impact of the proposed changes on students or other affected groups?

5. For a policy change or new initiative that affects students, what relevant resources and processes are available for collecting disaggregated data and assessing how the change impacts students? Who has access to that data? How will that data be made available to relevant participants in a way that removes personally identifying student information?

6. Who will be responsible for disseminating assessment results? How might participants ensure that data is shared in an organized, transparent way both to assess the change and to inform future work?

7. How can participants in the process ensure that assessment data will be used in an ethical and equity-minded way? What processes need to be in place to create a transparent process that will allow the institution or program to make subsequent changes based on results of the assessment process?

WORKS CITED

Baer, Linda. "Connecting the Dots: Accountability, Assessment, Analytics, and Accreditation." *Planning for Higher Education Journal*, vol. 46, no. 1, Oct.–Dec. 2017, pp. 1–16.

Bailey, Thomas R., et al. *Redesigning America's Community Colleges: A Clearer Path to Student Success.* Harvard UP, 2015.

———. "What We Know About Guided Pathways." *Community College Research Center*, 2015, https://ccrc.tc.columbia.edu/media/k2/attachments/What-We-Know-Guided-Pathways.pdf.

Bennett, Randy Elliot. "Formative Assessment: A Critical Review." *Assessment in Education: Principles, Policy, and Practice*, vol. 18, no. 1, Feb. 2011, pp. 5–25.

Cizek, Gregory, et al. *Formative Assessment: History, Definition, and Progress*. Routledge, 2019.

Dedman, Ben. "Equity Is Behind All of This." *Liberal Education*, 7 July 2021, www.aacu.org/liberaleducation/articles/equity-is-behind-all-of-this-how-community-colleges-are-strengthening-guided-pathways-and-ensuring-students-are-learning.

Diamond, Robert. "Why Colleges Are so Hard to Change." *InsideHigherEd*, 8 Sept. 2006, www.insidehighered.com/views/2006/09/08/why-colleges-are-so-hard-change.

Dunican, Brian, et al. "Exploring Resistance to Change and Intolerance to Ambiguity in Higher Education Institutions." *International Journal of Leadership and Change*, vol. 7, no. 1, 2021 pp. 41–47, https://digitalcommons.wku.edu/cgi/viewcontent.cgi?article=1078&context=ijlc.

Eisenberg, Avigail. "Education and the Politics of Difference: Iris Young and the Politics of Education." *Educational Philosophy and Theory*, vol. 38, no. 1, 2006, pp. 7–23.

Eubanks, David. "A Guide for the Perplexed." *Intersection*, Fall 2017, pp. 4–12.

Higher Learning Commission. "Policy Title: Criteria for Accreditation." *HLC*, www.hlcommission.org/Policies/criteria-and-core-components.html.

Horst, S. Jeanne, and Caroline O. Prendergast. "The Assessment Skills Framework: A Taxonomy of Assessment Knowledge, Skills and Attitudes." *Research and Practice in Assessment*, vol. 15, no. 1, 2020, pp. 1–25.

Jenkins, Davis, et al. "How to Achieve More Equitable Community College Student Outcomes: Lessons from Six Years of CCRC Research on Guided Pathways." *Community College Research Center*, Sept. 2021, https://ccrc.tc.columbia.edu/media/k2/attachments/equitable-community-college-student-outcomes-guided-pathways.pdf.

Lane, India. "Change in Higher Education: Understanding and Responding to Individual and Organizational Resistance." *Journal of Veterinary Medical Education*, vol. 34, no. 2, 2007, pp. 85–92.

McNair, Tia Brown, and Lucie Bonneville, editors. *Paths to Success: How Community Colleges Are Strengthening Guided Pathways to Ensure Students Are Learning*. American Association of Colleges and Universities, 2021.

Minnesota State University Mankato. "University Policy Development." https://admin.mnsu.edu/organizational-information/policies-procedures/university-policies/university-policy-development/.

Young, Iris Marion. *Justice and the Politics of Difference*. Princeton UP, 1990.

Chapter 7

Conflicts in Shared Governance and Policy Development

GUIDING QUESTIONS

1. Shared governance and deliberative discussion can be valuable opportunities to hear from a wide range of people and perspectives. What are best practices for facilitating these exchanges in productive, transparent, and forward moving ways?
2. What strategies work best for moving past impasses in deliberative discussion?
3. What are some recommendations for distinguishing conflicts that emerge from poorly defined jurisdictions and those that are the product of "personality clashes"?
4. What are some tools for surfacing underlying assumptions or issues that may be fomenting conflict?
5. Frequently there is a clash between "how it has always been done" and what might be a more effective engagement in shared governance. How might individuals navigate this tension?

This chapter focuses on the kinds of conflicts that emerge within governance bodies in the context of colleges and universities. We discuss types of conflict, strategies for negotiating direct and indirect conflict, and strategies for facilitating difficult conversations, as well as the role of emotional and affective labor within the work of academic governance. Given how centered so much of the rhetoric of shared governance is on "debate" and the accompanying rules that are spelled out in much of parliamentary procedure, it may be counterintuitive to assert that much of the actual decision making that takes place in shared governance can be sorted out outside of meetings or through carefully curating what should

DOI: 10.4324/9781003257974-7

be the focus of group discussion. The history of classical rhetoric has focused on persuasion—that the job of a "good person speaking well" is to convince others of their point of view, sometimes regardless of the positionality the listener them-self embodies, values that imbue academic operations and culture. Of course, the missing component of this understanding of classical rhetoric is the role that the audience plays. Rhetoric that does not appeal to the audience is failed rhetoric, and rhetoric that does not adjust and respond to the needs and interests of inter-locutors is unethical rhetoric.

Shared governance asks all participants to listen and understand their audience—in this context, colleagues, coworkers, students, and administrators—and seek the best outcome according to that which governs the situation. These are never the outcomes that best suit one individual person, but rather the group, the institution, and the stakeholders. Shared governance leaders that focus on persuasion only will miss out on opportunities for collaborative, productive, and sustainable decision mak-ing. In this chapter, we discuss some of the common types of conflict that can emerge in the course of policy or practice discussions, as well as strategies for navigating conflict (and for managing the affective labor that such negotiation can often require).

A note about where conflict foments: in higher education, the line between personal and professional can be blurry and this can create an overreliance on backchannel communication because of interpersonal intimacies across friend-ships, partnerships, and enmities. As in many workplaces, people are not just colleagues, they are friends, and in situations that include tenure, people might spend upwards of 30 years in the same environment. At the same time, histori-cally, academics rarely see themselves as workers in an organization but rather they are passionately called to their profession—or, in some cases, their ego and identity are deeply invested. These characteristics of higher education govern-ance participants can be a good thing, but they can also create a false sense of the stakes of the conflict being higher than they actually are.

A brief query that includes the terms "conflict resolution" and "higher educa-tion" results in nearly 3 million hits each. There are journals dedicated to conflict management such as *Conflict Resolution Quarterly*, and there are entire disciplines such as industrial and organizational (I/O) psychology that specifically study human behavior in the workplace. This chapter is not an overview of conflict management in higher education. It is instead focusing on the ways in which shared governance and policy-making leadership gives a framework for managing conflicts in the educational environment.

WHAT IS CONFLICT AND HOW DOES IT MANIFEST?

Conflict can be large or small, it can be sudden and surprising, or predictable and irksome. Conflict usually occurs in one of two ways: lateral or hierarchical. For conflict not to forestall the positive change work attempted, it is necessary to understand the structures of the system AND the potential sources of and nature of the conflict that may come about. Being prepared for this conflict with a few communication strategies can help faculty and staff effectively participate in shared governance. To develop these strategies, it can be useful to first understand the nature of the conflict.

Lateral Conflict

Conflict can manifest in multiple ways within and between governance groups, sometimes emerging from places that stakeholders may not fully understand. This is called "lateral conflict." Consider, for example, an institution where there are senates, councils, or other governance groups that represent different employment types—faculty, staff, students, etc. While one group may value certain resources and information (e.g., documents from the American Association of University Professors, which is treated as the gold standard of governance policy), another group, such as students or staff, does not see their work and values represented in those resources. Alignments and realignments can happen across groups (staff and students, faculty and staff, students and administration) in ways that make it challenging to find common ground across groups. Because the needs of staff or students are left unaddressed by the guiding documents for faculty, there may be, in this example, a perception that faculty are ignoring the other groups. This breeds lasting conflict and resentment and makes it less likely that the groups will collaborate.

A good example of lateral conflict is when it comes to following or using existing policies, particularly when it comes to the interpretation of policy language. In this kind of situation, discussions can become more like legal haggling, with competing interpretations of a governing document (a state-level policy on hiring, credentials, employment conditions, or the responsibilities of an individual or group). Seeking clarity or precision where perhaps there is none, such conflicts may hinge on the connotations of a specific word, or of language that is general and does not offer a pathway for action. In such situations, the leadership of that particular body must create a series of check-ins to keep the group goal oriented. What is the point of the activity? Haggling over precision can matter but at what point does it stall out the benefits of the activity? In many ways, lateral conflict requires more leadership because it is among workplace peers.

Hierarchical Conflict

Also common in higher education are conflicts between individuals or groups at different levels in a hierarchy. Think here of faculty senates and provosts and presidents or chancellors and system-level officials. In 2022, for example, the University of Wisconsin System planned to distribute a survey on free speech (see Kremer 2022), but objections between the university's State System office and the next layer of leadership—chancellors—resulted in the resignation of a chancellor and delay of the survey (Zahneis 2022). Media coverage from multiple sides of the political spectrum, including the Foundation for Individual Rights in Education, a free speech watchdog organization, critiqued the situation, arguing that both resistance to research and coverage of such conflicts "actively impede the gathering of knowledge, and if we let ourselves concede that the act of *gathering data* about free speech only serves evil, we condemn ourselves to a willful ignorance that is unfit for the academy and antithetical to its aims" (Goldstein, et al. 2022). The survey was eventually successfully launched, with wide student participation after many weeks of additional work to address conflict.

Hierarchical conflicts can be large and encompass an entire university system or small and result in the staff of a particular office undermining the function of that office because they don't get along with the administrator, chair, or administrative assistant in charge. Another example of hierarchical conflict comes when organizations try to make changes to existing policies or to create new policy. In fact, changes to the existing policy are nearly guaranteed to produce differing opinions and perspectives, with stakeholders bringing to bear their own views, experiences, and positions, some of which are better or less well served by an existing policy. This might include responses from a loud but politically motivated minority of the community in which the university or college is located that does not serve anyone well on campus but has, perhaps, come up on the news as the latest foci of outrage.

Both types of conflict result in the same thing: an inability to successfully and safely do work, an inability to progress, to learn, and to address issues that arise. The inability to navigate disagreement represents the core failure of rhetorical listening—in order to move at all we must listen, and, hopefully, act. In their book, Ratcliffe and Jensen outline four tactics of rhetorical listening, two of which are building cultural logics and listening pedagogically (see the discussion of listening in Chapter 3). Building a cultural logic is particularly applicable to university governance because the culture of a university is something that is celebrated for students, in particular, constantly. Each a complicated concept in its own right, we can think about cultural logics as the often-invisible scripts that govern the processes that guide our actions. How do we know to jump up and cheer for our team at a game but remain in our seats when listening to a particularly effective conference paper: the cultural logics of the spaces we inhabit that guide our beliefs, patterns, dispositions, and actions. Listening pedagogically can be understood as audience awareness that locates resistances that prevent learning. The word pedagogy might be tricky here. Usually, we think of pedagogy as teaching, but it's not only about teaching others, it's about teaching ourselves. A skilled leader or participant in a governance setting listens with a will to learn within the framework of understood and recognized cultural logics.

NEGOTIATING CHANGE

There are formal and informal settings in which deliberative discussions within an organization or group can take place. Though organizational psychology and all its accompanying scholarship is part of what we integrate into this chapter, ultimately we rely on rhetorical strategies for thinking about solutions. Institutions are notoriously slow to move, particularly in higher education, but strategic action on behalf of the members of the institution can be highly effective in moving policy forward to meet the needs of stakeholders.

In broader conversations within higher education, there is often a desire to reach a consensus. This is a goal articulated by multiple parties and used throughout higher education leadership scholarship. However, we invite readers to reframe this thinking not because we do not value consensus but because consensus is neither attainable nor desirable in every instance. Sometimes the issues of consensus, or being a consensus builder, can permanently forestall action because of the objections of a small group. Alternatively, consensus seeking can uphold a harmful status quo, particularly in cases with marginalized or multi-marginalized members of the university or college community. Within shared governance groups, the desire to fully hear all perspectives and ensure that decisions are as inclusive as possible is an important underlying principle. The key is to reach a decision (which is not the same as achieving consensus). Resolving conflicts, in this case, means:

1. Identifying a goal or decision to be reached
2. Gathering feedback
3. Providing opportunities for discussion and conversation for perspectives to be heard
4. Acknowledging concerns and issues raised
5. Preparing a plan for addressing concerns, if needed
6. Arriving at a decision and a course of action

It's also crucial for shared governance participants to critically evaluate the nature of concerns or issues. We have all had colleagues who abuse deliberative dialogue by demanding an inequitable amount of speaking time or dominating email discussions, or who seem largely interested in imposing their perspective on what should happen in the group rather than seeking a mutually agreeable solution to a problem. Resistance to solving a problem or delaying action is not the same as consensus or consensus seeking and, in fact, will ultimately accomplish nothing but maintaining the status quo and silencing productive voices of difference.

STRATEGIES FOR MANAGING DIRECT CONFLICT

Shared governance within the context of rhetorical listening and deliberative discussion can provide valuable opportunities to hear from a wide range of people and perspectives. At the same time, navigating in-person or remote discussions with a balance of formality and flexibility can present challenges. There are a range of strategies that have been used in higher education and large institutions for a long time such as Robert's Rules of Order (RRO; see Robert, et al. 2020) or Sturgis's *Standard Code of Parliamentary Procedure* (see Sturgis 2000). These parliamentary procedures provide a process through which formal organizational deliberation can take place and are used in many formal governance structures. The more groups lean into using parliamentary procedure the less flexible conversations and deliberations can be (there are time limits enforced in certain procedures, for example); however, without procedural rules, conversations can be so free flowing that decisions might not be made. Reflect on questions and possibilities such as the following.

When Is It Best to Enforce Parliamentary Procedure Systems Such as Robert's Rules or Sturgis's?

RRO is a logic for how to create the ideal conditions for decision making to happen. It provides logistics for managing the flow of a meeting. The nature of a contentious issue may clarify when it is important to adhere to the parliamentary procedure; for example, if there is a complex issue that is expected to surface a wide spectrum of perspectives, then adhering to a fixed time for speaking (for example, two to three minutes) may help circulate as many views and perspectives as possible. Limiting speakers to two speaking turns can also ensure that as wide a range of participants as possible can contribute. That being said, open debate of this formal nature can sometimes inhibit people from marginalized groups from contributing, if the ethos is framed as "debate" and not "sharing perspectives." The timing and stage of a decision can also provide guidance on this question. For example, at a final decision-making stage where a clear vote on a specific motion is at hand, having a collective time period for discussion (rather than individual time limits) can be effective. It's important to consider the purpose for shaping the discussion; as a tool, the rules and regulations of parliamentary procedure provide guard rails that can be held for the purpose of creating space for multiple voices to participate, rather than whoever has the most energy, status, or influence. If the conventions are available to all those who aim to participate (in an accessible way), then parliamentary procedure can democratize discussion.

When Is It Best to Exit Parliamentary Procedure and Have a Structured or Semistructured Discussion?

In the same way that parliamentary procedure can create the conditions for a conversation to be equitable, it can also be weaponized to silence underrepresented voices. RRO (Robert, et al.) is difficult, dense, and requires a somewhat steep learning curve. To engage in RRO, or in any parliamentary procedures, participants must all understand the rules and, frankly, RRO has an exception to every single rule—which even the most skilled parliamentarian may not know. There are a number of quick guides available free online with a quick search, and keeping those on hand can be a useful way to develop the language around parliamentary procedure. In the meantime, experience with such rules leads to comfort but sometimes suspending the rules allows for a better conversation. Having a semistructured conversation under "suspended rules" can allow people to speak more freely and not be silenced due to formal rules of engagement that may not serve the body of participants.

When Is It Useful to Have Someone With an Authority Role (a Chair, Dean, Director, Administrator) Manage the Discussion?

We encourage readers to recognize that this situation—when it involves a specific governance unit, a department, a college, or a program—is highly shaped by the structure of a specific institution. For example, in some situations, the unit may be very explicitly positioned as advisory to an administrator (a department head, for example) while in another context, a faculty member serving as a department chair is responsible for aspects of leadership within the body but may have little formal authority. In situations where there is a long, toxic history that seems to color many conversations, an administrator can be a helpful counterbalance to what may be a series of unproductive discussions. When a group seems to be continuously retreading the same ground or spinning wheels, that can be an opportunity to bring in someone with a higher level of responsibility to bring a big-picture perspective to the conflict.

For some readers, RRO may be something unfamiliar even though it is the most commonly offered solution to problems that arise with deliberative discussion. Many times, groups will institute a policy around using Robert's Rules or having a parliamentarian, so that conflict can be measured and professionalism enforced. A healthy governing body may benefit from and in fact thrive in situations governed by RRO; however, needing a system that is unfamiliar to so many participants may also indicate a problem with goodwill actions among members of the group and/or a willingness to compromise to move issues forward. If RRO or some set of rules adopted by a body feels necessary, then it is incumbent upon the person leading that body to provide time, space, and some form of compensation (even if it's coffee) for everyone to learn the operating procedures. Thinking something is a good idea and steamrolling people into that idea are two very different things. Supporting people and making them feel as if they are valued and their time is important can go a long way in building the goodwill that a group needs in order to focus on the goals at hand.

EXTERNAL STRATEGIES FOR FACILITATING DIFFICULT CONVERSATIONS

When Is Help Outside of the Unit or Department Needed to Facilitate Discussion?

It is possible to get mired in issues that continue to resurface, or that seem to influence nearly every discussion that a group might wish to undertake, for example, a procedural violation, a bad hire, a student's exit from a program, or a mistake from an administrator that haunts those who remain. There are too many examples of campuses or departments that simply cannot independently move beyond past harm or trouble that was not satisfactorily resolved, or that continues to be brought up in decision-making conversations. In this case, consider the following questions:

- What processes and procedures are already in place in the organization (external department review, accreditation, strategic planning processes) that might be leveraged to deal with a longstanding issue?
- Does your campus have an ombudsperson or Ombuds office whose responsibility is helping to manage culture or climate issues?
- Are there resources accounted for in a union contract or bargaining agreement that provide for conflict resolution, for example, an appointed intermediary from outside the affected unit who can be tasked with addressing the conflicts?
- Is the issue specialized, such that an external consultant or mediator needs to be tapped to help the group navigate the issues?

Institutional literacy accounts for a large portion of navigating these external strategies—what resources are available in the organization or institution to help achieve the goals at hand and best serve multiple stakeholders? While procedures and resources matter and are there to be leveraged, gathering a group of supportive individuals is a necessary part of any direct conflict. Finding allies can help individuals navigating any form of direct conflict. In so doing, direct conflict can point to and is often grounded in indirect conflict. It is, in fact, interestingly the case that the bulk of conflicts will happen in indirect situations rather than direct issues that arise from procedural violations or mistakes.

STRATEGIES FOR MANAGING INDIRECT CONFLICT: SCENARIOS AND APPLICATION

Indirect conflict, or what we would also label as "backchannel"' conflict can manifest in a myriad of different ways. Consider the following scenarios.

Scenario 1: Curricular Work

Curricular work taking place through a senate is repeatedly derailed by a special appointee that the provost has given reassigned time to create documents for the degree. The special appointee calls other faculty at home one evening to complain that the elected academic staff (non-tenure-line) instructor chairing the senate policy committee (which has responsibility for putting curricular changes into policy) is unqualified to do the work.

In scenario 1, the person about whom there is a conflict is not actually privy to the specific complaints and only discovers it secondhand. There is no written evidence of the "behind-the-scenes" counterefforts, and the initiating complainant does not demonstrate direct, interpersonal hostility to the individual who is being complained about. This kind of backchannel conflict is not worth addressing. Though the political dynamics of the appointment—and the unprofessional behavior of the appointee—is frustrating, ultimately the actions do not rise to the occasion of a policy violation, nor will they ostensibly affect the governance work taking place, which has to follow particular steps in a process through the work of elected (not appointed) faculty and staff regardless of the personal irritations of someone operating outside of the governance structure.

There is not necessarily a way to prevent this kind of under-the-table communication. However, those in leadership positions can work to provide opportunities upfront for channels of communication. This can be an email address or listserv created specifically for gathering feedback, regular end-of-meeting check-ins on concerns or issues that have surfaced, or ways to provide anonymous feedback in an online form that can be deployed regularly to understand what is happening not just out front of a service or governance group but also behind the scenes. Leaders can also make it clear what is considered "out of bounds" behavior and establish boundaries for when and how the group's business can be done.

In such a scenario, actions may include:

- *Transparency*—If every aspect of the work being done is visible, backchannel conflict and personality run-ins (bullying) have a limited impact on the process. Backchannel conflict might still exist and make the individuals in the know uncomfortable, but the more visible the work and processes are, the less likely it will be that individuals can derail the work.

- *Communication*—Put everything in writing and provide check-ins that are included in the minutes as well as anonymous feedback forms at several steps throughout the process, even if it is a short timeline so that a record of work and interactions can be maintained.
- *Strategic planning*—in this particular case, if one individual is delaying outcomes based on their role, offer up a draft of the item they are responsible for after collecting feedback from all of the members of the group or committee. With a drafted document in hand, the work is practically done and therefore any additional stalling tactics will be very visible to the rest of the organization. Visibility and transparency impact conflict in positive ways.

Scenario 2: University-Level Program Outcomes

Revision of university-level program outcomes is continuously sabotaged by members of a particular college within the university who object to new accountability expectations for course approval. Several particularly vociferous faculty send multiple emails to the faculty senate to insist the work be delayed or halted, but never contact the committee chair directly.

In scenario 2, the conflict is somewhat more public—initiated by more than one person and being directed to a university- or college-level body. This behavior has implications for the development of university policy and, to a lesser extent, reporting that is necessary to the relevant accreditor about the development of the new policies and practices. This scenario is a slightly more complex situation, and actions depend on the specifics of the person in each role. In all cases, however, transparency is the best course forward.

For example, if you are a senate leader who is being asked to manage the backchannel complaints, then asking the complainants to express their concerns directly to the committee chair is the right course of action. Whenever possible, communication about issues should be "above board" rather than behind the scenes. This does not mean that the governance group should adjudicate the issue or take it on as an item of public business. Instead, the disgruntled individuals should be encouraged to communicate their concerns fairly and clearly to the committee. It would not be inappropriate to facilitate a meeting of the affected parties to try to diplomatically navigate the key issues. In the case that you are the committee chair, or on the receiving (but perhaps unknowing) end of the complaints, there is a less clear course of action. If at some point the committee is made aware of the concerns, then explaining the rationale for the decision, communicating in a public context about the issues that have been raised, holding a listening session, or circulating an anonymized short feedback form are all ways to surface what issues exist and strategize ways to address them.

This scenario has multiple layers of conflict and decisions in relation to that conflict. The complexity of the situation may mean that there is no single strategy to prevent such issues from emerging. Existing networks and relationships within universities—particularly since many faculty are colleagues for years if not decades—can shape to whom and how they express frustration or complaints. It can be challenging to disrupt these established patterns. Knowing how an institution is structured (thinking back to the definition of *institutional literacy* in Chapter 2) is a foundation for circumventing at least some of the "who you know" models of operating in higher education.

Existing relationship patterns can also function in the opposite way—the length of such relationships may mean that a faculty or staff member has a long (bad) history with a colleague (or has a colleague whose reputation precedes them), which means that they simply will not feel comfortable approaching that person directly with a concern. Colleagues may also be operating in bad faith, knowing that the channel they have selected to offer the feedback is not the appropriate one. As in scenario 1, though, providing multiple channels and opportunities for feedback (both formal and informal) is essential for resolving conflict. It can be typical for governance bodies and groups to operate in rigid timelines, such as annual reports, or communicate once a month through detailed and sometimes impenetrable meeting minutes. Think carefully about intentionally constructing ways of sharing information and gathering feedback that minimizes the temptation to prevail upon personal relationships to get things done.

In such a scenario, actions may include:

- *Transparency*—Strive for a "user-friendly" organization that makes deadlines, processes, procedures, contact information, and records of decisions as accessible and user friendly as possible.
- *Communication*—Use procedures and timelines to the advantage of organization members and make them scrutable.
- *Strategic planning*—Avoid assumptions. There is an old adage about assumptions and it remains true. Assumptions will build on bad feelings, bad faith, and misunderstandings.

Scenario 3: Faculty Search Committee

A department search committee chair hiring for a new faculty position realized in the middle of the search that two candidates for the two open positions are being courted personally by the department's chair and spouse (also a faculty member in the department). They are invited to stay at the department chair's home and to attend family recreation activities of department members who are hoping the preferred candidates will be hired. The search committee chair is concerned that raising the issue with higher-ups could result in a failed search or grievance because one of the candidates is a member of a protected class.

Scenario 3, while happening in private or nonacademic spaces, has legal and human resources implications. The search chair is not observing the inappropriate forms of interaction between department members/leaders and candidates directly but has been entrusted with overseeing a fair, equitable, and legally compliant search for the positions. At the same time, the department chair and their spouse have supervisory or evaluative authority over the search chair.

There is no question in this scenario— or any scenario that involves potentially unethical behavior around screening, interviewing, and hiring candidates (all of which are governed by relatively inflexible federal employment laws and regulations)—requires immediate intervention at the administrative level. This may mean a dean, a human resources administrator, or even relevant legal consultation if the campus or system has legal counsel retained. Issues that have the potential to create liability for the institution have to be addressed immediately at a higher level than department or interpersonal conversations.

As the most clearcut (and yet perhaps most challenging on an interpersonal level) scenario, there are obvious ways to prevent these kinds of unethical behaviors: most campuses offer detailed training sessions via the HR department for search committee chairs and members. Because of legal mandates, an institution's HR policy is almost always publicly accessible and relatively rigid, with specific steps that have to be followed at each stage of the process. Individual units can ensure that issues such as conflicts of interest or prior relationships are disclosed at the start of a screening process, and approval language in governing documents such as committee operating guidelines or bylaws codify those expectations. If, as in this scenario, departments are responsible for running a search, all members of that committee should review the hiring policy or hold a meeting with an HR representative to understand the structures in place around hiring.

The governance challenges at an interpersonal level are, of course, rooted in power. A department chair has, depending on the location, varying levels of power over faculty in the department and their behavior must be transparent and above board. In this scenario, their behavior is unethical, bordering on illegal. As such, they may need to be removed from the chair by the university, which will create contention in the department. Open communication about expectations of behavior is a key aspect of handling a difficult situation, and legal rights and responsibilities outweigh any interpersonal conflicts.

In such a scenario, actions may include:

- *Transparency*—Establish the presence of clear language and expectations within governing documents and policies that can guide conduct.
- *Communication*—Report out to required offices, including a series of conversations that are not private and include offices such as the dean, HR, an ombudsperson, or a Title IX coordinator, as well as union or faculty senate representatives, if necessary.
- *Strategic planning*—Create and maintain accountability measures for everyone involved in a process.

157

Notice that all these scenarios find resolution through a combination of three things: transparency, communication, and strategic planning. It is simply true that a healthy organization will operate under and leverage these aspects of the institutional organization for its benefit. Being as transparent as possible and making decisions in visible and policy-guided ways results in equity, means that no one's individual feelings are driving a scenario, and creates a process that all the best experiments thrive in. If stakeholders in an institution know that they will be communicated with openly and honestly and that the information they are presented is trustworthy and consistent, the organization will thrive. Transparency and communication function hand in hand. Backchannel negotiations are not transparent. Hallway conversations among a few people are not transparent. Going off book (constitution, contract, policy, etc.) is not transparent and creates a situation in which people vie for being heard rather than developing institutional literacy together. If institutional literacy is built to achieve shared goals, strategic planning can happen safely, with consensus, and with an eye toward the goals of the many rather than the few.

EMOTIONAL AND AFFECTIVE LABOR

What is often underestimated in the work of shared governance (whether a senate, a department governance structure such as a faculty body, a national committee, or beyond), is the emotional or affective labor that goes into either clarifying and reinforcing existing policy or identifying and implementing needed changes to improve the experience of stakeholders within that context as policy changes are developed. For the purposes of this chapter, we use Carlson, et al.'s 2012 definition of emotions labor: "the management or alteration of emotion in carrying out job duties" (849), and contrast this definition with that of affective labor, which Bessette and McGowan (2020) explain more fully: "Emotional labor is what we are asked to manage within ourselves, while affective labor involves managing other people's emotions" (137). Emotional labor within higher education may be required in response, for example, to what Carlson, et al. call "abusive supervision," which they define as "a form of nonphysical aggression" and note "is a reality of today's organization. Abusive supervision affects an estimated 13.6% of the U.S. workforce" (849) because abusive supervision (not unusual in the highly hierarchical system of colleges and universities) requires deference to higher status individuals, whether an administrator, department or unit chair, or simply a faculty member with more employment security or higher status. For example, public meetings such as department-wide meetings, committees or senates can be sites for workplace gatherings where abusive supervision not only takes place but is fully visible and includes "'subordinates' perceptions of the extent to which leaders engage in the sustained display of hostile verbal and nonverbal behaviors, excluding physical contact." Examples of abusive supervision are rudeness, tantrums, public criticism, and inconsiderate action" (850).

As much a discussion with others in differential status roles, or about controversial topics can require the management and display of negative emotions, so, also can the labor of managing *other people's* emotions fall on shared governance leaders: department chairs who need to cool tempers in a tough department meeting; a director who has to handle a personnel problem with an evaluation committee; a senate chair who must shepherd a complex policy through the governance group they chair. Of emotional labor, Lawless (2018) writes, "understanding labor as embodied shifts a general understanding of labor [which] is traditionally conceptualized as dull, hard, paid, useful, and productive (in the sense that a product results from the work)" (25–26). Labor that is both emotional and affective may be useful and indeed even productive, but it is less visible because the product is sometimes difficult to see (or it can be the absence of something else, such as conflict, stonewalling, withdrawal, or drama). It can also be the process itself of navigating emotional minefields, which is the product.

It is impossible to discuss emotional or affective labor without acknowledging the role that people of color and marginalized or multi-marginalized individuals play in carrying far and away the largest burden in higher education. Women, people of color, and LGBTQIA+ people bear the brunt of emotional and affective labor. This happens in sometimes small ways that can snowball into driving marginalized people out of their jobs. Affective labor is rooted, largely, in the effectiveness of the organization. For example, we know that "the gender composition and rules of a deliberative body dramatically affect who speaks, how the group interacts, the kinds of issues the group takes up, whose voices prevail, and what the group ultimately decides" (Karpowitz and Mendelberg 2014). Scholarship on affective labor is largely in the wheelhouse of feminist work on labor; however, the recent explosion of scholarship in the diversity of emotional and affective labor is something anyone interested in equitable shared governance should familiarize themself with. In the culture of academia, where there is a privileging of logic and evidence in the guise of research (that can manifest itself as tone-policing), there is an often-implicit understanding that if someone expresses too many feelings they are dismissed. Credibility relies upon the lack of emotionality, which is harmful. However, affective work is part of the participation of academic bodies and this is a strength in feminist, BIPOC, and LGBTQIA+ scholarship: the recognition that bodies at work contain emotions, difference, and value all at the same time.

In the spirit of rhetorical listening, we encourage particularly our white readers to enter into this section with an openness to understanding the conditions and cultural logics that govern the bulk of higher education institutions in the United States: whiteness. Turner, et al. (2011) use the term "whiteness-at-work" to analyze "white participants' moves to produce and protect their own comfort, advantage, and stability, thereby reifying the social structures of power in which white comfort, advantage, and stability take root. In these studies, whiteness-at-work continued to use the language of politeness and strategies of erasure to depoliticize and delimit differences (Nishi 2021; Sarcedo 2021; Tevis et al. 2022)" (31). These racialized disparities are compounded by gender. Gannon, et al. (2015) observe that traditional relational work of caring, networking, and being "friendly" and "supportive" in universities continues to be performed by women, and this labor is expected of women formally through workload allocations and informally through work processes and interpersonal interactions. So, while it appears that affective labor is recognized and allocated to women, which in turn undermines women's work as it is gendered, racialized, and classed, it seems that affective labor creates a series of byproducts that must also be accounted for in any discussion of equitable work. Whitney (2018) frames affective labor in terms of reduced subjectivity, hierarchies of identity, and marginalization.

STRATEGIES FOR MANAGING EMOTIONAL LABOR
Managing Your Own Emotions

In case it bears repeating: "The management of emotions is part of the work role" (Gabriel et al. 2015, 863). Ignoring emotions or pretending that they have no bearing in the workplace is directly located in the toxic masculinity that reifies feminized labor and displaces individuals that do not present as white, heteronormative, masculine, and classed in specific ways. This can, for example, appear in different forms: normalizing only the expression of particular kinds of emotions (anger versus sadness, for example), or tone policing the way that emotions are expressed, or expecting that emotional management will be a gendered and assumed responsibility of others.

An organization that participates in suppressing emotions is unhealthy. Though there are key governance strategies that have been shared throughout this book to make changes in productive and inclusive ways to an organization or institution, emotional labor is personal and must be managed within the context of your organization, whether or not it is healthy. In organizational management, the term for managing personal emotions has been referred to as "display rules": "[M]ost jobs have display rules, whether formal rules or informal norms, requiring employees to suppress undesirable emotions that may arise from negative events" (Carlson 852), as one article explains.

While we are not psychologists, we have all been in high-stakes and highly emotional workplace situations. Multiple vignettes included throughout this book point to boundary setting. We have also pointed to additional boundary setting. Like any relationship that requires being around other people, emotional

160

labor is, in no small way, setting boundaries that help you as a worker experience your work with minimal burnout in the matrix of expectations, power, identity, and disciplinary vs. local standards.

The simplest way to think about managing emotional labor is to establish, through the building of institutional literacy, the expectations for labor that are in the institutional contract and plot those out. These expectations will change depending on career stage and leadership involvement, and so too must a faculty member's expectations evolve in terms of self-care, and how relationships with colleagues, students, staff, and administrators play out. Teams and groups are impacted by individual emotional states, and while everyone is human and entitled to bad days, if the bad days outweigh the good because of overcommitment or frustration, emotional labor needs may need reevaluating.

Strategies for Managing Emotional Labor in Service and Governance

- Establish an understanding of institutional expectations and personal expectations that individuals or groups may be bringing into the space.
- Use institutional literacy to explicitly chart workload and adjust as needs arise, making sure that people have an understanding not only of their own roles and responsibilities but also those of others.
- Think about work longitudinally: Is labor assessment annual? Every three years? Every five? Goal set and include in those goals emotional boundaries.
- Structure in time before and after potentially stressful or difficult conversations or meetings to collect your thoughts or to chat with a colleague.
- Create a reflective journal to write out (rather than express or send) feelings of frustration and that tracks your internal responses over time to troubling situations and helps plan next steps.
- Create a habit around managing and processing emotional reactions within the context of the labor. This might include taking a pause, cultivating a group of friends that understand academic labor and provide a safe space for venting, or watching an old and enjoyable movie. It might be talking to a therapist.
- Creating a toolkit for the emotions we experience will enable us to be healthy as we engage in our labor.

MANAGING AFFECTIVE LABOR
Other's Emotions

Developing working relationships in any organizational setting takes time. In the academy, though the institution is slow to move, the people in it are diverse, invested, and have many different backgrounds, perspectives, and styles of communication. There is also, as discussed above, a unique sort of complexity to the relationships in higher education, and in that matrix, emotions can be highly charged and long lasting. Affective labor means, simply put, immaterial labor (Hardt and Negri), or caring or "pink-collar" labor (Słoniowski 2016). Indeed, affective labor has been recognized, particularly since 2020 as a "legitimate part of our work and workplace" (Bessette and McGowan 2020). For individuals who have spent their lives in academia, this can be a very challenging concept. In some ways, we are proposing a new idea, but a new idea that is grounded in the often-invisible labor of women, BIPOC, and LGBTQIA+ individuals: service requires affective labor.

We are not proposing that it is the job of a faculty member or shared governance leader to manage other people's emotions. However, developing a skill set that helps people to name and locate their emotions is a powerful tool and talent to cultivate. As Marjorie Hass (2021) writes, "In order to manage conflict well, you have to be able to tolerate someone else's negative feelings" (47). Higher education, particularly faculty participation in higher education, is largely defined by the process of work but not the people doing the work. This is discipline dependent. Those of us in applied fields who work closely with first-year students, returning students, veterans, or who mentor master's students, or who advise PhD candidates in an increasingly tricky market understand the ways in which affective labor is part of the job. However, it is important to recognize that this labor is underperceived, underprivileged, and rendered mostly invisible and indefinable by the discourses of the academy.

Our workplace context privileges intellectual labor. Intellectual labor is typically designated as different from (sometimes the opposite of) affective labor. But the data produced in research and the people producing that data are different things. In order to do affective labor well, and there is no such thing as perfect or easy affective labor, it can be helpful to shift an orientation of academic workload to complex emotional processes. In other works, recognize that sometimes the ways in which people frame their emotions as they communicate is to try to erase them.

Strategies for Managing Affective Labor in Service and Governance

There is no one way to manage other people's emotions and, in fact, there is no way to manage people's emotions at all. That is their responsibility. As faculty leaders in shared governance, we recognize that there is no way to compartmentalize emotion or emotional displays, but it is useful to maintain a focus on the fact that academics are people. We may exist in a culture that rewards intellectualism and productivity, but academics are human first. So we provide the following template as a useful strategy:

- *Validate emotions*—It's ok to feel angry, scared, worried, frustrated, over-worked, exhausted, or sad, and recognize that even within governance and service contexts that are about seemingly innocuous or straightforward workplace issues, negative emotions can arise frequently and quickly.
- *Name it*—Give people a way to name the emotion, the issue, or the problem. Identifying and offering a name for something that isn't part of the process being engaged in is a powerful tool. By naming the thing, all parties can recognize, perhaps for the first time, that the task is difficult, challenging, or different. This might be identifying feeling worried, threatened, upset, angry, sad, afraid, resentful, or overwhelmed.
- *Practice rhetorical listening*—Create spaces across face-to-face and digital interactions that leave time for listening. Let people vent, recognize people's achievements, and try to find the currents beneath the frustration. More often than not, anger is provoked because of fear.
- *Try not to internalize anger or attacks*—There is almost never a case where an initial burst of anger is actually personal, particularly in a service or shared governance setting.

These processes and recommendations will never be perfect or easy, but they are tools that can be used to create a healthy culture engaged in emotional, affective, and intellectual labor.

Kate McCahill at Santa Fe Community College describes how boundary management is a key component of managing conflict (internal and external) as well as workload.

VIGNETTE FROM KATE MCCAHILL, SANTA FE COMMUNITY COLLEGE

One thing I've learned about college service is that it risks being thought of as something like "Monopoly Money"—a currency in use that actually doesn't have value. Sometimes, our administrators defer to offering college service hours for projects as they arise, without taking into account the fact that folks' service quotas might already be full. Depending on the importance of the project and the workload therein, college service is not adequate compensation. When service hours are offered in exchange for work on projects, task forces, and committees enough times, the value of the hours becomes practically meaningless—and the quality of the work diminishes. At a certain point, faculty need to be compensated extra for the work that they do instead of absorbing any and all work outside of the classroom as "service"—and that balance is something my institution hasn't yet achieved.

The most important lesson I've learned about service, and my service participation, is that it's critical for me to protect myself against "work creep" in the form of excess service. When I started teaching full time in my late twenties, I didn't mind grabbing extra projects and participating wherever I could. I was just grateful to have a job! But after having a baby, I realized I'd set up a pattern of overextending myself, and I'd come to be relied upon as someone who always said "yes." Saying "no" instead was hard at first, but when I could document that I was doing my requisite service, it became easier. My service has changed a lot—I've moved from participating in meetings and task forces to working independently on projects I can complete and manage on my own time, without collaboration. Once you're able to tailor your service to your skill set and time restraints, it becomes less onerous and much more doable.

It can be hard to turn down requests to serve more, especially when you're new, but faculty need to trust their instincts—and rely on their more seasoned colleagues and their union representatives, if they have them, to establish a service workload that feels comfortable and reasonable. Don't be afraid to ask a colleague what's normal and what's not—and make sure you're clear on what your colleagues are doing for their service requirements, if you can. At the community college where I serve, faculty teach 15 credits—4 or 5 classes. Most faculty serve on one committee or task force, and that counts as their service. We also earn service hours by attending faculty senate and attending department meetings—and it's important to keep track of your work as the semester goes along, and not just tally it up at the end. You're bound to miss something if you aren't keeping track on a spreadsheet or simple document you keep close at hand, and you'll be surprised at how the little "odds and ends" add up. My advice? Familiarize yourself with what counts as service at your institution and what doesn't, and make a plan that will work for you.

SCENARIO FOR APPLICATION

An example: a newly elected chair of a curriculum committee is tasked with adjusting a university-wide curriculum requirement. The chair begins their work in consultation with their committee, but receives a series of increasingly irate emails from colleagues across campus accusing them of maliciously cutting courses or programs. In this scenario, both emotional and affective labor come into play. Emotional labor requires the committee chair to take a step back, to pause, to take a deep breath, and to recognize that though these emails feel like and are personal attacks, that is not the real issue. A lot of times adults, like children, act out because they have feelings that they can't identify and don't know how to name. In higher education that might be because there is no space for people to express their concerns or their fear and so they compartmentalize their emotions and simply lash out. Recognizing that though an attack feels personal, it may be more about the process and less about the people involved is an invaluable tool in affective labor. Consider the following aspects of this scenario.

Emotional Labor at Work in This Scenario

A human response might include the committee chair getting very upset sitting in their office reading these emails. This emotion might build the more they read. They will feel attacked, unappreciated, and threatened. They might think about quitting, about lashing out in return, about writing up a heady and wordy justification for the work they are doing that would take time away from their teaching, research, or other service responsibilities while simultaneously escalating the conflict into a series of accusatory and time-consuming emails. The step here of emotional labor means, however, engaging in *emotional self-regulation*: identifying the source of the negative feelings, reflecting on and assessing why the feedback has resulted in this emotional reaction, and using those personal insights to determine the best way forward to manage the conflict.

Affective Labor at Work in This Scenario

The affective labor that could take place in this example might include the chair naming what they understand as the cause of the anger being directed at them. This approach is simple and builds out emotional literacy in the process. A response to an angry colleague might include the phrase, "It seems like you feel worried about your program based on some of these proposed changes." Or "This must feel hard since it is a big change." Or "I'd be happy to work with your department to think about how your courses fit into this revision. That can be challenging work." This is a tool that therapists will refer to as validation. It costs nothing for the chair to validate the emotions underlying the angry email. Naming an emotion can be a powerful tool, especially in the academic culture of learned emotional deficiency and performed objectivity.

In this example, both scenarios can and will happen, but sitting in the emotional response without doing emotional labor will potentially allow for a continuation of bad feelings that override the goal of the work. In the affective labor component, though the angry faculty members may remain angry, the chair recognized that other people's emotions belong to them and created a context in which emotions could be named, identified, and safely dealt with as a part of the curricular process.

CONCLUSION

We began this chapter by acknowledging that conflict is unavoidable, complex, grounded in intersectional histories of labor, and difficult. We end this chapter with the same acknowledgment. Conflict is inevitable, even in the healthiest organization, but there are a number of strategies available to navigate conflict in productive ways. It is important to note that "faculty working conditions are student learning conditions" (Kottner 2022, 174). If the goal of higher education is to educate, then the workers responsible for student learning must be given the space to recognize and develop conflict management strategies that include emotional and affective labor.

APPLICATION

- Consider a recent lateral conflict that you have experienced. This might be small or large in scale. Navigate the strategies around emotional and affective labor in the context of that conflict and think about reactions that might have been improved upon.
- Consider a recent hierarchical conflict at your institution. Review the principles of transparency, communication (rhetorical listening), and strategic planning. In the context of those principles, how might that conflict have been shaped differently?

QUESTIONS FOR CONSIDERATION

1. What are some tools or strategies in this chapter that are useful at surfacing underlying assumptions or issues that may be fomenting conflict?

2. Frequently there is a clash between "how it has always been done" and what might be a more effective engagement in shared governance. How might individuals at your institution or in your unit navigate this tension?

3. Think about a recent conflict and consider the following:
   a. What is not negotiable?
   b. What is negotiable?
   c. How and in what ways might the strategies offered around emotional and affective labor impact this conflict?

WORKS CITED

Barry, Bruce, et al. "An Ethical Analysis of Emotional Labor." *Journal of Business Ethics*, vol. 160, 2019, pp. 17–34, https://doi.org/10.1007/s10551-018-3906-2.

Bessette, Lee Skallerup, and Susannah McGowan. "Affective Labor and Faculty Development: COVID-19 and Dealing with the Emotional Fallout." *Journal on Centers for Teaching and Learning*, vol. 12, 2020, pp. 136–48.

Carlson, Dawn, et al. "Abusive Supervision and Work-Family Conflict: The Path Through Emotional Labor and Burnout." *The Leadership Quarterly*, vol. 23, 2012, pp. 849–59. https://doi.org/10.1016/j.leaqua.2012.05.003.

Castro, Erin L. *Understanding Equity in Community College Practice*. New Directions for Community Colleges 172. Jossey-Bass, 2015.

Dorfield, Natalie, editor. *The Invisible Professor: The Precarious Lives of the New Faculty Majority*. The WAC Clearinghouse, UP of Colorado, 2022, https://doi.org/10.37514/PRA-B.2022.1589.

Gabriel, Allison, et al. "Emotional Labor Actors: A Latent Profile Analysis of Emotional Labor Strategies." *Journal of Applied Psychology*, vol. 100, no. 3, 2015, pp. 836–79. https://doi.org/10.1037/a0037408.

Gannon, Susanne, et al. "Uneven Relationalities, Collective Biography, and Sisterly Affect in Neoliberal Universities." *Feminist Formations*, 2015, pp. 189–216.

Goldstein, Adam, et al. "By Delaying Free Speech Survey in Response to Criticism, University of Wisconsin System Errs." *FIRE: Foundation for Individual Rights in Education*, www.thefire.org/by-delaying-free-speech-survey-in-response-to-criticism-university-of-wisconsin-system-errs/?fbclid=IwAR3RCok6GAIZomLaFl0DmtV9NRZJ9LHi_ZQ3z-nPPCPyRkTHFq_LaG3V0Tk.

Hardt, Michael. "Affective Labor." *Boundary 2*, Summer 1999, pp. 89–100.

Hardt, Michael, and Antonio Negri. *Empire*. Harvard UP, 2000.

Hass, Marjorie. *A Leadership Guide for Women in Higher Education*. Johns Hopkins UP, 2021.

Hass, Majorie. *A Leadership Guide for Women in Higher Education*. Johns Hopkins UP, 2021.

Ito, Aki. "'My Company Is Not My Family': Fed Up with Long Hours, Many Employees Have Quietly Decided to Take It Easy at Work Rather Than Quit Their

Jobs." *Business Insider*, 2022, www.businessinsider.com/overachievers-leaning-back-hustle-culture-coasting-employees-work.

Karpowitz, Christopher, and Tali Mendelberg. *The Silent Sex: Gender, Deliberation, and Institutions*. Princeton UP, 2014.

Kottner, Lee. "Breaking Up with Higher Ed." *The Invisible Professor: The Precarious Lives of the New Faculty Majority*. Edited by Natalie Dorfield. The WAC Clearinghouse, UP of Colorado, 2022, https://doi.org/10.37514/PRA-B.2022.1589.

Kremer, Rich. "UW System to Survey all Students about Campus Free Speech." *WPR*, 2022, https://www.wpr.org/uw-system-survey-all-students-about-campus-free-speecha.

Lawless, Brandi. "Documenting a Labor of Love: Emotional Labor as Academic Labor." *Review of Communication*, vol. 18, no. 2, 2018, pp. 85–97.

Micciche, Laura. *Doing Emotion: Rhetoric, Writing, Teaching*. Heinemann Publishing, 2007.

Nadasen, Premilla. "Domestic Work, Neoliberalism, and Transforming Labor." *S&F Online*, 2013, pp. 1–2, https://sfonline.barnard.edu/domestic-work-neoliberalism-and-transforming-labor/.

Nishi, Naomi W. "White Racial Bonding-At-Work in Higher ed STEM." *International Journal of Qualitative Studies in Education*, vol. 35, no. 2, 2021, pp. 1-19. https://doi.org/10.1080/09518398.2021.1983882.

Oksala, Johanna. "Affective Labor and Feminist Politics." *Signs*, vol. 41, no. 2, Winter 2016, pp. 281–303.

Ratcliffe, Krista, and Kyle Jensen. *Rhetorical Listening in Action: A Concept-Tactic Approach*. Parlor Press, 2022.

Robert, Henry M. III. *Robert's Rules of Order, Newly Revised*. 3rd ed. Public Affairs, 2020.

Robert, Henry M. III, et al. *Robert's Rules of Order, Newly Revised*. 12th ed. Public Affairs, 2020.

Sano-Franchini, Jennifer. "'It's Like Writing Yourself into a Codependent Relationship with Someone Who Doesn't Even Want You!' Emotional Labor, Intimacy, and the Academic Job Market in Rhetoric and Composition." *College Composition and Communication*, 2016, pp. 98–124.

Sarcedo, Geneva L. "Accepting Educational Responsibility for Whiteness in Academic Advising: Moving Towards Anti-Racist Advising Practices." *International Journal of Qualitative Studies in Education*, vol. 35, no. 4, 2021, pp. 1–15. https://doi.org/10.1080/09518398.2021.2003899.

Sloniowski, Lisa. "Affective Labor, Resistance, and the Academic Librarian." *Library Trends*, vol. 64, no. 4, 2016, pp. 645–66. *Project MUSE*, http://doi:10.1353/lib.2016.0013.

Sturgis, Alice. *The Standard Code of Parliamentary Procedure*. 4th ed. McGraw Hill, 2000.

Tevis, Tenisha et al. "Disrupting White Hegemony: A Necessary Shift Toward Adopting Critical Approaches Within the Teaching and Learning Environment." *International*

Journal of Qualitative Studies in Education, vol. 35, no. 1, 2022, pp. 1–15. https://doi.org/10.1080/09518398.2022.2035453.

Turner, Caroline Sotello Viernes, et al. "Faculty Women of Color: The Critical Nexus of Race and Gender." *Journal of Diversity in Higher Education*, vol. 4, no. 4, 2011, pp. 199–211.

Wharton, Amy. "The Sociology of Emotional Labor." *Annual Review of Sociology*, vol. 35, 2009, pp. 147–65, www.jstor.org/stable/2870073.

Whitney, Shiloh. "Byproductive Labor: A Feminist Theory of Affective Labor Beyond the Productive-Reproductive Distinction." *Philosophy and Social Criticism*, vol. 44, no. 6, 2018, pp. 637–60.

Wong, Kathleen. *Emotional Labor of Diversity Work: Women of Color Faculty in Predominantly White Institutions*. Arizona State UP, 2007.

Yoon, Irene H. "Justice-in-the-Doing: An Epilogue on Whiteness-at-Work in Higher Education." *International Journal of Qualitative Studies in Education*, vol. 35, no. 4, 2022, pp. 438–52.

Zahneis, Megan. "A Free-Speech Survey in Wisconsin Sparked Concerns: So a Chancellor Quit." *Chronicle of Higher Education*, 5 Apr. 2022, www.chronicle.com/article/a-free-speech-survey-in-wisconsin-sparked-concerns-so-a-chancellor-quit.

Chapter 8

Conclusion
Collective Action, Individual Effort

As this book, along with the stories of the contributors in it, has demonstrated, there's no single recipe for effective service and shared governance. Participating in a faculty council or senate may require a different set of skills than chairing that same group. Advocating for a marginalized group's needs (a club, resource center, or activist group) requires different knowledge of the institution, policy architecture, and personalities than chairing a search and screen committee or leading a reaccreditation self-study. What we ultimately hope readers leave this book with is a set of tools and strategies that they can select from and deploy depending on their role or needs. What is universally true about academic service is that it is not and never will be a solely individual effort. In this final chapter, we address issues for further consideration on national contexts shaping education and the role of shared governance in advocating for change.

As we've illustrated throughout this book and gestured toward at the outset, the landscape of higher education is changing. The idea of neoliberalism—or the privatizing of what used to be a public good—has, as Nadasen (2012) argues, "created a new political, economic, and cultural context through deregulation, privatization, securitization" (Nadasen). Some evidence of that includes the increase in casualization of labor (growth in part-time positions versus tenure-line or full-time benefited positions) and skyrocketing costs of college attendance.

This context has impacted how we think about labor while simultaneously pulling forward the old scripts and erasures of women, people of color, and LGBTQIA+ individuals. With a focus on deregulation, privatization, and individualism within a global community, embodiment gets erased in the constant focus on speed and productivity, and profit and money within a narrative of constant crisis that rests on precarity. Precarity keeps the worker in constant crisis and creates an environment in which the lived experiences, embodiment, dignity, and emotion of the worker can be ignored.

DOI: 10.4324/9781003257974-8

The reality of the underfunding of public higher education in the United States, paired with rocketing debt for students, and a less engaged workforce has led to proliferation of books such as *Vocation* (Berg and Sadler 2021), *Just Work for All* (Preiss 2020), *The Slow Professor* (Berg and Seeber 2016), *College Disrupted* (Craig 2015), *The Athena Doctrine* (Gerzema and D'Antonio 2013), which attempt to recognize bodies in the same moment that we understand how gender, race, and class are deeply relevant to the "ways labor is felt, experienced, and enacted" (Lawless 19). If we look for parallels to outside of the academy, the "quiet quitting"/"acting your wage" movement has some similar roots and contours: narratives of precarity and neoliberal ideologies that push productivity. The conversation around quiet quitting was encapsulated by Aki Ito (2022) who discusses it as a strategic "dialing back at work" (np). In human resource terms this is called quitting in place. Labor organizers might refer to this as "working to rule" (*Secretary of State for Employment v. Associated Society of Locomotive Engineers and Firemen,* No. 2), and social media has picked up the term "acting your wage" (@DadaBaseThough). In July 2022, the hashtag #quietquitting had 8.2 million views on TikTok (Kilpatrick). Barry et al. (2019) discuss the rights (autonomy, well-being) and duties (fidelity and nonmaleficence) that employees and employers have and that these rights and duties can come into conflict. The quiet quitting movement is one that exemplifies the ways in which well-being and projected notions of fidelity to an institution or organization can create conflict for the individuals employed by the institution.

Within the academy, then, quiet quitting/acting your wage is a refusal to work outside of the expectations of the contract, and the reduction in force of contracted employees who actually have service and governance components of their contract is diminishing rapidly. What this movement exposes is, of course, just how much free labor is expected in most industries to sustain the status quo. Education is particularly guilty, like any labor that might be classed as carework, of relying on free labor or employees going above and beyond, and doing so without complaint. What we emphasize at the close of this book is not a call for exploiting underpaid workers or working beyond contract; in fact, it is a call to those whose contractual responsibilities do include shared governance and service to take up several imperatives:

- To perform these activities effectively, responsibly, and with integrity
- To use the work that takes places in those spaces to advocate for just working conditions for academic workers within the institution
- To use those spaces to advance equity and inclusion within higher education for students at multiple levels
- To create, maintain, or revise structures such that they acknowledge and allow for embodied and multiperspective contributions to the academic working environment

ENGAGING AND REWARDING GOVERNANCE AND SERVICE

A key theme throughout this book has been that engagement in service such that this work is equitably distributed and effectively performed are inherently important goals for universities and colleges. We want to reinforce through some of the data from the American Council of Education how critical to equity, inclusion, and justice the distribution of this work is for the well-being of academic workers.

In *Equity-Minded Faculty Workloads: What We Can and Should Do Now* (2021), O'Meara and colleagues thoroughly document several evidence-based conclusions about the distribution of labor within the academy:

> "Women spend more time on teaching and service than men"
> "Women spend less time on research than men"
> "Faculty from historically minoritized racial groups spend more time on mentoring and diversity-related work than faculty who are white"
> "Women are asked more often to engage in less promotable or career-advancing tasks"

> (5)

Engaging all contractually obliged academic workers in service and shared governance—and appropriately rewarding that labor—is essential to equity in higher education. Likewise, finding ways to reward participation in and compensate academic workers who do not have contractual obligations for service and governance is a way to make sure that all stakeholders who are affected by a decision are able to make their voices heard without relying on "psychic rewards" or good will as a substitute for remuneration.

ADVOCATING FOR CHANGE

Though we describe many different kinds of change work and policy development in this book, we want to emphasize at the close the importance of advocacy work within these contexts that also centers on labor equity. Amy Lynch-Biniek, in the concluding chapter to the 2021 edited collection: *The Invisible Professor: The Precarious Lives of the New Faculty Majority*, explains the importance of the "how" in advocating for change:

> While I have long and loudly argued that tenured faculty members especially have a moral obligation to do this work, I have also come to understand that this work must be intersectional and collective, uplifting and protecting the most vulnerable among us. The work of organizing for workplace equity should be the responsibility of all faculty members, not simply the purview of

the most vulnerable; at the same time, those most empowered by the current, broken system should not center themselves . . .

(221)

This sentiment stands out to us as core to what effective shared governance and service do. They recognize that participation from those in the community who are affected by decisions is essential, not just because it's just, but because without that participation, decision makers don't actually have complete knowledge of the issues at stake. If an administrator makes a unilateral decision without input from faculty on a topic that affects them, that is an incomplete picture. If tenure-line faculty come to a decision about parts of the program that are largely taught by non-tenure-line instructors, then they also do not have a full understanding of the issues at play. The same goes for staff, students, or any other group that is governed without input and expected to comply with expectations that they had no say in shaping.

The common thread among the chapters in this book is that, ultimately, higher education is a public good. Most institutions claim to be committed at least in some way to community engagement, to equity, diversity, and inclusion, and to participatory and dialogic decision making. Likewise, access to and success in higher education shapes the social and economic mobility of the average person in ways that are well documented (see Ma, et al, "Education Pays," 2019 a report by the College Board, for extensive data on the advantages conferred by college degrees). To do effective service and shared governance, the institution must align the practices within a campus of labor equity, invitations to engage, and value attached to that participation in this mission and aspiration.

CONCLUSION

Though the focus of this book is on effective participation in sites of higher education service and shared governance, we want to close with some takeaways that distill the goals of academic work. The conclusions offered here are meant to summarize and illustrate the ways in which academic work is a dynamic and shifting institutional activity that is nonetheless manageable and doable. Though we have emphasized throughout this text that each institutional context is different, the landscape of higher education shares broad similarities through which we might engage in good governance efforts.

First, effective participation in an institution of higher education requires believing in the goals of higher education. Shared governance participation requires believing that students can learn, teachers can develop, colleagues can adapt, and institutions can grow. This disposition is a precursor for change work and requires, as we have emphasized throughout the guidebook, a focus on equity, inclusion, and, perhaps most importantly *belonging*. To understand oneself as a member of the institutional community is a powerful tool and an important starting place for building institutional literacy and growing a set of justice-oriented leadership skills.

Second, while *participation* in service and governance is essential, we also need *responsibility* and *accountability*. Showing up at a meeting, sharing opinions, or listing a committee on an activity report is not enough (spoiler alert: it never was). Academic workers both have the responsibility to participate and must be accountable for outcomes. A heuristic for engagement might include these questions:

- Do shared governance and service outcomes make students safer, smarter, more included, or healthier?
- Do they make our campuses more welcoming places?
- Do they increase students' civic, academic, and social engagement with the world around them?
- Do they create equitable labor conditions for all employees regardless of their professional statuses and roles in the institution?
- Do they result in functional processes that give faculty and staff manageable and equitable workloads?
- Do they develop and maintain pathways for all stakeholders to have a voice and participate in inclusive decision-making processes?
- Do they result in practices that reflect the needs of the communities that an institution serves?

These are the questions we must ask to have accountability in higher education.

Third, we do not mean accountability to groups like donors and legislators (those voices are often the most likely to demand it and there are policy, funding, and legal ramifications that require institutional accountability procedures to be in place). Rather, we mean accountability to ourselves, our colleagues, and our students for having accomplished something that contributes to the greater good of the academic community. That good work will look different depending on the context in which one works; however, as we have highlighted throughout this book, there are systemic inequities in higher education, such as an extreme overreliance on contingent labor, that require all of our best efforts to address.

As we conclude this book, we reaffirm that effective shared governance creates a foundation for functional and equitable higher education practices. It provides pathways for faculty, staff, administrators, and students to give input in the decisions that affect their conditions for working, teaching, learning, and living. It ensures that the voices and experiences of stakeholders with diverse social identities are included in decision-making processes in ways that draw from collective expertise, build community, and strengthen the outcomes of governance processes and institutional change. And finally, when shared governance is truly shared, it fosters a sense of belonging in higher education and allows participants to become their best professional selves.

WORKS CITED

@DadaBaseThough. 2022, https://twitter.com/DadaBaseThought/status/15606287 64953890816.

Barry, Bruce, Mara Oleklans, and Laura Rees. "An Ethical Analysis of Emotional Labor." *Journal of Business Ethics*, vol 170, 2019, pp. 17–34.

Ito, Aki. "'My Company Is Not My Family': Fed Up with Long Hours, Many Employees Have Quietly Decided to Take It Easy at Work Rather Than Quit Their Jobs." *Business Insider*, 2 Mar. 2022, www.businessinsider.com/overachievers-leaning-back-hustle-culture-coasting-employees-work.

Kilpatrick, Amina. "What is 'Quiet Quitting,' and How it May be a Misnomer for Setting Boundaries at Work." *NPR*, 2022, https://www.npr.org/2022/08/19/1117753535/quiet-quitting-work-tiktok.

Lawless, Brandi. "Documenting a Labor of Love: Emotional Labor as Academic Labor." *Review of Communication*, vol. 18, no. 2, pp. 85–97.

Lynch-Biniek, Amy. "Labor-Informed Graduate Education." *The Invisible Professor: The Precarious Lives of the New Faculty Majority*. Edited by Natalie M. Dorfeld. WAC Clearinghouse, 2022, pp. 217–22.

Ma, Jennifer, et al. "Education Pays 2019: The Benefits of Higher Education for Individuals and Society." *College Board*, https://research.collegeboard.org/media/pdf/education-pays-2019-full-report.pdf.

Nadesen, Premilla. "Domestic Work, Neoliberalism, and Transforming Labor." *Scholar and Feminist Online*, vol. 11, no. 1–2, Fall 2012–Spring 2013, https://sfonline.barnard.edu/domestic-work-neoliberalism-and-transforming-labor/#:~:text=Neoliberalism%20has%20created%20a%20new,dismantling%20of%20the%20welfare%20state.

O'Meara, Kerryann, et al. *Equity Minded Faculty Workloads: What We Can and Should Do Now*. American Council on Education, 2021, www.acenet.edu/Documents/Equity-Minded-Faculty-Workloads.pdf.

Pyle, Christian. "Statusism: How Adjunct Exploitation Isolates and Divides College Faculty." *The Invisible Professor: The Precarious Lives of the New Faculty Majority*. Edited by Natalie M. Dorfeld. WAC Clearinghouse, 2022, pp. 71–78.

Secretary of State for Employment v. Associated Society of Locomotive Engineers and Firemen No 2. ICR 19, 1972.

Contributors

Kathryn Blakeman is secretary to the Common Council at the University of Wisconsin-Stevens Point. A native of Northern Virginia, she is well versed in government and bureaucracy. She has worked at several universities, including the University of Virginia and Baylor University.

David M. Grant is an associate professor in the department of Languages & Literatures at the University of Northern Iowa. He is coeditor of *Decolonial Conversations in Posthuman and New Material Rhetorics* (University of Pittsburgh) and is currently exploring the rhetorical role of consideration in working across incommensurability and difference.

Sheila Amin Gutiérrez de Piñeres is dean of the Burnett Honors College at the University of Central Florida (UCF) and professor of public administration. Dr. Piñeres joined UCF in May 2018 following her role as executive vice president for academic affairs and dean of faculty at Austin College in Sherman, Texas. She is a founding member of the University of Texas System Academy of Distinguished Teachers.

Marjorie Hass is the first female president in the 65-year history of The Council of Independent Colleges. Dr. Hass began her tenure as president of Rhodes College in 2017. Previously, she was president of Austin College for eight years and provost of Muhlenberg College (Pennsylvania), where she spent more than 16 years as a member of the philosophy faculty. She is the author of *A Leadership Guide for Women in Higher Education* (2021). Dr. Hass earned bachelor's, master's, and doctoral degrees in philosophy from the University of Illinois at Urbana-Champaign.

Seth Kahn is a professor of English at West Chester University of Pennsylvania, where he teaches writing and rhetoric courses, does union work for the Association of PA State College and University Faculties. and researches academic labor organizing. Recent publications include "From Activism to Organizing; from Caring to Care Work" with Amy Lynch-Biniek (*Labor Studies Journal*, July 2022); "What Do We Mean by Academic Labor (in Rhetorical Studies)?" with Amy Pason (*Rhetoric and Public Affairs*, July 2021); and "We Value Teaching Too Much to Keep Devaluing It" (*College English*, July 2020).

Isaac Kamola is an associate professor of political science at Trinity College, Hartford, Connecticut. His research examines critical globalization studies, the political economy of higher education, and African anticolonial theory. He is author of *Free Speech and Koch Money: Manufacturing a Campus Culture War* (with Ralph Wilson, 2021) and *Making the World Global: US Universities and the Production of the Global Imaginary* (2019). He is the creator of Faculty First Responders, a program that monitors right-wing attacks on academics and provides resources to help faculty members and administrators respond to manufactured outrage.

Kate McCahill is assistant professor of English at the Santa Fe Community College (SFCC), where she serves as faculty advisor for the *Santa Fe Literary Review,* SFCC's nationally and internationally distributed literary magazine. She is an alumna of Wellesley College (BA) and the Vermont College of Fine Arts (MFA, Writing). Her book is *Patagonian Road: A Year Alone Through Latin America.* Her fiction, poetry, and nonfiction have been published in *Vox, The Millions, and elsewhere.*

Nerissa Nelson is a librarian/professor at the University of Wisconsin-Stevens Point. She just completed her two-year term as chair of the campus governance body, the Common Council, and has spent 20 years in various shared governance roles.

Molly Secor, PhD, RN, FSAHM is the associate dean for research and professor in the Mark and Robyn Jones College of Nursing at Montana State University. Prior to this role, she served on the School of Nursing and Department of Health faculty at North Dakota State University. While there she served as Faculty Senate president, cochaired the university Strategic Planning Committee, and was active in other faculty governance leadership roles. In recognition of her leadership and contributions in the field of adolescent health research, she is a fellow in the Society for Adolescent Health and Medicine.

Glossary

affective labor: Bessette and McGowan explain ". . . affective labor involves managing other people's emotions" (137).

constituencies: employee groups defined in 101.1 who are represented by governing bodies such as Faculty Senate, Staff Senate, or Student Senate.

diversity: in shared governance representation, means having a variety of people with different identities involved in governance processes in ways that fully represent the social and cultural backgrounds of an institution or organization. Diversity in representation also means that people from different professional backgrounds, functional units, and employment statuses have an opportunity to participate in processes that affect their working conditions and work lives.

educational opportunity gap: describes the differences between students who have adequate access to financial and social resources to support their pathways toward a degree (or other attainment of their own educational goals) and students who lack those privileges, which reduces the opportunities that they receive on their pathways toward going to college, staying in college, and receiving a degree.

emotional labor: Carlton, et al.'s definition of emotional labor is ". . . the management or alteration of emotion in carrying out job duties" (849).

equity: in higher education refers to institutional, program-level, and individual practices that create equal opportunities for students, faculty, and staff regardless of their social and cultural backgrounds or statuses within an institution. Equitable practices in a workplace directly address and actively resist bias and discrimination. In shared governance, equitable practices create equal opportunities for participation in decision-making processes and ensure that both individuals and groups within an organization have equal access to fair treatment and resources.

equity-minded: shared governance actively that acknowledges and seeks to address structural inequities and discrimination that exist within organizations, institutions, and society in general. It recognizes, as O'Meara, et al. note, that "Faculty workload systems are not strategically designed. There are few benchmarks or standards to acknowledge exemplary performance or to hold faculty members accountable when they do not perform" (1).

ex officio: someone in a particular role on campus whose expertise is seen as relevant to the work of a governance group, who can be part of the group to provide necessary information (see discussion of "Institutions" in Chapter 2); they serve as a member of a group "by virtue of" their position.

governance groups (see Chapter 1 on "Shared Governance and Service"): any formally constituted body with jurisdictions outlined in bylaws and/or a constitution that has oversight and decision-making authority about a specific university function, policy, or process (for example, an academic department, a senate, or senate committee).

inclusion: in higher education, means that students, faculty, and staff with diverse social and cultural identities are valued and supported on a campus, within learning environments, in a department or program, in a profession, and in other online and in-person spaces where they do work. Inclusion in shared governance creates conditions in which people with diverse identities and backgrounds have a sense of community, belonging, and a voice within an institution. The perspectives of individuals are valued and included as part of decision-making processes regardless of their employment statuses. Inclusivity emphasizes the "shared" aspect of governance—in other words, that governance belongs to all members of an organization and stakeholders within an institution, program, or department.

inclusive leadership: means "doing things with people, not doing things to people" and "promotes fairness of input and output to all" (Hollander 3; and see discussion in Chapter 2).

institutional integrity: the degree to which its stated values are aligned with the decisions that administrators, faculty, and staff make. We take *integrity* to be perhaps even more literally in its etymology. *Integrity* evolved from the Latin word *integer* which means "intact" (see Chapter 2).

institutional literacy: knowledge of the institutional communicative and sociocultural practices, as well as understanding of structures, processes, and policy architecture that shape a higher education institution (see "Do your homework," Chapter 3).

shared governance: a collaborative decision-making process that meaningfully involves all groups with a stake in decisions that affect their educational and work environment.

stakeholders: any person or constituency group that is affected by university decisions.

transparency: visibility of the rationale, thinking, and information that is considered as part of institutional decision making to the greatest extent possible within the context of policy.

voting versus nonvoting membership: within the context of a formal governance group, some members are granted voting rights while others are nonvoting. This distinction might be articulated in bylaws or a constitution; some ex officio members may be voting and some may be nonvoting. Often, nonvoting members have been identified in the process of constituting the group as having special expertise on the topic of interest to the group but is not in an employment category that allows for participation in governance.

Appendices

APPENDIX A: RESOURCES BY STATE

Resources on Governance and Policy

A variety of national organizations or consortia have resources to offer academic workers about (1) how higher education is organized, (2) what the priorities are nationally for a range of higher educational contexts, and (3) how to accomplish meaningful service and governance work.

The **American Association of Colleges and Universities** (www.aacu.org) is "a global membership organization dedicated to advancing the democratic purposes of higher education by promoting equity, innovation, and excellence in liberal education." They provide published and publicly available resources on a range of topics, including liberal education, assessment of student learning, undergraduate STEM education, curricular transformation, and community-based and global engagement.

American Association of University Professors (www.aaup.org/) is a "nonprofit membership association of faculty and other academic professionals." The association has a range of functions, including facilitating collective bargaining units on some campuses, serving as an umbrella organization for state or institution-specific chapters, producing reports and research, and conducting investigations on campuses that have violated traditional protocols of tenure, academic freedom, and shared governance.

The **National Association of Concurrent Enrollment Partnerships** (www.nacep.org/) "works to ensure that college courses offered by high school teachers are as rigorous as courses offered on the sponsoring college campus. As the sole accrediting body for concurrent enrollment partnerships, NACEP helps these programs adhere to the highest standards so students experience a seamless transition to college and teachers benefit from meaningful, ongoing professional development." For resources on relationships and formal program partnerships between high schools and colleges, this is a useful body.

The **Association of Governing Boards** (https://agb.org/) describes itself as ". . . the premier organization focused on empowering college, university, and foundation boards to govern with knowledge and confidence." Their Knowledge Center contains a wealth of resources on topics ranging from tenure and academic freedom to athletics, risk management, mergers, and other topics.

The **Association of Public Land Grant Colleges and Universities** (www.aplu.org/) describes itself as ". . . a research, policy, and advocacy organization dedicated to strengthening and advancing the work of public universities in the U.S., Canada, and Mexico. The association's membership consists of more than 250 public research universities, land-grant institutions, state university systems, and affiliated organizations."

The **American Council of Learned Societies** (www.acls.org/) is a nonprofit federation of 79 scholarly organizations. This group describes its mission as supporting "the creation and circulation of knowledge that advances understanding of humanity and human endeavors in the past, present, and future, with a view toward improving human experience."

We provide here links to the public systems of higher education in US states, including state-level offices and/or university system boards of regents or trustees. These are the primary sources of policy and practice authorities and typically have pages or links to policy manuals or "policies and procedures" documents on their websites.

Alabama:
- Alabama Commission on Higher Education

Alaska:
- www.alaska.edu/alaska/

Arizona:
- Arizona Board of Regents
- https://highered.az.gov/

Arkansas:
- www.uasys.edu/leadership/board-of-trustees/
- https://adhe.edu/

California:
- https://regents.universityofcalifornia.edu/
- www.cde.ca.gov/

Colorado:
- https://cdhe.colorado.gov/

Connecticut:
- www.ctohe.org/

Delaware:
- www.doe.k12.de.us/domain/226

Florida:
- www.fldoe.org/schools/higher-ed/
- www.flbog.edu/

Georgia:
- www.usg.edu/

Hawaii:
- www.hawaii.edu/
- www.hawaii.edu/policy/index.php?action=home&policySection=rp

Idaho:
- https://boardofed.idaho.gov/

Illinois:
- www.ibhe.org/
- www.bot.uillinois.edu/

Indiana:
- www.in.gov/che/
- https://trustees.iu.edu/

Iowa:
- www.iowaregents.edu/plans-and-policies/board-policy-manual

Kansas:
- www.kansasregents.org/about
- www.kansasregents.org/about/policies-by-laws-missions

Kentucky:
- https://cpe.ky.gov/
- https://systemoffice.kctcs.edu/about/leadership/board-of-regents/index.aspx

Louisiana:
- www.ulsystem.edu/
- www.louisiana.gov/government/executive-branch-higher-ed/

Maine:
- www.maine.gov/doe/learning/highered
- www.maine.edu/board-of-trustees/

Massachusetts:
- www.umassp.edu/bot
- www.mass.edu/home.asp

Michigan:
- https://regents.umich.edu/regents/
- www.mtu.edu/bot/
- https://trustees.msu.edu/
- www.mcca.org/board-of-directors

Minnesota:
- https://regents.umn.edu/
- www.minnstate.edu/board/index.html

Mississippi:
- www.mississippi.edu/board/
- www.mississippi.edu/commissioner/welcome.asp

Missouri:
- www.umsystem.edu/curators
- https://dhewd.mo.gov/

Montana:
- https://mus.edu/board/
- https://mus.edu/che/

Nebraska:
- https://ccpe.nebraska.gov/
- https://nebraska.edu/regents

Nevada:
- www.nevadaregistry.org/ece-resources/ nevada-system-of-higher-education/
- https://nshe.nevada.edu/regents/

New Hampshire:
- www.education.nh.gov/who-we-are/state-board-of-education
- www.usnh.edu/trustees

New Jersey:
- www.state.nj.us/highereducation/
- http://njascu.org/about-us/

New Mexico:
- https://hed.nm.gov/
- https://regents.unm.edu/

New York:
- www.highered.nysed.gov/
- www.cuny.edu/about/trustees/the-board-of-trustees/
- www.suny.edu/about/leadership/board-of-trustees/

North Dakota:
- https://ndus.edu/state-board-of-higher-education/sbhe-policies/

Oregon:
- https://trustees.uoregon.edu/
- www.oregon.gov/highered/Pages/index.aspx

Pennsylvania
- www.passhe.edu/Pages/default.aspx
- www.passhe.edu/inside/BOG/Pages/default.aspx

Puerto Rico:
- www.uprm.edu/cms/index.php/page/1241
- www.pupr.edu/about/board-of-trustees/

Rhode Island:
- www.ride.ri.gov/boardofeducation/overview.aspx
- www.riopc.edu/page/Council%20overview/

South Carolina:
- www.che.sc.gov/
- https://sc.edu/about/offices_and_divisions/board_of_trustees/members/index.php

South Dakota:
- www.sdbor.edu/administrative-offices/infogovtrelations/Pages/South-Dakota-Higher-Education-Institutions.aspx
- www.sdea.org/who-we-are/higher-education

Tennessee:
- https://tennessee.edu/
- https://trustees.tennessee.edu/

Texas:
- www.utsystem.edu/offices/board-regents
- www.highered.texas.gov/

Utah:
- https://ushe.edu/board/about-the-board/
- https://ushe.edu/

Vermont:
- www.vsc.edu/
- https://education.vermont.gov/vermont-schools/school-operations/post-secondary-programs

Virginia:
- https://bov.virginia.edu/
- www.virginia.gov/agencies/state-council-of-higher-education-for-virginia/

Washington:
- www.washington.edu/regents/
- https://wsac.wa.gov/colleges-and-institutions-washington

West Virginia:
- www.wvu.edu/about-wvu/wvu-system
- www.wvhepc.edu/

Wisconsin:
- www.wisconsin.edu/
- www.wtcsystem.edu/about/wtcs-board/

Wyoming:
- www.uwyo.edu/trustees/
- https://communitycolleges.wy.edu/
- https://edu.wyoming.gov/

APPENDIX B: 5 STEPS TO PLAIN LANGUAGE

Five Steps to Plain Language

https://centerforplainlanguage.org/learning-training/five-steps-plain-language/

A communication is in plain language if its wording, structure, and design are so clear that the intended readers can easily find what they need, understand what they find, and use that information.

Our five-step checklist will guide you through the plain language process and help you develop content that's right for your organization.

Step 1: Identify and describe the target audience

Define the target groups that will use the document or website

- List and prioritize top tasks by audience group
- List what people need or need to know to complete the task
- List characteristics of the groups that should influence design (for example, age, computer experience . . .)

The audience definition works when you know who you are and are not designing for, what they want to do, and what they know and need to learn.

Step 2: Structure the content to guide the reader through it

- Organize the content so that it flows logically
- Break content into short sections that reflect natural stopping points
- Write headings that help readers predict what is coming up

The structure works when readers can quickly and confidently find the information they are looking for.

Step 3: Write the content in plain language

Keep it short and to the point

- Write short but logical sentences
- Present important information first in each section, subsection, and paragraph
- Include the details that help the reader complete the task
- Leave out details that don't help or may distract readers, even if they are interesting
- Use transitions to connect ideas, sentences, paragraphs, or sections

Set a helpful tone

- Use a conversational, rather than legal or bureaucratic tone

Pick the right words

- Use strong verbs in the active voice
- Use words the audience knows
- Make titles or list elements parallel (for example, start each with a verb)
- For websites: Match the link wording to landing page names

The language works when readers understand the words and grasp the intended message quickly and confidently.

Step 4: Use information design to help readers see and understand

- Use headers and sub-headers to organize the information
- Use typography (font size, color, bold, etc.) to guide the reader's attention
- Use whitespace to organize the information
- Use images to make content easier to understand

The design works when users notice and use the signposts to move through the information efficiently.

Step 5: Work with the target user groups to test the design and content

Test the design at multiple points

- Were audience needs, such as top tasks, prioritized based on user research?
- Did you test navigation labels and information organization for predictability?
- Did you test the content for readability and understandability?
- Did you test the final product?

Use evidence-based testing strategies

- Were the participants representative of the target groups?
- Did you test your design and content with enough people?
- How was understanding and ability to act measured?
- Was there a before-and-after comparison to demonstrate improvement?

Check that the final product is useful and usable

- Ask readers to describe who and what the document or site is intended for
- Have them show you how they would find the information they want or need

188

- Ask them to describe key concepts or processes in their own words
- Observe whether target users can finish key tasks easily and confidently
- Note where they stumble or misunderstand and rethink those parts of the site or document

The document or site works when target users can find what they need, understand what they find, and act on it confidently.

Additional Resources for Policy Writing

Be sure to seek out any directive policy writing guidance within your own institution.

- "Writing Policy Documents." University of Wollongong Australia. https://documents.uow.edu.au/about/policy/write/index.html
- "Writing Policies and Procedures." University of Texas at Austin Center for Professional Education. https://professionaled.utexas.edu/writing-policies-and-procedures
- "Policy Writing Tips." Michigan Technological University. www.mtu.edu/policy/tips/
- "Guidance for Writing Policy." Oregon State University. https://policy.oregonstate.edu/resources/guidance-writing-policy
- "Policy Writing Guidance." Boise State University. www.boisestate.edu/policy/policy-writing-guidance/
- "Instructions for Writing a University Policy." University of Southern Queensland. https://policy.usq.edu.au/documents/13705PL
- "User Guide to Writing Policy." University of Colorado. www.cu.edu/sites/default/files/APSwritingguide.pdf
- "Guide to Writing Policy and Procedure Documents." University of California-Santa Cruz. https://policy.ucsc.edu/resources/images/GuidetoWritingPolicy.pdf
- Office of University Compliance and Integrity. "Tips for Writing a University Policy." The Ohio State University. https://policies.osu.edu/assets/docs/Tips-for-Writing-a-University-Policy.pdf
- "Guide to Writing and Maintaining Campuswide Administrative Policy." University of California Davis. https://manuals.ucdavis.edu/sites/g/files/dgvnsk1766/files/inline-files/Guide%20to%20Writing%20Policy_2.2020_0.pdf
- "Policy Writing Style Guide" Administrative Services Gateway. University of Buffalo. www.buffalo.edu/administrative-services/policy1/develop-policy/policy-writing-style-guide.html

APPENDIX C: EXAMPLE OF GUIDING PRINCIPLES FOR SHARED GOVERNANCE

Guiding Principles for Shared Governance

SBHE 305.1.4.a states, each President shall ensure effective and broad-based participation in the decision-making process from faculty, staff, student, and others in those areas in which their interests are affected.

The purpose of this document is to outline and clarify the collective understanding of shared governance operations at NDSU. Shared governance has long been a hallmark of higher education's internal governance model. It is a collaborative process involving relevant stakeholders creating, implementing, and upholding policies that affect the educational and working conditions here at NDSU. With shared governance, stakeholders share both the benefits and the responsibilities of governing NDSU.

NDSU affirms its commitment to shared governance, and while the exact processes involved with shared governance may change over time, four fundamental aspects will always be critical to effective shared governance:

(1) transparency: stakeholders will share accurate and relevant information with the other stakeholders about both decisions and the processes that supported those decisions;
(2) responsibility: stakeholders understand that the institution is obligated to be a good steward of its resources;
(3) good faith: the stakeholders will enter into the process with good intentions, making an ethical commitment to seeing processes through;
(4) respect: stakeholders participate in deliberations and dialogue with care and regard for the perspectives of other groups.

Each stakeholder, represented by a governance group, has the right to propose new policies and, adjust, or amend existing policies, through the appropriate process, as outlined in policy 714—Senate Coordinating Council. As stated in the policy, the Senate Coordinating Council "does not approve or disapprove policies but facilitates the policy review process by the various Senates." Policy 714 covers the responsibilities and procedures for our shared governance model at NDSU.

Additionally, all faculty, staff, and students are encouraged to use their voices and actively participate in the existing governance structure to inform decision making at the university as it seeks to fulfill its mission. It is the prerogative of the faculty, staff, and student governance representatives to voice the concerns of the respective groups they represent in good faith and fair dealing with the administration, and vice versa.

Shared governance means each governance body has the responsibility to inform, educate, and share with its constituents how shared governance is defined at NDSU and the mechanisms by which they can participate in the work. This may require different approaches for different groups of stakeholders.

Rights and Responsibilities

Governance bodies elect representatives for the purposes of reflecting principles for representation of reflecting the view of constituent groups. Therefore, we affirm that senators in each of the groups should adhere to the following:

- as part of their participation in governance activities, consider their role as a representative of the diverse constituencies whom they represent.
- regularly communicate the activities of the governance group to constituents
- •identify multiple clear and transparent opportunities for represented constituents to share views on upcoming items

I. Definitions

A. The stakeholder groups **(administration, faculty, staff, and students)** are those defined in NDSU Policy Manual Section 101, "Personnel Definitions" and NDSU Policy Manual Section 101.1 "Employee Group Definitions."

B. **Stakeholder** refers to any person or constituency group who is affected by university decisions.

C. **Constituency** refers to employee groups defined in 101.1 who are represented by governing bodies such as Faculty Senate, Staff Senate, or Student Government.

D. **Governance body** refers to any formally constituted body that has oversight and decision-making authority about a specific university function, policy, or process (for example, an academic department, a senate or senate committee).

E. **Transparency:** In the context of governance, transparency means the visibility of the rationale, thinking, and information that is considered as part of institutional decision-making to the greatest extent possible within the context of policy.

F. **Consultation** is defined as the process of engaging the appropriate stakeholders or groups in feedback-gathering activities prior to the finalizing of a decision. Consultation should be focused on gathering perspectives that meaningfully inform the final outcome. Consultation shall occur whenever reasonably possible and appropriate. In instances where consultation has not taken place due to constraints (e.g. legal or budgetary), administration shall share its rationale with the appropriate governance group.

APPENDIX D: SAMPLE DOCUMENTS FOR STREAMLINING SHARED GOVERNANCE COMMUNICATION

Sample Agenda

Faculty Senate
Executive Meeting SAMPLE Agenda
[Date and Time]
[Location]
[Link to online meeting space]

Tl;dr (Or Summary in Brief): [Topic for the meeting, major points, what was discussed in summary]

1. Reports
   a. President
   b. Vice President
   c. Treasurer
   d. Committees
      i. Assessment
      ii. Budget
      iii. Curriculum
      iv. Faculty Development
      v. Planning
      vi. Research
      vii. Unit representatives
      viii. Caucuses
2. Consent Agenda
   a. Approval of minutes from [Date, last meeting]
   b. No-contest voting to fill open spots on committees
      i. [Position Name], [Volunteer Name, Affiliation with link to volunteer statement]
3. Discussion/Action Items
   a. Review of faculty senate operating procedure 3 [with link to operating procedure revision in question], [Name of Presenter]
   b. Assessment Cycle [Name of Presenter], **time certain 4:00 p.m.** [with links to necessary documents]
   c. Committee charge review: Budget Committee [Name of Presenter, links to the old charge and the new draft charge]
   d. Social Event for Faculty Senate members [Name of Presenter]

4. Open Committee Positions
   a. Committee Name
      i. [Name of Volunteer, Affiliation] (e.g., Juan Rios, College of Business)
      ii. [Name of Volunteer, Affiliation]
      iii. [Name of Volunteer, Affiliation]
   b. Special Appointment to Faculty Development Committee (1-year replacement)
      i. [Name of Volunteer, Affiliation]
      ii. [Name of Volunteer, Affiliation]
      iii. [Name of Volunteer, Affiliation]
      iv. [Name of Volunteer, Affiliation]
5. Volunteers Needed for Committee Positions
   a. Committee Name, Affiliation Needed
      i. Brief description of duties, time commitment, and expectations
   b. Committee Name, Affiliation Needed
      i. Brief description of duties, time commitment, and expectations
   c. Committee Name, Affiliation Needed
      i. Brief description of duties, time commitment, and expectations

Please Note

This is an example of an agenda that can be sent out with a meeting invitation on a system calendar. Reports are hyperlinked and can be clicked on so that each reporter during the meeting can use their time to highlight key issues. As the meeting progresses, the appointed notetaker can make a copy of the agenda and annotate it so that a record of all decisions is kept. Both the agenda and the minutes, as well as the reports, should be kept in a common and accessible online folder using something like Microsoft Teams so that they can be easily found after the fact by any interested faculty member.

Sample Minutes

Faculty Senate
Executive Meeting SAMPLE Minutes
[Date and Time]
[Location]
[Link to online meeting space]

Tl;dr (Or Summary in Brief): [Topic for the meeting, major points, what was discussed in summary]

Members in attendance:

1. Reports
   a. President
   b. Vice President
   c. Treasurer
   d. Committees
      i. Assessment
      ii. Budget
      iii. Curriculum
      iv. Faculty Development
      v. Planning
      vi. Research
      vii. Unit representatives
2. Caucuses
   i. Disability
   ii. Faculty of Color
   iii. Feminist Issues
   iv. LGBTQIA+
3. Consent Agenda
   a. Minutes from [Date, last meeting] approved by vote [#] yay [#] nay [#] abstain
   b. No-contest voting
      i. [Position Name], [Volunteer Name, Affiliation] approved by vote [#] yay [#] nay [#] abstain
4. Discussion/Action Items
   a. Review of faculty senate operating procedure 3 [with link to operating procedure revision in question], [Name of Presenter]
   b. Assessment Cycle [Name of Presenter], **time certain 4:00 p.m.** [with links to necessary documents]
   c. Committee charge review: Budget Committee [Name of Presenter, links to the old charge and the new draft charge]
   d. Social Event for Faculty Senate members [Name of Presenter]
5. Committee Positions to be Filled
   a. Committee Name **Volunteer ii elected** [#] yay [#] nay [#] abstain
      i. [Name of Volunteer, Affiliation] (Ex: Juan Rios, College of Business)
      ii. [Name of Volunteer, Affiliation]
      iii. [Name of Volunteer, Affiliation]
   b. Special Appointment to Faculty Development Committee (1-year replacement) **Volunteer iv elected** [#] yay [#] nay [#] abstain
      i. [Name of Volunteer, Affiliation]
      ii. [Name of Volunteer, Affiliation]

  iii. [Name of Volunteer, Affiliation]
  iv. [Name of Volunteer, Affiliation]
 6. Volunteers Needed for Committee Positions
  a. Committee Name, Affiliation Needed
   i. Brief description of duties, time commitment, and expectations
  b. Committee Name, Affiliation Needed
   i. Brief description of duties, time commitment, and expectations
  c. Committee Name, Affiliation Needed
   i. Brief description of duties, time commitment, and expectations

Please Note

This is an example of a document that can be sent out with a meeting invitation on a system calendar. Reports are hyperlinked and can be clicked on so that each reporter during the meeting can use their time to highlight key issues. As the meeting progresses, the appointed notetaker can make a copy of the agenda and annotate it so that a record of all decisions is kept. Both the agenda and the minutes, as well as the reports, should be kept in a common and accessible online folder using something like Microsoft Teams so that they can be easily found after the fact by any interested faculty member.

Sample Report

Faculty Senate
Executive Meeting
[Date and Time]
SAMPLE Report by [Name], Unit Representative for the College of
Humanities and Social Sciences

Brief Summary Statement
 Detailed Report [with embedded hyperlinks to information as necessary]

Index

Note: Page numbers in *italics* indicate figures and those in **bold** indicate tables.

196

Made in the USA
Las Vegas, NV
09 August 2024

93589256R00118